Regional Networks, Border Regions and European Integration

European research in regional science

1   **Infrastructure and regional development**
    edited by R W Vickerman

2   **Sustainable development and urban form**
    edited by M J Breheny

3   **Regional networks, border regions, and European integration**
    edited by R Cappellin, P W J Batey

Pion Limited,

Regional networks, Border Regions and European Integration

Editors   R Cappellin, P W J Batey

Series editor   P W J Batey

European research in regional science

ISBN 085086 162 4
ISSN 0960-6130

British Library Cataloguing in Publication Data
A CIP catalogue record British Library.

published by Pion Limited, 207 Brondesbury Park, London NW2 5JN

Printed in Great Britain by Page Bros (Norwich) Limited

Contributors

S Bodson — University of Louvain la Neuve, 1 Place Montesquieu-Bte 14, 1348 Louvain la Neuve, Belgium

P Brenner — European Centre for Regional Development, 20 Place des Halles, F67000 Strasbourg, France

R Cappellin — Department of Economics, Bocconi University, Via Sarfatti 25, 20136 Milan, Italy

A M Figueiredo — Oporto Faculty of Economics, Rua de Estefania 251, 4100 Porto, Portugal

R H Funck — Institute for Economic Policy Research, University of Karlsruhe, PO Box 6980, D-76128 Karlsruhe, Germany

B Guesnier — Institute of Regional Economics, University of Poitiers, 93 Av. du Recteur Pineau, 86022 Poitiers, France

A J Hingel — Commission of the European Communities, 200 rue de la Loi, 1049 Brussels, Belgium

G Horváth — Hungarian Academy of Sciences, Centre for Regional Studies, PO Box 199, H-7601 Pecs, Hungary

J S Kowalski — Institute of Economics, University of Münster, am Stadtgraben 9, 4400 Münster, Germany

J S Pedersen — Department of Socioeconomics and Planning, Roskilde University, PO Box 260, 4000 Roskilde, Denmark

A Pimpão — University of the Algarve, Campus da Penha, P-800 Faro, Portugal

M Quévit — University of Louvain la Neuve, 1 Place Montesquieu-Bte 14, 1348 Louvain la Neuve, Belgium

R Ratti — Office of Economic Research, Stabile Torretta, 6501 Bellinzona, Switzerland

P Rietveld

*Department of Regional Economics, Free
University, De Boelelaan 1105,
1081 HV Amsterdam, The Netherlands*

M Steiner

*Department of Economics, University of Graz,
Schubertgasse 6a, A-8010 Graz, Austria*

D Sturn

*Institute for Regional Development, Joanneum
Research, Steyrergasse 17, A-8010 Graz, Austria*

A van der Veen

*Department of Public Policy and Public
Administration, University of Twente,
PO Box 217, 7500 AE Enschede,
The Netherlands*

N Veggeland

*NordREFO, Store Strandstræde 18, DK-1350
Copenhagen K, Denmark*

R W Vickerman

*Centre for European, Regional and Transport
Economics, University of Kent at Canterbury,
Canterbury, Kent CT2 7NF, England*

Contents

Interregional Cooperation in Europe: An Introduction   1
R Cappellin

Part 1 A borderless Europe
The Prime Role of Regional Cooperation in European   21
Integration
A J Hingel

The Border Region Challenge Facing Norden: Applying New   31
Regional Concepts
N Veggeland

Transport and Communication Barriers in Europe   47
P Rietveld

How can Existing Barriers and Border Effects be Overcome?   60
A Theoretical Approach
R Ratti

Part 2 The economics of cooperation
Interregional Cooperation and the Design of a Regional   70
Foreign Policy
R Cappellin

Theory and Practice of Cross-border Cooperation of Local   89
Governments: The Case of the EUREGIO Between Germany
and the Netherlands
A van der Veen

Theory and Practice of Interregional Cooperation and Urban   96
Networks in Economically Lagging Regions: The Experience
of Galicia and the North of Portugal
A M Figueiredo

Part 3 The policy of cooperation
The Channel Tunnel and Transfrontier Cooperation   116
R W Vickerman

The Baltic Region and the New Europe   135
J Storm Pedersen

Restructuring and Interregional Cooperation in Central Europe: 157
The Case of Hungary
G Horváth

Interregional Cooperation and Transborder Activities in a   177
Middle European Context
M Steiner, D Sturn

Transborder Cooperation and European Integration: 191
The Case of Wallonia
M Quévit, S Bodson

Transnational Networks and Cooperation in the New Europe: 205
Experiences and Prospects in the Upper Rhine Area and
Recommendations for Eastern Europe
R H Funck, J S Kowalski

The Atlantic Arc: The Small and Medium-sized Enterprises   215
and the Transfer of Technologies
B Guesnier

Transborder Cooperation: Regional and Business Development   231
A Pimpão

What Makes an Interregional Network Successful?   239
P Brenner

Index   245

Interregional Cooperation in Europe: An Introduction

R Cappellin
University of Calabria and Bocconi University

1 Introduction

Until recently, interregional cooperation in Europe had not been identified as a major issue by public opinion and national policymakers. However, the process of fragmentation of many national entities, as has occurred in Eastern Europe, and the gradual removal of national barriers in Western Europe highlight the increasing importance, or even the necessity of, interregional cooperation as a factor promoting the process of European integration.

In fact, the recaptured political freedom and the process of internationalisation lead to a resurgence of ethnic and cultural values so long repressed. On the other hand, the internationalisation of national economies only apparently implies a shift of power to supranational institutions, and leads instead to a greater specialisation of each regional economy in its comparative advantage and to the need to mobilise endogenous resources and to rediscover regional identities, as regions are spaces where a higher internal solidarity may help in facing the challenges of international competition. In particular, interregional cooperation favours a greater autonomy from national institutions and it provides a response to the aim of coping with the interregional spillover effects created by the increasing interdependence between regional economies, while avoiding a concentration of power in supraregional or national organisations.

The economic literature on this subject is still not extensive and that which does exist is fragmented in various contributions presented at different conferences, mostly of a regional or national character. It seemed useful, therefore, to ask a selected number of European experts in this field to contribute to this book—to illustrate the results of their research on this topic. This has certainly required a greater effort from authors, but it has also enabled an updated framework to be created for the state of the art of interregional cooperation in Europe. The choice of papers has been guided by two complementary criteria, as the aim has been both to cover the various geographical areas in Europe, from the Nordic to the Mediterranean countries, and to analyse interregional cooperation experiences from various functional perspectives, ranging from technology, to transport infrastructures, to institutional issues.

The book is organised into three major sections. The first section includes chapters in which the authors highlight (a) the role of borders as barriers and as an interface between the various countries and regions and (b) the impact on the structure of the European territory that a reduction in these barriers may have. The second section contains chapters which are focused on (a) the various factors which justify interregional cooperation from an economic perspective and (b) the institutional and organisational characteristics of cooperation schemes between regions. Finally, the third section includes various chapters in which the actual experiences of interregional cooperation in various policy fields are analysed and stimuli and obstacles to interregional cooperation are illustrated.

As all the authors deal with very similar issues, although from different perspectives, rather than summarise each individual paper, it seems more useful to highlight the most important issues which have been raised by the various authors and which indicate that a substantial degree of consensus exists among them.

2 New regions in a borderless Europe

The removal of national barriers within the European Community, and the development of economic and political relationships with the European countries external to the EC, imply a new geo-economic order in Europe and a change in the hierarchical relationships between the various regional and urban production systems (CEC, 1991). As indicated by Hingel and Veggeland, interregional cooperation will lead to a change in the spatial organisation of Europe. However, there are different criteria which may be adopted for a redefinition of the regional concept in a European perspective. Therefore, next to the criteria of economic, social, and ethnic homogeneity, or that of polarisation and accessibility (which, as indicated by Rietveld, are traditionally relevant for defining regional units), a new regionalisation criterion may be represented by the sharing of a joint strategy of future development, as this may be a crucial factor favouring a common sense of regional belonging.

Thus the European territory may be subdivided into various types of regions, such as:
(a) actual administrative regions, which define the spatial framework of regional powers of self-government;
(b) historical regions, which are based on the principle of homogeneity and, to a large extent, correspond to the 18th-century city-region states. They may define the spatial frameworks which have common cultural values and have common regional identity and thus may also have a specific common 'image' to be promoted at the European level;
(c) new meso-regions, which are based on network relationships among various urban centres and indicate new development trends.

Meso-regions are characterised by a relative spatial contiguity and may comprise regions which are 500 km to 800 km apart from one another. They are also to a certain extent based on a common identity, on reciprocal trust, and thus on a common sense of belonging; factors which represent a precondition to defining a common development strategy.

A peculiar characteristic of an interregional approach is the fact that it is leading not to new rigid boundaries but to a patchwork pattern of overlapping jurisdictions or to a variable geometry of multiple transnational cooperation networks, as indicated by Hingel, Cappellin, van der Veen, and Figueiredo. In fact, the increasing cooperation between firms within the European economic system and the need to create modern infrastructural networks between the various European urban centres and regions is linked with the identification of new groups of regions and countries at a transnational scale; groups which represent new transnational meso-regions within the European economy. These meso-regions are characterised by a higher than average internal level of economic integration, and this justifies the creation of cooperation schemes or alliances between the various regions which belong to them. On the other hand, global competition concerns not only individual firms but also the various national and regional production systems.

Thus, the European economy may be interpreted as an urban system made up of a combination of various urban networks or large European meso-regions which have a transnational dimension (Cappellin, 1988; 1989), as indicated in figure 1. Within these urban networks, cooperative relationships based on the specialisation and complementarity of each individual urban centre or region prevail, whereas competitive behaviour prevails in the relationships between these individual urban networks or meso-regions at a European scale.

In particular, each national area can be subdivided into two or more areas which can belong to different European meso-regions. Moreover, each meso-region can be defined in a way that includes regions belonging to three or more nations. Therefore, the fact that a region belongs to a specific national community does not exclude, and may on the contrary be complementary to, the fact that this region also belongs to a large interregional transnational community. In fact, the creation of European meso-regions is a factor conducive to a greater integration of the various national economic systems at a European level.

These meso-regions suggest new strategic frameworks in the promotion of regional development. They are abstract ideas, symbols, visions, or strategic instruments which aim to mobilise resources in order to solve common problems. They do not correspond to existing territories but may indicate future territories and certainly correspond to the actual tendencies that may be perceived by an expert analyst.

These large meso-regions identify new development axes which insure a greater European cohesion in territorial terms, and are of special importance from the perspective of a policy of 'amenagement' of the European territory. Vickerman illustrates the impact of large transportation projects on interregional cooperation, and many of the other authors in this volume underline the fact that national authorities design infrastructure networks

4   R Cappellin

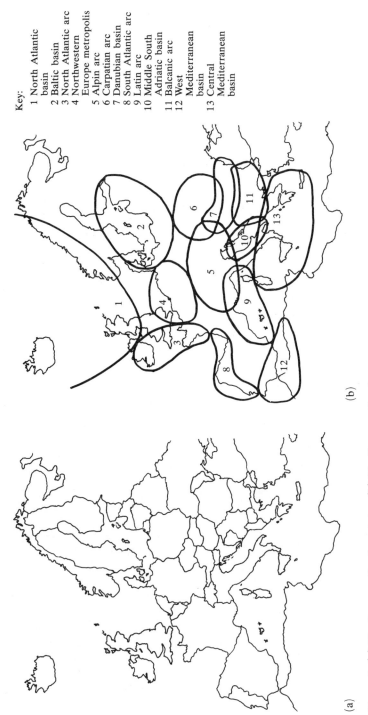

Key:
1 North Atlantic
   basin
2 Baltic basin
3 North Atlantic arc
4 Northwestern
   Europe metropolis
5 Alpin arc
6 Carpatian arc
7 Danubian basin
8 South Atlantic arc
9 Latin arc
10 Middle South
   Adriatic basin
11 Balcanic arc
12 West
   Mediterranean
   basin
13 Central
   Mediterranean
   basin

(b)

(a)

Figure 1. (a) The Europe of nation-states. (b) The Europe of regions.

in their own national interests and that reducing transport barriers is a major objective of cooperation between border regions.

Within each meso-region each individual urban centre should develop infrastructural links and economic, financial, and technological relationships with the other urban centres of that meso-region, as well as with other European meso-regions. This seems a precondition for a meso-region to represent an internally integrated subsystem which could compete at the European level with other European transnational regions, or could develop positive relationships with other neighbouring countries and regions both in Europe and in the Mediterranean basin.

The chapters by Pedersen, Horváth, and Funck and Kowalski indicate that interregional cooperation schemes may represent a key strategy in promoting economic growth, and that these schemes have been initiated or are at least discussed even in Eastern Europe, where nationalism seems to have been an almost inevitable consequence of recaptured freedom after the removal of the Iron Curtain and of the social tensions created by a fast transition to a market economy.

Many chapters, such as those by Figueiredo, Vickerman, Quévit and Bodson, Pimpão, and Brenner refer to EC regional policy and especially to recent programmes such as INTERREG (for development in border regions) and RECITE (Regions and Cities for Europe). An open question is still whether the EC is willing and able to perform the role of network incubator, or if it can play only the more limited role of supporter of specific projects by already existing networks.

3 Three international organisational paradigms

A transnational interregional perspective represents a challenge to two traditional views of the process of European integration. In fact there is an increasing consensus that it is too restrictive to base an approach to European integration on only the creation of a *European Single Market*, or a European economic space, characterised by:

(a) the abolition of the various obstacles to the international movement of goods, services, capital, and people;

(b) the creation of a common legal framework which would ensure equal competitive conditions for all firms;

(c) a monetary system which would ensure the stability of exchange rates; and

(d) a convergence of the inflation rates and of other macroeconomic indicators, which would ensure a stable framework for exports and international investments of the firms.

On the other hand, another conception of the political and institutional development of European integration, which differs from the previous one in its greater attention to microeconomic aspects and in its dependence on the need for specific public interventions in the process of European integration, is the traditional conception. This has been elaborated since

the 1950s and is a *European Community*, characterised by:
(a) the overcoming of those national conflicts which had given rise to two world wars;
(b) the mass-production model;
(c) the power of multinational firms:
(d) the harmonisation of national regulations and their replacement with a European legal system;
(e) the homologation of local cultures and the overcoming of national diversities;
(f) the development of a European culture;
(g) the development of a European identity and of a European nationalism;
(h) the development of supranational institutions with a hierarchical power with respect to those of individual nations;
(i) a decrease in the powers of national institutions;
(j) an instrumental alliance with regional institutions; and
(k) the gradual extension of the powers of the EC even in those fields in which regional institutions are competent.

However, this conception of European integration also seems increasingly to conflict with the actual trends in European economy and society. In fact, since the 1980s a new conception has gained strength; namely a *Europe of regions*, or the European federalism, characterised by:
(a) the internationalisation and innovation process in the individual regional and national productive systems;
(b) a model of flexible production;
(c) the development of network organisational forms, not only at a local level but also at an interregional level;
(d) the increasing role of small and medium-sized firms in international markets;
(e) the increasing integration or internationalisation of regional and national productive systems;
(f) the claim of autonomy and self-government by regional institutions and the increasing consensus on the principle of subsidiarity;
(g) the increasing perception of the value of regional and national diversity;
(h) the discovery and development of transnational historical, social, and cultural identities;
(i) a flexible geometry of interregional and international cooperation relationships;
(j) the development of nonhierarchical relationships based on partnership between national institutions and regional institutions in joint programmes; and
(k) the development of specific European programmes, additional to, rather than instead of, regional and national programmes.

The typically federalist perception of the Europe of regions differs from that of the European Single Market in that interregional flows are not perceived in a functional way or as controlled by a global system of multinational or transnational firms, but as the effects of the interdependence and integration between the different regional productive systems. On the other hand, the Europe of regions is a concept which is different from that of a supranational European Community, as regionalism and the claim for regional self-government are based on the belief that economic development in individual areas depends mostly on the capability of local initiatives and on the exploitation of synergies among the local resources.

As indicated in the papers by Hingel, Veggeland, Cappellin, Pedersen, Horváth, and Steiner and Stern the process of interregional cooperation has profound implications for the very characteristics of European integration. Interregional cooperation implies a bottom-up or grass-roots approach to European integration. This seems to justify a thorough analysis of the characteristics of concepts such as those of regional administrative autonomy, regionalism, federalism, or nationalism which are often used in a rather contradictory manner.

In abstract terms, the distinction between the three different concepts of a European Single Market, a European Community and the Europe of regions is similar to that between the three different organisational forms of the modern theory of the firm, but also to the three principles at the base of liberal-democratic thinking. Therefore, it is possible to identify three different organisational–institutional models or paradigms, each of which is characterised by an internal logic, implying a tight interaction between concepts related to the organisation of relationships between firms and to the forms of political and institutional relationships as indicated in table 1.

In particular it is worth underlining the tight relationship between federalism and modern organisational forms of the economic system and of the individual firms. Federalism or regionalism correspond to a paradigmatic transformation of the structures of society, economy, and production technologies in Europe (Cappellin, 1990; 1992). Federalism ensures a greater decentralisation in the decisionmaking process and therefore represents an institutional form, which is more suited to a socioeconomic system that is more articulated, culturally more advanced, and technologically more complex. Therefore, whereas federalism is typical of an 'open system' logic, centralism is typical of a 'closed system' logic.

The internationalisation of economies or the integration of local and national production systems, on the one hand, and regionalism and federalism in the government structures of economy, on the other hand, are complementary phenomena. In fact, it is typical of regional economies to imply a tight integration not only of product markets but also in terms of the flow of production factors. Thus the internationalisation process transforms nation-states into large regions which are highly heterogeneous, and this leads to the need for a regionalisation of individual national systems.

It also seems important to underline the tight complementarity between the concepts of regionalism or federalism and those of cooperation and solidarity which, being based on individual consensus, seem rather distinct from those of an equity imposed by a superior authority and of legal rights to public transfers. Moreover, separatism is more like centralism or nationalism than regionalism. In fact, centralism implies opposition to developing those flexible forms of integratoin which are a typical characteristic of regionalism and the oppression of ethnic minorities, and this may lead to separatism, which is in fact a form of micronationalism. Thus the centralistic power of the nation-state not only is the main factor of the lack of unity at European level, but also is often the factor which leads to division of the individual national communities.

Table 1. Organisational forms and models of institutional integration.

	Free market model	Centralistic model	Federalist model

Organisational forms	market
	atomistic
	  competition
		hierarchy
		mass production
			cooperation
			flexible
			  production

Organisational principles	initiative responsibility efficiency	authority legal rights economies of scale	self-government synergy flexibility

Interaction logics	competitivity
	monetary
	  exchange
	interdependence
		homogeneity
		control/
		  dependence
		coordination
			differentiation
			influence/
			  leadership
			negotiation

Geographical
  framework
	homogeneous
	  space
		administrative
		  units
			territorial
			production
			  systems

Negative effects	hegoism economicism liberalism	bureaucracy assistance dirigism	conflicts assemblearism veto power
Political ideals	liberté	egalité	fraternité
International relations	free trade	mercantilism	complementarity
European integration	Single Market	supranational community	interregional federation

Negative developments	economic/political
	  disequilibria
		nationalism/
		  separatism
			confusion/
			  impotence

4 The principle of subsidiarity

The economic foundation of federalism is represented by the principle of subsidiarity, according to which each function should be attributed to the lowest efficient decision level within the hierarchical system of relationships between regions, nation-states, and the EC. Therefore, functions should not be transferred to a superior level when they can be efficiently exercised at a lower level.

The subsidiarity principle, on the one hand, implies a limitation of powers of national governments and of the EC and, on the other hand, can lead to greater efficiency in national government, and in the EC, which, being free from disparate competences, may gain in terms of greater flexibility and may concentrate efforts in policy fields which have a specific national or European dimension.

In particular, the policy fields for which the regional level seems to be the optimal decisionmaking level in a modern economy typical of that of most European countries are:

(a) territorial planning, infrastructure, and environment;
(b) vocational and higher education, and applied research; and
(c) industrial and innovation policy for small and medium-sized economies.

In fact, the ineffectiveness and inefficiency of national administrations in these policy fields is demonstrated by a long-term record in most countries.

As the extent of regional autonomy according to the subsidiarity principle depends on the criteria of efficiency, the actual solution may be rather ambiguous and depends on the specific country and region concerned, and especially on the different approaches adopted in the specific policy fields considered. Thus a traditional industrial policy based on financial incentives may be managed more efficiently at the national level, whereas a modern industrial policy based on innovation promotion and on intersectoral technological interdependencies could be more efficiently organised at the local level. Therefore, there is a mutual interdependence between changes in the approach to economic policy and changes in the optimal institutional solution to the relationships between regions and nation-states.

However, a further limit of the subsidiarity principle, apart from its relative ambiguity, is its hierarchical character, as it explicitly takes into account only vertical relations between the regional, the national, and the EC levels. Therefore, it would imply a shift to higher levels of all competences related to problems which have a superregional dimension. This is a serious limitation, as most problems have clearly interregional spillover effects across regional boundaries. On the contrary, interregional cooperation, both in a bilateral and in a multiregional framework, seems an institutional and organisational solution that is more efficient than simply creating new 'authorities' to tackle those cases of policy interventions which, despite having a superregional dimension, do not in fact have a clearly national relevance.

This may be the case when only a limited number of regions in a given country have a common interest in the problem considered. A further typical case is that of relationships between border regions, as the coordination of respective national administrations, which are much less familiar with the concrete problems at hand, would often imply greater problems than direct negotiation between the regional governments of the regions concerned.

This problem is illustrated by figure 2, where the various functions are organised according to a hierarchical principle starting from those which imply a smaller planning geographical unit to those which, for their efficient management, imply a larger territorial framework. The horizontal axis indicates various location points, which correspond to different regional administrations.

Thus, for some functions the relevant areas do not intersect and total autonomy can be allowed to each regional administration. On the other hand, in the case of superregional problems (for example, when the required planning minimal units overlap, as is indicated by the areas D, E, and F) bilateral or multilateral cooperation schemes may be more efficient solutions rather than the complete delegation of power to a superregional or national authority. According to this approach, power should be delegated to a superregional or national authority, which may have its own legitimacy and act autonomously from the various regional governments considered, only when the area of overlap between the regions concerned represents the largest portion or is just greater than half of their territory.

Thus, the principle of interregional cooperation is consistent with a bottom-up decisionmaking process and it appears as a logical extension of the principle of subsidiarity. In fact, the impulse to cooperate comes from the individual local governmental units as much as from individual firms and local lobbying groups. Interregional cooperation is both the effect of and an instrument aimed at promoting the active participation of local actors.

A thorough analysis of the different characteristics of national borders and their relationships with interregional cooperation is developed by Rietveld, Ratti, van der Veen, Pedersen, and Steiner and Sturn. According to Ratti, borders represent a favourable element in the determination of a supporting space for the firms of the individual regions, and this allows the creation of a transborder economy characterised by a common technological regional system.

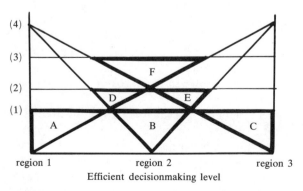

Figure 2. Functions and efficient decisionmaking levels.

The chapters by Cappellin and Pimpão underline the close similarity between the processes of interregional cooperation and of internationalisation of private firms and the applicability to interregional cooperation of concepts elaborated by modern industrial economics and the theory of the firm. Although interregional cooperation is suggested mainly for reasons of allocative efficiency, and analysis is concentrated on the supply side, it can also be justified in theoretical terms by an analysis of the demand side, as indicated by van der Veen. In fact, reference to the literature on fiscal federalism may be useful in indicating the roles of different local tastes, the production of local or cross-border public goods, and external effects, and because it may guide the search for an optimal spatial jurisdiction and aid in the analysis of the implications for fiscal autonomy and interregional transfers of fiscal resources.

5 The development of interregional cooperation
The design of a new interregional framework from a European perspective leads to new types of relationships between nation-states and regional governments. This is especially important for land-border regions, which are highly contiguous, but it is also true for sea-border regions and more generally for those regions which may be considered a member of a large transnational meso-region.

Border regions are the most severely penalised by the existence of various obstacles which may be defined as territorial costs of the non-Europe, according to the terminology used in the construction of the European Single Market. Thus, they deserve greater attention from EC institutions and national governments aiming to promote a greater cohesion of the European economy. This explains why the EC Commission has recently supported, although with what are still inadequate financial allocations, the development of cooperation schemes among regions through the INTERREG programme and the RECITE initiative.

In particular, cooperation between border regions may be consistent with the achievement of three different objectives:
(1) to remove the barriers between the two regions concerned and solve bilateral problems and conflicts:
(2) to represent an interface area or a gateway in the relationships between the two countries; and
(3) to represent an overall transnational region which may play a role in international competition with other European meso-regions.

It must be underlined that there are advantages and costs in the process of transnational cooperation between border regions. First of all, the relationships between border regions have been, and still often are, relationships of conflict for various reasons, such as the existence of ethnic minorities, fear of immigration, fear of unfair competition, negative environmental spillover effects, and so on. However, conflictual relationships may be transformed into relationships of cooperation, whenever bilateral relationships are interpreted in a larger European perspective (Maillat, 1990; Nijkamp, 1993).

In some cases, the survival of national barriers may represent an advantage not only for the capital regions where the national administrations is concentrated but also for some border regions, which benefit from a form of rent position because they are the location of customs administration, various international transport and financial activities, and of military installations, and may receive considerable subsidies from national governments.

Several chapters, including those by Cappellin, Guesnier, and Brenner, underline the fact that interregional cooperation cannot be based on mere goodwill. On the one hand, there are economic reasons for creating an alliance and, on the other hand, there are operative requirements to be satisfied in order that an alliance can be effective. In particular, according to the contributions in this volume, the benefits of regional integration may be summarised as follows:

(a) the development of joint historical–cultural values and regional differences;

(b) the exploitation of complementarities of regions;

(c) the exploitation of network economies in the circulation of information and know-how;

(d) the exploitation of common natural resources taking into account external economies and diseconomies;

(e) the exploitation of economies of scale and the overcoming of indivisibilities in the production of specific important public services and infrastructures;

(f) increases in the flexibility of the regional economy, more-timely reactions to market changes, the stimulation of innovation, and a reduction of risk;

(g) the exploitation of economies of scope in the planning of tightly complementary services which require a large territorial basin, and the exploitation of economies of scale in the joint planning of these services;

(h) a reduction in the transaction costs which hinder the cooperation of firms in the various regions;

(i) a reduction of the competition between the regions concerned and of those conflicts due to the existence of national borders;

(j) the promotion of joint coordinated actions and the sharing of the international contacts in order to sustain the challenges created by some external 'enemy', such as the competition of other European meso-regions or the centralism by respective national authorities, and the advocacy of greater regional autonomy.

A number of authors, such as Pedersen, Horváth, Steiner and Sturn, Quévit and Bodson, Funck and Kowalski, and Guesnier, consider interregional cooperative initiatives in the field of new technology and the support of small and medium-sized firms. From this perspective new 'soft' infrastructures, such as industry and technology parks, may be a useful instrument in order to promote technology transfers. However, most of the authors also indicate that interregional cooperation can be important in the development of service sectors and in increasing the efficiency of local public administrations.

However, the development of cross-border cooperation may imply various costs, such as: transaction costs in interregional negotiations; the displacement of firms, or of production, into neighbouring regions; and greater immigration from neighbouring regions.

The development of a strategy of interregional cooperation is also hindered by a series of obstacles which in some cases may represent either a constraint, which can scarcely be overcome, or a precondition for the start of a strategy of interregional cooperation. Obstacles to interregional cooperation have been identified even in the most central of EC regions, as indicated by Vickerman, and Quévit and Bodson, and they are even more important in the case of border regions with Eastern Europe, as indicated by Pedersen, Horváth, and Steiner and Sturn.

Among the obstacles which have most often been identified in the previous experience of interregional cooperation are the following:
(a) a different technological or development level;
(b) different institutional competences;
(c) inadequate financial resources;
(d) different languages;
(e) different working methods;
(f) weak knowledge and reciprocal trust, as cooperation is a gradual interactive learning process;
(g) inadequate specification of respective interests;
(h) inadequate identification of respective strengths, complementary resources, and specific knowledges;
(i) inadequate identification of respective weaknesses and bottlenecks;
(j) a lack of engagement and motivation;
(k) the length of time required for preparing joint activities;
(l) insufficient stability in objectives and of the persons responsible for the individual projects;
(m) the inadequate development of a networking process between regional actors; and ·
(n) an inadequate design of those efficient institutional forms which are required for managing the cooperation scheme.

In addition, the urban structure of a region may favour its degree of openness to the international economy and municipal authorities may have a very active role in promoting interregional cooperation initatives, as is indicated in the chapters by Cappellin, Figueiredo, Steiner and Sturn, Funck and Kowalski, and Pimpão.

Cappellin emphasises that the creation of an agreement is not a sudden occurrence but resembles a gradual learning process. Thus, as well as the conditions which may lead to the creation of an agreement, are the factors leading to its continuity and success or interruption which may be even more important.

The existence of different competences is not a crucial obstacle for the creation of successful cooperation schemes. What clearly matters is the behavioural logics of the various regional administrations, as interregional cooperation requires a pragmatic logic of public entrepreneurship or a project-design capability, rather than the formal respect of bureaucratic competences.

Funck and Kowalski underline the interdependent relationships between economic structure and institutional architecture. Thus, whereas the existence of sound economic factors is supporting the effort to a greater regional autonomy and the promotion of effective schemes of interregional cooperation, the change in the institutional framework implied by interregional cooperation is fostering economic development in peripheral regions.

As indicated by Vickerman and Guesnier, interregional cooperation has profound implications both for policy design and for policy implementation by local authorities, and it is an instrument capable of leading the identification of innovative projects and to the mobilisation of an enterprising spirit and of external and internal resources. Thus the case of the Atlantic Arc, described by Figueiredo and Guesnier, has become a paramount example of the success of interregional cooperation as an instrument in the lobbying of action at the EC level.

According to Hingel, Cappellin, and Figueiredo, interregional networking and cooperation has an implicit hierarchical or selective character. It also implies the existence of regions performing the role of leaders, especially in preparatory phases and the creation of specific structures or contractual provisions which will ensure coordination in implementation. In particular, there is a close relationship between the capabilities at the interregional scale and those at the regional level. In fact, the development of interregional cooperative relationships clearly implies the capability of the individual regional governments to establish cooperative relationships with the other regional institutions and organisations, such as professional associations, individual private firms, cultural and research institutions, and so on, in order to design joint projects which may promote the international role of the overall regional production system.

As indicated by Veggeland, Figueiredo, and Guesnier, interregional cooperation is not limited to local public administration but is closely related to internally networking within the individual regions, as may be anticipated by or as may lead to the mobilisation of political leaders and of other local specialised actors, which may have a crucial role in developing cooperation in various new specialised fields. Therefore, the existence of an integrated local production and innovation system represents both a strong point and a prerequisite in order to participate in more complex initiatives of networking at an interregional level.

Interregional cooperation may represent a stimulus to the recognition of the importance of regional policies in countries where economic policy seems to be directed towards only sectoral or macroeconomic issues, or to change outdated approaches in regional policies such as those still followed in many economically lagging European regions. Interregional cooperation varies according to the nature of the economic problems affecting the various neighbouring regions. Thus, in the case of less-developed regions not only is it addressed at different objectives, as indicated by Pedersen, Funck and Kowalski, and Pimpão, but it should also face particular obstacles and it should imply a different role by public institutions.

In the case of the economically lagging regions of the EC, interregional cooperation initiatives are hindered by the lack of a project-oriented mentality, which is the effect of the prevailing centralist and 'dependent development' model. In these regions it is still not widely recognised that interregional cooperation may also be a business for private organisations.

According to Figueiredo, regional administrations are facing a lot of difficulties in order to involve entrepreneurial organisations in cooperation strategies. Local actors aim only at the financial incentives to be granted by public authorities within the framework of these initiatives and refuse to take a more active role in the organisation of cooperation projects. Thus it is necessary for cooperation initiatives to be promoted first of all by the various regional administrations with technical assistance and financial help from national and EC institutions.

The centre–periphery logic is negative, as it leads to the focusing of effort on the direction of the development of further centripetal relations between each peripheral region and a supposed centre, instead of developing horizontal relations of interregional cooperation. In fact, it is typical of EC economically lagging regions and also of Eastern European countries to compete with each other in order to attract resources and to achieve the best position in the process of economic integration with the 'central' countries and regions in the European economy.

The development of a strategy of interregional cooperation would allow a centre–periphery logic, which is prevailing in economically lagging regions, to be overcome and would stimulate these regions to adopt a polycentric logic. According to this logic, regions peripheral with respect to a supposed centre of the European economy may also become central in a different geographical perspective, which may be enlarged to include countries which do not belong to the EC, such as those of Eastern Europe or of the Mediterranean basin.

Thus, the logic of interregional cooperation has a selective or hierarchical character, as the regions which are most capable of participating in a networking process at the European level are the most developed ones.

This may lead to an increase in regional disparities, unless national and EC institutions help economically lagging regions to escape from their relative closure and to increase their awareness of the need of each region to develop its international relations.

6 New tasks for EC regional policies

The objective in EC economic policies is to achieve a greater cohesion between European regions and countries. However, 'cohesion' is an ambiguous expression which may be interpreted according to three different definitions which refer to three very different policy fields:
(a) the convergence of macroeconomic indicators;
(b) reequilibrium in regional development disparities; and
(c) the development of integration/interdependence between the various regional and national production systems.

Although the first two concepts refer to the concept of a European monetary union and of a supranational community having a large fiscal autonomy, respectively, the last definition is the most important from the perspective of a European policy of 'amenagement du territoire' and of the creation of a Europe of regions. This last definition of cohesion should be considered in the design of a new strategy in EC regional policy (Cappellin, 1991b; Cappellin and Molle, 1988).

In fact, it seems necessary to complement the traditional strategy of EC regional policy, which was aimed at promoting economic development in various types of problem regions, with a second objective. This involves the removal of all the obstacles having a territorial dimension and hindering a greater economic and social integration of the regions and countries of the EC, just as the programme for the European Single Market has done in the case of obstacles created by various national regulations.

Therefore EC regional policy could be articulated in two different objectives, as indicated in table 2: (a) programmes for economic development; and (b) programmes for regional European integration. These two objectives lead to two different approaches to regional policymaking. The first mainly implies a bottom-up strategy based on the paradigm of endogenous development, whereas the second suggests a top-down strategy based on the paradigm of interregional networks (Cappellin, 1991a; Konsolas, 1990).

A policy aimed at promoting regional economic integration should not necessarily adopt the typical centralist and technocratic approach based on multiple and often conflicting programmes organised according to a strict functional logic, the definition of different macroregions for each particular programme, the creation of various high authorities for each programme, and the vertical negotiations between EC institutions and each individual national and regional authority. This approach clearly contrasts with that based on interregional cooperation which, as indicated by cooperation between the Nordic countries, relies on the principle of bottom-up development and does not require the creation of strong international authorities, having their main competences in the design and implementation of measures in the different fields of intervention. In particular, the development of EC and national programmes aimed at a greater integration of the European space should lead not only to large-scale physical networks, as in the case of major transport investments, but also to the creation of flexible or 'software' networks between the various local, regional, and national institutions.

Table 2. Two complementary strategies in EC regional policy.

Regional development	European integration
1. Development model	
Economic development is promoted by the interdependence between endogenous and exogenous factors	Innovation and competitiveness is promoted by interregional network and interregional cooperation
2. Spatial framework	
Individual problem regions. Concentration in EC regions.	Networks of regions. Extension to non-EC regions.
3. Policy strategy	
Intersectoral integrated programmes. Partnership between local actors. Promote local entrepreneurship.	Tackle European common problems. Promote interregional cooperation. Decrease transaction costs in inter-regional relations.
4. Policy design	
Mainly bottom-up. Local authorities propose specific projects. EC elaborates general regulations and evaluates project proposals.	Mainly top-down. EC elaborates strategic plans. Local authorities contribute with specific projects.
5. Financing	
EC financing has a complementary role. Coordination of regional, national, and EC programmes.	EC funding has a principal role. Interregional cooperation. Public – private partnership.
6. Institutional procedures	
Hierarchical principle. Vertical coordination. Cooperation between regions, states, and the EC Commission.	Subsidiarity principle. Horizontal coordination. Cooperation between regions. Concertation between an assembly of European regions and the EC.
7. Relations between regional and nonregional policies	
Regional policy aims at cohesion as regional disparities decrease. Each policy aims at different and often conflictual objectives. Regional policy has mainly a redistributive and compensatory character.	Regional policy aims at cohesion as European integration increases. Regional and nonregional policies aim at common and complementary objectives. Regional policy contributes to achieve the objectives of other policies.

Thus, relations between EC institutions, and national and regional governments may be designed according to a network model and may be based on the principle of partnership and negotiation, rather than on the principle of a clear-cut separation of competences. A network structure has the advantage of being flexible and of promoting the power or the duty of defining strategic directives by national and EC institutions and the power or the right of initiative by regional institutions.

According to an interregional cooperation approach, interventions by EC institutions should be characterised by the definition of meso-regions based on a sense of belonging, the creation of interregional working communities within the various regional governments, the definition of interregional planning contracts among groups of regions and the EC institution, the creation of joint ventures or 'Sociétés Mixtes', and other forms of public – private partnership on various specific projects. EC regional policy should support interregional cooperation schemes both in the case of the economically developed regions and in the case of the economically lagging regions. The first type of measure is often that most needed, because of the central role these regions have in promoting European integration and of their function as interfaces between the various countries of the EC. These measures should be supplemented with measures addressed to economically lagging regions in order to avoid an increase in regional disparities as a result of the lower capability of these regions to develop active relations with foreign regions and countries.

In particular, national and EC regional policies should recognise the need to attribute a greater importance, also in financial terms, to programmes of interregional cooperation to be integrated within the traditional regional policy schemes elaborated for the economically lagging regions, such as the European Community Frameworks. This may require a simplification of procedures and specific financial incentives for the promotion of exploratory contacts and the design of cooperation in operational projects.

EC policies should not support only the cooperation schemes between the economically lagging regions and developed regions. In fact, these schemes have the same shortcomings as the traditional national policies of technology transfer and of cooperation with less-developed countries. On the contrary, it is necessary first to promote cooperation schemes among contiguous economically lagging regions. These schemes may be considered as a precondition in order to establish cooperation with the more-developed regions based on a more balanced distribution of the decisionmaking power. In fact, only through a greater internal integration within large European meso-regions may economically lagging regions be capable of sustaining the competition of the developed regions.

In this framework, the role of national governments and of the EC is initially that of ensuring the institutional framework that would allow cooperation between the various European regions by removing outdated regulations hindering international relations between regional and local institutions within an integrated community. Second, they may guarantee those financial incentives required to overcome the transaction costs in the development of interregional cooperation and can offer various forms of technical assistance and take a leading role in promoting innovative initiatives of interregional cooperation.

7 Conclusions

The contributions to this volume indicate that the gradual development of schemes of interregional cooperation is a powerful instrument for the promotion of European integration, in the case of central and developed regions and in that of peripheral and economically lagging regions, and also between EC regions and between these regions and those external to the EC. Although national authorities have a vested interest in the preservation of international differences, the creation of new large transnational regions based on interregional cooperation may promote the overcoming of national barriers.

National and EC institutions should have a clear interest in promoting cross-border cooperation not only as an effective way to promote a more integrated European territory but also for equity reasons, as interregional cooperation represents an effective strategy in promoting regional development in peripheral regions. A greater role assigned to interregional cooperation is a factor favouring the adoption of a new regional development strategy in economically lagging regions, based on the endogenous approach, the responsibility of local actors, and the development of internationally competitive activities.

Interregional cooperation, especially with regions of former socialist countries, is instrumental in strengthening democratic institutions and thus in reinforcing political stability in Europe. However, interregional cooperation may also be of fundamental importance in reinforcing the powers of local governments, trust in its own capabilities, the sense of responsibility, the values of democratic accountability, and the efficiency of local public administrations in many less-developed regions of Western Europe. In conclusion, I wish to express the hope that, although they may appear preliminary and fragmented, the experiences of interregional cooperation illustrated in this book may stand as a laboratory for a process of overcoming national differences and conflicts in Europe with a bottom-up or federalist approach.

Acknowledgement. Although I have been responsible for the choice of the theme of this book and for collecting the various contributions, I am very grateful to Peter Batey who, in his function as coeditor, has stimulated the completion of this book and has carefully revised the English texts of various chapters.

References

Cappellin R, 1988, "Transaction costs and urban agglomeration" *Revue d'Économie Régionale et Urbaine* **2** 261 – 278

Cappellin R, 1989, "International linkages among cities: a network approach", paper presented at the 29th European Congress of the RSA, Cambridge, 1989; published in Italian as "Networks nelle città e networks tra le città", in *Gerarchie e Reti di Città: Tendenze e Politiche* Eds F Curti, L Diappi (Franco Angeli, Milano) pp 71 – 97

Cappellin R, 1990, "The European internal market and the internationalisation of small and medium size enterprises" *Built Environment* **16** 69 – 84

Cappellin R, 1991a, "International networks of cities", in *Innovation Networks: A Spatial Perspective* Ed. R Camagni (Belhaven Press, London) pp 230 – 244

Cappellin R, 1991b, "Patterns and policies of regional economic development and the cohesion among the regions of the European Community", in *The State of Social and Economic Cohesion in the Community Prior to the Creation of the Single Market: The View from the Bottom-up* Ed. R Leonardi (Commission of the European Community, Bruxelles)

Cappellin R, 1992, "Theories of local endogenous development and international co-operation", in *Development Issues and Strategies in the New Europe* Ed. M Tykkylainen (Springer, Berlin) pp 1 – 19

Cappellin R, Molle W, 1988, "The coordination problem in theory and policy", in *Regional Impact of Community Policies in Europe* Eds W Molle, R Cappellin (Avebury, Aldershot, Hants) pp 1 – 22

CEC, 1991 *Europe 2000: Outlook for the Development of Community's Territory* (Commission of the European Communities, Bruxelles)

Konsolas N (Ed.), 1990 *Local Development: Regional Science Studies in Southern Europe* Regional Development Institute, Athens, Greece

Maillat D, 1990, "Transborder regions betwen members of the EC and non-member countries" *Built Environment* **16** 38 – 51

Nijkamp P, 1993, "Border regions and infrastructure networks in the European integration process" *Environment and Planning C: Government and Policy* **11**(4) forthcoming

The Prime Role of Regional Cooperation in European Integration[†]

A J Hingel
Commission of the European Communities

1 Europe: from *space* to *territories*

The Treaty on European Union was agreed upon in Maastricht, as a conclusion of more than forty years of debates, negotiations, and compromises between a 'federalist' and a 'functionalist' project for Europe. The first referendum in Denmark, which gave a narrow 'No' to Maastricht, the French referendum with its just as narrow 'Yes', and the parliamentary turmoil in the United Kingdom have already initiated a prolonged period of reflection.

In fact, it is useful to consider what European integration is all about. Should we be aiming for Tönnies's (1926) 'gesellschaft' ideal type where interest constellations are the only cause of development and motive of agreements? Have we dismissed the importance of a genuine community— 'gemeinschaft'—of people who, in solidarity, believe that they belong together? Is 'Europe' merely a common project between people who want to 'do things together' or between people who want to 'be together' (*faire ensemble/être ensemble* —see Pisani, 1993).

In the first case we imagine a *space* in the form of a marketplace which provides the optimal conditions for utilitarian and sectorial projects. In the second case we imagine a *territory* of peoples who believe they belong together in solidarity—that they belong to the same global social reality (Pisani, 1993).

In fact, both of these images constitute the reality of European integration. On the one hand, a 'European space' is being created by the Internal Market; the social space by the European Monetary Union. Products, services, capital, and labour will circulate within a European economic area with 380 million inhabitants and covering 43% of world trade. On the other hand, European integration is an integration of national, regional, and local territories.

The central question to answer is, therefore, not doctrinal—for or against a Europe of space or of territory—but pragmatic: will European integration not, by necessity, be a (hopefully peaceful) process where *territories in Europe* change by expanding, combining, and deepening in response to the possibilities that the *European space* without borders provides for boosting communication and exchange? And, may this process of integration not

---

[†] The viewpoints here are those of the author and not necessarily those of the Commission of the European Communities.

ultimately result in a Europe of unified territories which relate to a common European destiny and to a common European cultural project of future development, where the future of the territories is perceived by their citizens not as disconnected—as territories that happen to be in Europe—but in an integrated global manner as genuine *European territories*? The overall question is therefore: what influence does the European space have on the development of territories in Europe and what is the role of local actors?

2 Approaching European territories

The processes of European integration have mostly been studied and understood in terms of macroexpressions—*macroeconomic integration*. We know much less about the *microeconomic integration*, where the key factors of integration dynamics are the *strategies of actors* (social, economic, and institutional). Here cross-national cooperation comes to the fore.

In order to approach the development of European space and territories, it is central to look at the emergence in Europe of still-more-dense networks of cooperation, especially in the fields of science, technology, and innovation (Hagedoorn and Schakenraad, 1988). We are concerned here with what has been named *network-led integration*, which shows European integration as a twin process of changes in *spaces of flows* and in *spaces of places* (Bressand and Nicolaidis, 1990).

In fact, still-more-dense *spaces of flows* are being generated which increasingly ignore the limits of geographical and institutional borders of local communities, regions, countries, and the Community. These are flows of interaction, communication, cooperation, and information between socioeconomic actors and institutions. They are part of the general process of globalisation and internationalisation (Petrella, 1991). However, the importance of *spaces of places* as anchor grounds for the participation in the integration process—the process of regionalism and the importance of the regional economy, local production and innovation systems, industrial and technological districts—is amplified (Gaffard et al, 1993; Lundvall, 1992; Mlinar, 1992).

To approach these complex processes of European integration I will focus upon three dimensions, drawing on the results of a series of research studies which the FAST programme of the Commission of the European Communities has initiated in the fields of 'science, technology, and social and economic cohesion in the Community' (Hingel, 1992). First of all I will discuss the *spatial dimension* of integration by examining the indicators of spaces of flows and spaces of places as well as the regional faculties for participating in, and drawing benefits from, integration. Following this, I shall explore at the recent development of *regional cooperation* and its role in the integration process.

2.1 The spatial dimension of European integration

In order to understand the spatial dimension of European integration and its dynamics, I will identify, on the basis of available regional statistical data, the geographical areas in the EC which are characterised by a relatively high level of homogeneity. I shall then identify the participants in scientific and technological cooperation networks, their locations, and the network boundaries. Finally, I will measure, by statistical indicators, the faculties of the Community regions for participating in, and drawing benefits from, the integration process. Put briefly, I am concerned here with understanding the dynamics of the integration process, with the elaboration of a map of European integration, and with considerations of the future spatial development of the Community.

2.1.1 *Regional clusters—or European integration by megaregions*

Clusters of regions in Europe, which are characterised by relative homogeneity, could provide important information on European integration. These areas could be interpreted as indicators of latent, if not manifest, territories.

Regional diversity in the Community has been studied in terms of social, economic, cultural, and attitudinal characteristics by the application of the regional socioeconomic data series from EUROSTAT and the Euro-barometer opinion surveys (Bauer and Schmitt, 1990). The data series concerned are about: labour-force structure, unemployment, education, migration, economic structure, population density, gross value-added, rurality, services, religion, church attendance, satisfaction with life, and political party attachment. Without me presenting the detailed statistical analyses here, which include a factor analysis because of the great number of variables, it would be important to precis by a regional cluster analysis cross-regional areas which are characterised by a relatively high level of homogeneity, or cohesion (variance between regions is minimised within the cluster and maximised with respect to outside regions).

Three main results emerge from the study.

(1) The regional clusters are mostly *plurinational*. When ten clusters are identified, only a small minority (10%) of the EC populations [those in Brussels, the three German city-states, Norte (Portugal), and the Greek islands] live in uninational clusters of regions. This is not affected by 'stopping' the cluster analysis at an earlier point, when for example thirteen clusters have been identified. At a very early stage of the analysis we find that the Danish regions, for example, are clustered together with the English regions of East Anglia and the South West. This is the same in the case of the Benelux countries.

(2) The regional clusters are mostly *contiguous spatial areas*. The clusters are thus not, in general, made up of a series of individual spatially dispersed regions. The biggest of the clusters covers the whole geographical centre of the Community including most of the regions in Germany,

France, and the northern part of Italy. Other spatially contiguous clusters are, for example, the centre region of Greece which is grouped with the Mezzogiorno regions (Italy), or the region Sul do Continente (Portugal) clustered with Noroeste (Spain).
(3) Cross-national regional clusters are almost as strongly correlated with people's attitudes as with the national unit. This is considered to be a highly surprising result, as opinions and attitudes are normally found to be very closely related to the national communication system.

The present quality of regional statistical data suggests that we should treat the results of this analysis with prudence. Nevertheless, the possible existence of cross-national adjacent regional areas in the Community—they have been called 'megaregions'—within which, because of relative socio-economic and attitudinal homogeneity, the integration process might proceed faster than with any region 'outside' the area, indicates the importance of valid information on these processes. These cross-national megaregions provide a first input to the European map of integration.

2.1.2 *Cooperation networks—or centripetal integration*
A second approach to the understanding of the spatial dimension of European integration would be to identify the boundaries of cooperation networks and the location of networking actors. One area where coopera-tion has flourished within recent years is in science, technology, and innovation.

The study *Archipelago Europe* (Hilpert, 1992) was carried out in all EC countries as well as in the USA and Sweden. One of the preliminary steps in the study was to identify the location of contractors in public research programmes [EC, national, and regional research and technological devel-opment (RTD) programmes] in biotechnology, artificial intelligence, aero-nautics, and space for the ten-year period 1981–92.

In all of the countries studied one finds a few 'islands': relatively small, and mostly urban, local areas with a high concentration of contracting enterprises and research laboratories. In the case of biotechnology in Germany, eight islands are identified, each accounting for more than 5% of the total public R&D funding in the country: Rhein-Ruhr, Frankfurt am Main, Braunschweig/Hannover, Hamburg, Berlin, Stuttgart, Mannheim, and Munich. These eight islands together have as much as 80% of the total R&D public expenditures (in the case of general technological and microbiology research) in the studied period. It is not only the local concentration and the limited number of national islands which are signifi-cant, but also their *high specialisation* within specific scientific subfields (for example, 'medical electronics' and 'professional electronics' within the field of electronics in Île de France, or 'gentechnology' within the field of biotechnology in Heidelberg/Ludwigshafen).

On the basis of interviews, Hilpert goes on to show that the research laboratories and enterprises in this European archipelago of a few islands work together intensively in a highly exclusive network cooperation. Very few cooperation opportunities exist for outsiders; that is, laboratories and enterprises from regions outside these major islands. Only 5% of all cooperation partners in Europe are located in the less-developed regions of the Community (Objective 1 regions).

One can further observe a very high concentration of the strongest of these islands defined according to four criteria: islands which each account for more than 20% of the total public R&D spending of the study area; islands which have a strong presence both of laboratories and of enterprises; islands which master more than one technoscientific specialisation (of the three studied); and islands which are central 'knots' in the European web of scientific and technological cooperation. The EC core, from these criteria, is made up of only ten 'major European islands' which are all located in the old industrial area of Europe: Southeast England, Rotterdam/Amsterdam, Paris/Île de France, Rhein-Ruhr area, Frankfurt am Main, Stuttgart, Munich, Lyon/Grenoble, Turin, and Milan. In these ten islands, we find up to 80% of all the laboratories and enterprises that participate in cross-national cooperation (depending on the technoscientific field) in Europe. Within these islands, in most cases, one can observe intensive local cooperation aimed at science-based innovation.

The quality of the cooperative links between the major European islands of innovation and their partners outside in periphery regions indicates a clear mechanism of *regional grading*. The additional laboratories and enterprises, which participate in cooperation with partners in the major islands, are located further outside the European core if it is more likely that they are laboratories rather than enterprises, the smaller and more specialised the projects become, and if it is more likely that the cooperation is initiated by the biggest enterprises in the EC core. These mechanisms of regional grading all point towards an ever stronger European core, constituted geographically by the major islands of innovation.

In the recent DATAR study on cities in Europe, where a large number of indicators for the performance of cities were used, there is the same concentration (Datar-Reclus, 1989). Whether we look for the strongest European cities in terms of communications, economics, culture, multinationals, finance, engineers, technicians, administrators, the press and publishing, or international relations, we find, in general, the old European centre which is situated in the area between the south of England and the north of Italy. This is the so-called 'Blue Banana' area.

In fact, this centre has existed since the empire of Charlemagne. The development of Romanesque Art (in the 10th century to the 12th century), the renaissance, print shops, the main cities, and the transport infrastructure in the 15th century can all be found within its borders. The industrial revolution was born in the same 'major islands' in the European 'backbone' countries and regions. Correspondingly, the European peripheral areas and countries have a history of periphery.

The study by Hilpert (1992) indicates that the new generic technologies in areas such as biotechnology or artificial intelligence do not lead us to question the strength of the old historical European core regions. On the contrary, new technologies are used more efficiently by the core to strengthen its position and in the restructuring of old industrial sectors.

Network-led integration, from the principles of links between the core and the periphery regions described above, will reinforce a centripetal integration movement, strengthening the local areas situated between London and Milan which might increasingly convert towards a common and extremely competitive cross-national mode of development and innovation. The mode of innovation becomes local and cross-national, rather than national. At the same time this integration mechanism will reproduce the peripheral status of other regions in the Community, together with their strategic dependency on the core and consequently their lower level of development.

2.1.3 *Regional faculties of integration*
Participation in European integration can be looked at as a regional faculty. Some regions are more prepared and equipped to participate in, and to draw benefit from, the integration process than are others. The FAST programme initiated a statistical study on these regional faculties in two dimensions: the regional level of *accessibility*—the physical possibility of getting access to innovative ideas, new technologies, and investments from outside the regions—and *receptivity*—the ability to take into consideration, apply, and draw benefits from the same (Cadmos et al, 1991). The study was carried out by the Netherlands Economic Institute (NEI) on the basis of twenty-nine statistical indicators which were combined into five areas: economic development and specialisation, agglomeration economies, labour market, innovation and research infrastructure, and external orientation and cultural cohesion.

The research results show that the regions with the highest levels of both accessibility and receptivity to innovative ideas, new technologies, and investments can be found in a few core regions of the Community: Noord-Holland, Brabant, Île de France, Köln, Darmstadt, Stuttgart, Hamburg, and Oberbayern. In addition there are areas outside this centre which have significant capabilities: cities such as Hamburg, the capital region of Denmark, and regions in the 'North of the South' (Lombardy, Catalonia, Rhône-Alpes, Provence A, and Piemonte). These regions are thus best equipped for participating in, and drawing benefits from, the integration process. Compared with the situation ten years earlier, in 1981, when the study was first carried out with the same methodology but less-rich data (Boeckhout and Molle, 1982), one sees a significantly improved accessibility in the southern regions of Germany and France and the northern regions of Italy and Spain, but also a deterioration of the position of some southern regions (Centro, eastern continental Greece, and several Spanish regions) as well as some northern regions in the Community (such as East Anglia, Friesland, Drente).

2.2 Regional cooperation—a chief constituent of European integration

We can observe a very rapid development of cross-national cooperation agreements among regions, cities, chambers of commerce and industry, local trade-union sections (the CSIs), and so on. These cooperations have, to a large degree, been initiated with 'Europe' as a frame of reference. In the EC RECITE programme (Regions and Cities of Europe), which was launched in 1991, some 200 regions and cities currently participate in nearly forty networks.

Studies showing the European core, in the now famous Blue Banana (Datar-Reclus, 1989), have been the subject of many strategic reflections in regions and have inspired regions to consider their positioning in the European integration and to engage in regional cooperation. For example, the 'Atlantic Arc' cooperation between twenty-two Atlantic-coast regions (the European *Finistère* in the DATAR study) and the complex cooperation networks around the Baltic Sea were based on 'Banana debates'.
Baltic Sea were based on 'Banana debates'.

The cooperations initiated by regional authorities share the following characteristcs:

(1) they are often agreements of *widespread cooperation* in many, if not all, possible fields (economic, RTD, social, education and training, culture, tourism, sports, infrastructure development, and so on);

(2) they are agreements where *RTD cooperation* often plays a major role; and

(3) they are what the actors concerned themselves call *agreements between friends*, between *companions of development*, between *regions of affinity*.

Such regional cooperations include:

Atlantic Arc (regions in Portugal, Spain, France, the United Kingdom, and Ireland);

Atlantic Arc South (regions in Portugal, Spain, and France);

Saar-Lor-Lux-Trier/Westphalz (EUR region-B, Luxemburg, Germany, and France);

Baltic Sea cooperation (regions in all Baltic countries);

North Sea (coast regions in the United Kingdom, Denmark, and the Netherlands);

COTRAO, Arge-Alpes, Alpes-Adria (trans-Alpine cooperations);

Four Motors for Europe (regions in Spain, France, Italy, and Germany);

Dreiländereck (regions in Germany, Poland, and the former Czecho-slovakia);

Carpathian cooperation (EUR region-Hon, the Slovak Republic, Poland, and the Ukraine).

Most of these agreements have been initiated solely among EC regions. However, local cooperation across the external borders of the Community are strongly developing in the Baltic area, in the Balkans, and across the

Mediterranean Sea. The promotion and support of these cooperation setups, which are often initiated by the local representatives and actors themselves, is a crucial challenge to the Community and the countries concerned (Hingel, 1993). In many cases they represent the most likely prospect of development.

4 The integration of European territories—prospects and potential dangers
European integration is, as microeconomic integration, based on the territories of today, but at the same time integration challenges them to change, expand, combine, and deepen. These changes are accompanied by the creation of local, often cross-national, spaces within which socioeconomic and cultural integration proceed especially fast. I have given above the spatial configuration of such spaces as concerns *spaces of places* and *spaces of flows*. The main messages can be captured in four points.
(1) European integration progresses by cross-national regional spaces of cohesion. These cross-national cohesive areas, with relatively high levels of socioeconomic and attitudinal commonality, are not identical to the existing territories defined on the basis of ethnic or linguistic characteristics, but they might be indicators of future territories. The relatively strong cohesion within these areas means that one could expect communication, information exchange, and the circulation of products, services, capital, and labour to flourish, creating a sense of increasing belonging among citizens and a process of territorisation.
(2) Network-led integration creates dense *spaces of flows* between actors located in a few local areas. The majority of the participants in network cooperation are located in small, mostly urban, local areas—islands. Cross-national cooperation is dominated by actors from the ten strongest islands in the central core of Europe. However, in the area of science and technology, actors in these 'islands' develop their capacity to participate in cross-national cooperation by means of dense local cooperation. The local system of innovation and technology transfer is, in most cases, a *sine qua non* for participating in national as well as cross-national network-led integration.
(3) The regional capacity to participate in, and to draw benefits from, European integration is relatively dispersed, but is highest in a few regions in the core of Europe. European integration as a process of increasing transfers, of best practices, new technologies, and new knowledge will strengthen the relative position of a few central core regions in Europe. Improvement of the regions' capability of drawing benefits from, and participating in, European integration would have two major effects, both of which are central to the future of the regions and the Community. First, it would provide grounds for *counterbalancing*, in the medium and long term, the relative strength of the core regions, but, second, it would also provide the less-favoured regions with the means to *draw the maximum benefits from the strong core regions*.

(4) All the known examples of cross-national regional cooperations in the Community involve regions which are neither part of the same cross-national space of cohesion (compare above) nor of a common territory of ethnic or linguistic characteristics. Regional cooperation seems, therefore, to be a chief constituent of European integration, which valorises the existence of diverse regional cohesive areas in the Community and which improves the capacity of the weaker regions to draw benefit from the integration process. Regional cooperation in the Community thus plays a primordial role as a demiurge that renders European integration of spaces of flows, spaces of places, and territories possible as a peaceful and solidary process.

The French historian Alfred Grosser pronounced recently the following on a Europe of regions:

"There exists a risk that regions will act to satisfy their own needs. By this, it would follow that we would be missing the opportunity that could make the regions a place where the necessary solidarity to construct Europe could be rediscovered. A Europe of regions will not be creative unless it shows the example of solidarity, beyond the frontiers and beyond interest and cultures" (Grosser, 1993, my translation).

These risks count for little, however, compared with the dangers that may be faced if the ethnic self-interests call on *Blut and Boden* instead of promoting European union as an integration between interdependent and solidary European territories.

References

Bauer P, Schmitt H, 1990 *S/T and Regional Socio/Economic and Attitudinal Diversity* FAST Dossier: Science, Technology and Community Cohesion (Commission of the European Communities, Brussels)

Boeckhout S, Molle W T M, 1982 *Technical Change, Locational Patterns and Regional Development* (Commission of the European Communities, Brussels)

Bressand A, Nicolaidis K, 1990, "Regional integration in a networked world economy", in *The Dynamics of European Integration* Ed. W Wallace (Frances Pinter, London) pp 27–49

Cadmos S A, Netherlands Economic Institute, Roland Berger, 1991 *European Scenarios on Technological Change and Social and Economic Cohesion in the Community* FAST Dossier: Science, Technology and Community Cohesion (Commission of the European Communities, Brussels)

Datar-Reclus, 1989 *Les Villes Européennes* (European Cities) (La Documentation Française, Paris)

Gaffard J-L, Longhi Ch, Quere M, Ravix J-L, Boronat Ph, Canard F, 1993 *Cohérence et Diversité des Systèmes d'Innovation en Europe* (Coherence and Diversity of Systems of Innovation in Europe), FAST Dossier: Continental Europe Science, Technology and Cohesion (Commission of the European Communities, Brussels) forthcoming

Grosser A, 1993 *La Lettre de la Fondation: Europe et Societé* (Letter of the Foundation: Europe and Society) May, page 12

Hagedoorn J, Schakenraad J, 1988 *Strategic Partnering and Technological Cooperation* (University of Limburg, Maastricht)

Henderson J, Castells M (Eds), 1987 *Global Restructuring and Territorial Developments* (Sage, London)

Hilpert U, 1992 *Archipelago Europe—Islands of Innovation: Synthesis Report* FAST Dossier: Science, Technology and Community Cohesion (Commission of the European Communities, Brussels)

Hingel A J, 1992 *Science, Technology and Community Cohesion—RTD Policy Recommendations* FAST Dossier: Science, Technology and Community Cohesion (Commission of the European Communities, Brussels)

Hingel A J, 1993, "Sam-udvikling på tværs af EF's ydre grænser" (Co-development across the external borders of the EC) *Samfundsøkonomen* 3 April, 21 – 24

Lundvall B Å (Ed.), 1992 *National Systems of Innovation: Towards a Theory of Innovation and Interactive Learning* (Frances Pinter, London)

Mlinar Z (Ed.), 1992 *Globalization and Territorial Identities* (Avebury, Aldershot, Hants)

Petrella R D, 1991 *Four Analyses of Globalization of Technology and Economy* (Commission of the European Communities, Brussels)

Pisani E, 1993, "Pour un aménagement du territoire européen" (On territorial development in Europe), in *L'Événement Européen* 21 203 – 211

Tönnies F, 1926 *Gemeinschaft und Gesellschaft* (Community and Society) (Berlin)

The Border Region Challenge Facing Norden: Applying New Regional Concepts

N Veggeland
NordREFO, Copenhagen

1 Introduction

There is every reason to believe that the current 'map of Europe' will have to be redrawn by the year 2000. Doubtless, national boundaries will still exist, but they will be less important, and the faint outline of a 'borderless Europe' will be discernible. Furthermore, new borders will also have become apparent, representing an embryonic 'Europe of regions'.

Current research is therefore focused on defining the character of the present regionalisation process and identifying criteria for establishing the new boundaries. As a result, the following questions may be posed. How are regions built? How do they develop? What patterns follow? Are they a result of governmental regional planning or spontaneous regional movements? When are they built as a result of top-down political factors or, alternatively, as a result of bottom-up dynamics? What gives European region-building its strength, durability, and variety? Too often we believe, perhaps overoptimistically, that even the immediate and mid-term future will be radically different from the present. It will not be. Catastrophes apart, future conditions will be a continuation of the past, even though they are evolving all the time.

But an important distinction should always be made between naive and complex heavy trends. Naive trends are based on rough extrapolations of quantifiable development tendencies, whereas complex-trend descriptions are based on a mixture of empirical facts and qualified, visionary options (Godet, 1987; Naisbitt, 1982). It is important to bear this in mind when one goes on to focus on heavy trends, especially when the subject matter embraces the evolution—and devolution—of Europe in terms of regionalisation. The future of Europe continues to be based on a legacy of heavy trends rather than on current political manifestations and agreements (Veggeland, 1992a).

Heavy trends have many aspects. In research they represent an empirical basis on which to construct hypothetical models which may later become paradigms. Scientists producing such paradigms select trends on which to justify them. Each period in history has its particular paradigms, bolstered by a suitable set of observed and confirmed trends. The paradigms are to serve the interests of society. However, as history evolves, events eventually lead to a break in the verity of long-accepted paradigms. New heavy trends set in as a result of new preferences, and therefore new paradigms have to be produced to explain the new state of affairs. This leads automatically to new sets of values and facts that come to be accepted by society (Kuhn, 1962).

It is vital to understand that trends within society are exceedingly complex phenomena and subject to vested interests and politics. Research sociologists choose trends as their basis for establishing facts, and this is by no means a neutral or unbiased process. Knowledge is motivated and guided by interest (Habermas, 1968), and herein lies the desire to change the direction in which society is going.

New times bring new trends. The situation may be comparable to the movement of wave formations. A wave builds up out at sea, moves landwards, and becomes exhausted on the shore. The process repeats itself again and again. Trends are similar to waves; they are produced again and again. However, the choice of the trend or trends on which to lay the foundation of new knowledge to influence the evolution of society is imperative.

Sociologists and politicians ought to accept the fact that old trends have to be left to history. However, the opposite is often true. Old trends, which still form the dominant paradigms, are usually only very slowly replaced, perhaps with great reluctance in some circles. History shows that a conflict always develops between old schools of thought and the new ideologists; a conflict between conservative forces and new progressive forces (Kuhn, 1962). This fact is apparent in the early 1990s and is related to the region-building process in Europe in which there is a heavy trend to replace the paradigm based on the nation-state by one based on regional power.

Before we move on, a distinction must be made between the terms 'nation-state' and 'nation'. A nation-state may consist of several nations and regions which it integrates and controls. Is the European nation-state about to become extinct; that is, become a paradigm of the past? It still represents the main framework of political, economic, and cultural administration. Likewise, are the 'new-wave formations' of internationalisation and regionalisation going to become the new heavy trends forming the new paradigms for fact-finding and political development? There are many experts who believe that this will be the case (Alemand, 1979; Cappellin, 1990; Gerner, 1990; Hedegaard and Veggeland, 1991; Veggeland, 1992b).

For the past two centuries, the nation-state has been the main expression of heavy trends, and has represented the dominant paradigm, shaping national and regional development. Other kinds of regions (ethnic, common language, or cultural regions) have been integrated into the nation-state and forced to accept its authority. The state system has evolved in a highly complex way, imposing its legitimacy upon its subjects as if its sovereignty was quite naturally and irrevocably predetermined.

However, a change is coming about. Today, society is evolving differently. Regional researchers show that a paradigm transformation with regard to national and regional development is under way.

The nation-state seems to be terminating its role as the omnipotent, universal, regional problem-solver. To wriggle out of this impasse, in an attempt to give credence to its survival, the European nation-state has created supranational organs, such as the European Community. However, this move is contradictory because of the irreversible weakening of its institutions and universal legitimacy.

On the other hand, dynamic regional movements and regionalisation are emerging as forces to be reckoned with. The apparent weakening of the nation-state does not mean that it will disappear entirely. It will continue long after the year 2000, but its role will alter in the new paradigm which will be based on an internationalised and regionalised Europe.

2 Three reasons behind internationalisation and regionalisation

2.1 Economic internationalisation

With regard to economic forces, much of the GNP of most European nation-state economies is already a result of an internationalisation process stretching back many decades. In economic literature, the following terms are well known: multinational companies, international network economies, flexible specalised production systems, industrial areas and clusters, international division of labour, and so on (Porter, 1990; Scott, 1990). This means that European industrial concerns, which are fundamentally dependent on export trade, have already undergone the international integration process. This part of the European economy knows no national boundaries.

The EC economy was already a vigorously functioning, internationalised entity long before recent political decisions on the Single Market were affecting it. International business cooperation and networks are the result of spontaneous, commercial, decisionmaking processes which are independent of political planning. The move by the EC to establish the Single Market, with its free movement of goods, capital, services, and labour to remove some practical hindrances, is more a political confirmation; or an attempt at giving politics a legitimate claim to being the real cause behind economic internationalisation (Cecchini et al, 1988).

Another opinion is that clusters, networks, flexible internationally distributed production systems, and the division of labour in Europe are located in specific areas, in industrial conurbations, for example. Such areas will be characterised by a mutually dependent relationship between particular economic activities and their high population densities. Likewise, the different European regions are intricately bound together and are very interdependent. They are actually forced to work in conjunction with each other as a result of the high degree of internationalisation inherent in the current European economy. It requires interregional regimes of a new character to function.

Moreover, herein lies the very development potential. The current heavy trends in Europe indicate that this fact ought to be an incitement to a strategic interregional development plan, with the construction of large functional regions. The point is that such strategic planning and cooperation will give a comparative advantage through the resulting common utilisation of resources and the realisation of the development potential. Quite simply, competitive advantage will be increased (Europe 2000, 1992; Stöhr, 1990).

2.2 Political internationalisation based on regional stimuli

As seen above, the economic integration in Europe is highly advanced. Whether this is also true of political integration is doubtful: "Europa Müde"—"Europe Is Tired"—read the recent headlines in the German newspaper *Die Welt* with regard to the latest stalling of the Maastricht Treaty. The Maastricht Treaty was apparently an attempt to make the political, cohesive integration of Western Europe a natural sequel to economic integration.

However, the whole problem is the result of the Maastricht Treaty and its inherent 'federal union' concept, being obviously made for the benefit of the nation-states involved. After all, it was created by them in the first place! The Danish 'No' to Maastricht in June 1992 highlighted the fact that, in a democratic country, a federation cannot just be *imposed upon* the citizens. Yet the Danish 'No' was not the root cause of the current 'malaise'; it was merely a symptom of the ancient, deeper-rooted, common democratic awareness that pervades many European societies. Many observers are quick to point out that a mental gap due to irreconcilable perceptions and beliefs, or lack of cohesion, exists between the political leaders and the citizens of certain European nations.

In spite of the outcry caused by the desperate attempt to bulldoze the Maastricht Treaty through the ratification process before the citizens realised what was happening, the main problems plaguing European integration have not yet been solved. There is a lack of social and economic cohesion in Europe. The list of problems is a long one: inefficient currency exchange-rate mechanism, rising unemployment, deficiencies in human rights legislation, lack of international coordination against rising crime, mounting environmental issues, and safeguarding security, to name but a few.

Many problems could be solved through international cooperation. Nevertheless, it would seem that the regional level is the best basis for future cooperation. Mobilising the regions can certainly compensate for the lack of cohesion at the nation-state level (Veggeland, 1993).

2.3 Ethnic and cultural impulses influencing integration

European social and cultural integration is highly unlikely—nigh impossible—this side of the year 2000. In fact the opposite is more likely to be the case as Europe is experiencing a resurgence of ethnic and cultural values, so long repressed. There are national, regional, and even very local demands for autonomy, as well as the need for greater legal recognition of the cultural and ethnic authenticity of identity groups. This movement represents the postmodernistic spirit (Harvey, 1990). The phenomenon has historical, cultural, and political roots. Nevertheless it stresses the new heavy trend towards regionalisation and region-building. This is occurring through regional movements which demand independence and autonomy from the nation-state in order to preserve unique cultures and identities.

3 Which regions?

A likely scenario for the evolution of European development towards the year 2000 is that regions will continue to emerge from their slumbers and play a greater role within the political, economic, and cultural arena. This will be in accordance with the heavy development trend mentioned above. Regional cooperation, alliances, and partnerships will answer the call made by an internationalised economy on infrastructure and official engagement. Furthermore, the role of the regions in the integration process will put them in a stronger position to control capital movements in accordance with the principles of subsidiarity.

The scenario describes increased regional integration which will reduce the lack of political harmony that continues to paralyse the nation-states of Europe in the post-Maastricht-Agreement era. Regions will cooperate on a sectoral and functional basis. They will solve the problems of collaboration now existing in trade, infrastructural development, environmental issues, and cultural matters.

The scenario implies that the heavy trend towards increased socio-cultural fragmentation in Europe requires regionalisation as the natural resolution level. This will satisfy those of the regional movements who are seeking to imprint their different identities on the map of Europe by winning autonomy, in contrast to the top-heavy, cumbersome apparatus of the nation-states.

The scenario therefore advocates a new paradigm on which to base region-building and regionalisation in Europe. European regional researchers ought to develop their new knowledge and fact-finding on the basis of this new paradigm. Yet, which regions will come to emerge within the framework of the new paradigm produced by the new heavy trend in development? What empirical evidence is available to enable the region-building of Europe to be categorised?

Based on a set of studies on European regionalisation, a simple model has been constructed to elucidate current processes (table 1) (Veggeland, 1992a; 1992b). The model is academic, but also constructive. It is a framework for policymaking and planning, today and tomorrow. The model is based on the regionalisation process in Europe and Norden being an empirical fact. Several points about the model are worth mentioning. *First*, it includes the well-known 'administrative regions' which have developed within the confines of the nation-state framework.

Administration regions have been used in the implementation and administration of laws and directives from the supranational EC Commission which occupies the top position in the hierarchy. The nation-state hierarchy includes local and municipal authorities, such as: the Nordic counties (fylker/län/amter), the UK counties, French départements, German Länder, and so on.

The hotly debated issue of the moment is about at which hierarchical level to apply the subsidiarity principle. Perception differs from country to country. It was the Maastricht Treaty which introduced the idea of the subsidiarity principle to give greater power to the lowest appropriate, competent level within the hierarchies of nations and regions in order to compensate for the increased decision power at the top; for example, the EC supranational level.

Moreover, the recent revelation of the inadequacies inherent in the Maastricht Treaty has intensified the desire to introduce the subsidiarity principle. The question is how? The EC Commission deems it best to apply subsidiarity by means of the existing hierarchical structure of the nation-state. In so doing, the nation-state will keep control of the decentralised decisionmaking. The EC is to guarantee the overall competence and maintenance of standards. The debate as to whether this is the correct path to follow resembles the debate prevalent since the 1970s in the Nordic countries concerning the tripartite, functional division of administrative responsibility between the state, counties, and municipal authorities (Amdam and Veggeland, 1991).

The burning need for decentralisation is based on the necessity to establish a broader decision-base and a more efficient, problem-solving, project-initiating apparatus. Lethargy in these areas has plagued the EC for years, but the transfer of resposnsibility and capital to regional actors will have a dynamic effect as it will automatically engender a mobilisation of local forces as soon as it is implemented.

Table 1. A model for future region building in Europe.

Type of region	Actors	
	top down the supranational EC	bottom up regional movements
Administrative regions Functional regions Identity regions	↓	↑
	Hierarchy Control Standardisation Economic growth	Autonomy Influence Variety Cultural aspects
	Politically dynamic	

Second, there are 'functional regions', identifiable on the basis of functional interaction and integration across territories. The functional interaction may be vertical through urban hierarchies, in which specialisation takes place and the large cities take on more important functions and preside over the lower settlement levels. The cities are connected and integrated by a comprehensive infrastructural network that makes them urban agglomerations. Such an organised hierarchy can, under certain conditions, generate growth and development, as described both in classical and in neoclassical central place theories (Christaller, 1966; Jacobs, 1985).

The result of this functional development based on the greater importance of certain locations may be seen in Europe today at its most highly complex level in the sprawling conurbations. On a map, they appear linked to one another over hundreds of kilometres. As many of these elongated, population agglomerations resemble a banana in shape, they have been dubbed 'bananas'. The best example is the 'Blue Banana' which stretches southwards from the English Midlands and London, through Belgium, the Ruhr, Frankfurt, and München, to Torino and Milano in northern Italy. This axis may be accepted as the European core, along which a substantial concentration of the European population is to be found. During the 1980s a further 'banana' was justly identified as a result of the enormous economic and industrial expansion of southern Europe since the Second World War. The 'Green Banana' stretches from the industrial zones of northern Italy, passes westwards through Marseilles, includes the Rhône corridor, and continues to encompass the boomtowns of eastern Iberia: Barcelona and Valencia (Illeris, 1992; Linzie and Boman, 1991; Veggeland, 1992a).

But functional cooperation between regions can also occur horizontally. Interregional alliances are formed by public actors (local municipal authorities, public utility networks, and cultural, scientific, and educational institutions) or by private actors (industrial concerns, the travel industry, financial bodies, business service organisations, and various companies responsible for basic services). Together they form a series of multifarious networks of widely differing spatial range, geographically and with regard to intensity. They create, in effect, 'functional regions'. They are independent of normal administrative boundaries. Therefore it is quite natural for them to cross one or more administrative boundaries.

A common identity, perhaps the result of a certain homogeneity or apparent advantages of interaction, has led to the establishment of functional regions in the European context; such as the cross-boundary cooperation between Holland and Germany (Euroregi region), or the work being carried out between 'the four motors of Europe'—Catalonia, Lombardy, Rhône-Alpes, and Baden-Württemberg. There are many others, and all of them are able to take economic advantage of the so-called EC Interregional Programme.

The dynamics behind the building of functional regions, with reference to Europe, is twofold. One aspect is the top-down initiative, which is typical of the administrative hierarchies in the nation-states; the other is the bottom-up initiative, which is typical of 'the four motors of Europe' as a result of a low-level, regional movement in which the advantages of economic collaboration are achieved without the loss of cultural identity and autonomy. The second initiative is typical of identity regions (see the third point below) that wish to develop an effective functionality within the 'regions of Europe' concept.

Third, it is possible to identify 'identity regions' on the basis of the historical and cultural homogeneity found within a specific geographical territory. The diversity of European identity regions is underlined by the fact that the continent has as many as sixty-seven different languages, whereas there are only just over thirty nation-states. Naturally, this fact causes dissatisfaction, particularly among minorities whose language and culture have been repressed for decades or even centuries; leading to strong nationalistic and regional movements in order to gain independence and autonomy. The language problem is exacerbated by differences pertaining to dialect.

Lord Tebbit, a leading UK Conservative Party politician, has been quoted as saying that "no folk will ever accept being governed by people speaking another language". That fact will become more apparent as the nation-states falter in their bid to retain complete control over their territories. Tragic consequences are already apparent in the Balkans as a result of fundamentalist regional movements. However, there *are* success stories, and these will shortly be focused upon. Constructive and positive forces influencing the regionalisation process must be cherished and nurtured, as they show the way forward (Östhol, 1991).

Constructive region-building can occur, based on the principles shown in table 1. It happens when an 'identity region' seeks to make its people's common identity the main potential for the development of functional regions and the acquisition of administrative powers; that is, in accordance with the subsidiarity principle, but without a hierarchical framework. Examples of how this positive development works in practice will now be given via three case studies from Norden.

4 Three case studies from Norden
4.1 The Baltic region: functional or identity region?
Great uncertainty exists with regard to the future development of the Baltic region, occasionally referred to as the Baltic Rim. Scenarios of potential regional development paths in the Baltic region must be based on a stable set of conditions in order to become a reality.

The first essential condition is political stability in the nasent East. Another prerequisite is economic support from the Western world to create economic growth in the region, and the acceptance by the Western world to be reponsible for a coherent development within its regional neighbours. Then, seen in a Northern European context, the region represents an enormous potential market for investment in business, infrastructure, and the environment. It will also become a major consumer market once its purchasing power rises.

We advocate development, and yet we are also aware of the need to protect the environment. We also know that the region has a high population density and a high degree of urbanisation (table 2). Concentrated within the north–south belt of land between Lappland County in Finland in the north and Kaliningrad in the south, there are seventeen million inhabitants; almost equal to the combined population totals of Denmark, Sweden, and Finland.

Taking these conditions as the starting point, the following may be said. The August Revolution of 1991 which dissolved the Soviet Union and created the conditions for the emergence of independent republics, including the Baltic States, has in fact not only created a 'new political Europe' but also opened up an enormous economic frontier zone. On account of its enormous dimensions, the Baltic region must be considered in the near future as a potential European-core area, seen from a European perspective. The regional growth rate, measured in GNP, may approach what we already experience in the southern regions of the European core (that is, in the 'Green Banana') because the need to develop the frontier areas is very great.

The nation-states that form the Baltic Region (Denmark, Germany, Poland, Lithuania, Latvia, Estonia, Finland, Russia, Sweden, and Norway) now have a representative body, the Baltic Council, which was established in Copenhagen in March 1992. The Foreign Ministers of the different countries signed the agreement. The former German Foreign Minister, Dietrich Genscher, advocated a 'Europe of regions' which included the Baltic region when he said, "Europe benefits from its regional diversity and the Baltic region is the latest contribution to increase this diversity". Declarations made at the end of the meeting included an agreement to tackle a series of tasks through regional cooperation: the development of the infrastructure, economic development, securing human rights, improving

Table 2. The East Baltic region: demographic facts, 1990 (source: Dellenbrant, 1991).

Area	Territory (1000 km²)	Population (thousands)	Density (km⁻²)	Urbanisation (%)
Karelia	172	796	5	82
St Petersburg region	86	6698	77	66
Estonia	45	1538	35	72
Latvia	65	2687	42	71
Lithuania	65	3723	58	68
Kaliningrad region	15	878	56	79

the environment, strengthening democratic institutions, and the eventual incorporation of all the Baltic member states into the EC.

Above all, the Baltic region will be defined and territorially divided on the basis of agreements made between the existing regions in the area, not the nations. The EC Commission's Directorate of Regional Policy, DG XVI, has apparently understood this need.

A series of impact studies on the future regional and spatial development in Europe will form the basis of a revision of the EC document on strategy: "Europe 2000" (the so-called 'Major document'). An obligatory task for the Nordic Impact Study Group, under the supervision of Nord-REFO, was to focus upon the interrelationship between Norden and the new-neighbour region to the east. The Baltic region will be described with a view to future cooperation and potential development towards the year 2000. The study is included in the work "The Impact of the Development of the Nordic Countries on Regional Development and Spatial Organization in the European Community" which was presented to the EC Commission in June 1993 (Veggeland et al, 1993).

What are the potential patterns of region-building in the greater Baltic region? Several questions need to be answered before patterns may emerge. Based on the political and economic conditions described above, what kinds of regional territories and regional development patterns within the Baltic region will ensure the region's political stability and sustained economic growth? What scenarios incorporate the factors and activities leading to the creation of functional regions? Is there reason or cause for the establishment of 'identity regions' based on a common language, common culture, and common history? How will the principle of subsidiarity, the need for regional partnership, and the development of infrastructure be applied to shape region-building in the Baltic region? What knowledge do we already possess to help answer all these questions and more?

First I will tackle the 'identity region' concept. It could be said that the Baltic states resulted from regional bottom-up movements which fought for their identity within the structure of the former Soviet Union. The product was the formation of identity regions which ended as independent nations. In other words, these regions have struggled for the right to define and organise themselves as functional and administrative units within a national framework.

Yet are there still other regional movements in the Baltic region which are fighting for national identity? One might identify the transnational Lapp groups in northern Scandinavia and Russia, or else the Åland Islands which, on the basis of their strong historical connection with the Swedish culture and language, already enjoy special rights within the framework of the Finnish constitution. However, these population groups are particularly small in number.

Of greater interest is the attempt to find a historical, territorial identity to rationalise the development of functional regions in the Baltic region. In his Swedish report, "The march towards doom for the past two hundred years of erroneous European development characterised by nationalism, racism and the territorial national state" (title translated), the historian Kristian Gerner attempts to define a functional region in the southern Baltic region based on historical identity (Gerner, 1990). His idea is based on the former territory controlled by the Hanseatic League whose towns were efficiently organised in a network partnership stretching from Bergen in the west to Novogorod in the east. Using modern terms, he seeks to legitimise the renaissance of this former 'functional Baltic region'.

It is only natural that the spirit of the old Hanseatic League fires the imagination when one considers region-building in the north. One strives to unearth historical ties. In the same way, one could hark back to the historical Pomor Trade which used to link northern Norway and northern Russia in the 19th century. This was also set up in order to inspire partnerships within certain regional frameworks such as Nordkalotten, which is a northern functional region based on partnerships which extended as far south as the Baltic Sea (see below). Evoking historical constellations is naturally inspiring and all very well, but what is most essential when labelling the Baltic area as a region in its own right is its future role as an area of functional cooperation, regional partnership, and network establishment. It is therefore this functional regional concept which is important, and thus the Baltic region must be considered as a functional region. It is also important to understand that the Baltic region itself may be divided into several functional subregions.

One impetus to the creation of functional regions in the Baltic area is the need to develop cohesion between the new regions of both its eastern and its western parts. The deep economic and social gap which divides the various Baltic subregions must be eradicated so as to guarantee fair cooperation. Today there is obviously a geographical cohesion due to the binding force of the Baltic Sea itself. A further cohesive element might well be the traditionally high standard of education in the region as a whole, but particularly at the university level, which has already been the basis of international university cooperation and ought to be the spring-board to even greater interaction and more-mature relations. But the economic and social cohesion is definitely unsatisfactory at present.

Thus a further impetus to functional region-building will depend on the willingness of the West to contribute to the anticipated economic growth of the 'new' Eastern Europe. European development, according to the works on 'the regions of Europe' (CEC, 1992; Linzie and Boman, 1991), is not just a question of nations fighting for market shares or growth factors. Regions compete as well, and they are becoming more important as central actors on the politico-economic scene.

A third source of energy to fuel functional region-building must come from the regional and local actors themselves. Evidence suggests that development in the Baltic region does not start with decisions made by the nation-states, but through pressure and lobbying at the grass-roots level and from enterprises and regional networks; in other words, subsidiarity in practice. Alternatively, cooperative relationships and partnerships may be established. In conclusion, it would be true to say that it will be local actors rather than the transnational Baltic Sea Council who will become the region-builders.

The final essential impetus to functional region-building in the Baltic area will be the improvement of the infrastructure: roads, railways, ferry and air routes, and telecommunications. The question remains: how, where, and when will this infrastructural unification occur?

Certain sections are already at the planning phase and the construction of certain road–rail connections is possible within this decade: the Øresund Bridge/Tunnel linking Denmark and Sweden, and the Fehmarn Sea Belt project linking Germany with Denmark. A planned motorway expansion in eastern Germany is the inevitable result of German unification. The motorway network will extend to the eastern Baltic area around the Gulf of Finland, centring on Helsinki/St Petersburg, as the 'Hanseatic Highway', 'Via Baltica', and road and rail development will take place all the way north to the Kola Peninsula. New ferry links will also be established in the Baltic Sea.

We know perfectly well that functional region-building can only be made on the basis of a responsible and efficient physical infrastructure. As yet, we do not know precisely how it will develop in the Baltic region. In summary, we may assume that as long as stable conditions exist for political and economic development, the Baltic region will clearly be a functional region which can become a new economic and cultural 'centre of gravity' in Europe, but its territorial extent is not well defined (Gerner, 1990; Veggeland, 1992b). Within its area, subregions will develop.

4.2 Åland: an identity region within the greater Baltic region

The Åland Islands, lying midway between the Swedish and Finnish mainlands in the Baltic Sea, belong to the Finnish nation-state. There are 25000 inhabitants. With the terminology used here, Åland complies at first sight with our concept of an administrative region. However, Åland is more than that. An international rights declaration, just after the First World War, allowed the islands to become an autonomous, demilitarised area within Finland.

Åland makes its own laws, shapes its own financial policies, tailors its industrial development, and enters into trade agreements. On the other hand, Åland is not allowed to make its own fiscal policy, but it does have the right to veto international agreements signed by Finland which come within the sphere of its legislative competence.

Historically and culturally, Åland is more closely related to Sweden than to Finland. Indeed, Swedish is the mother tongue. Åland is rather unique, and is justified in considering itself an identity region on the basis of several criteria.

Finland is currently applying for EC membership. This gives Åland the opportunity to strengthen its autonomy within an internationalising Finland. Åland aims at achieving special status within the EC. First, it demands the right to make its own fiscal legislation. Its strategic weapon is its veto right to opt out of international agreements made by the EC; a line of argument currently pursued by Finland as well. It should be mentioned that during the EEA Agreement, Åland was granted special rights on the basis of Article 26.

In table 1, Åland may be considered as a homogeneous identity region, its political aspirations indicated by the upward-pointing arrow on the right-hand side of the diagram. It is attempting to expand its horizontal powers within international society and thus metamorphose into a functional region. Compared with Finland, Åland has less unemployment because of its stronger economy. Its potential as a functional region in its own right cannot be denied.

Literally all Ålanders are intent on winning total autonomy for the region, both economically and culturally. Moreover, they are seeking to establish themselves as an independent, administrative region by gaining full legislative and administrative powers. Now (1993), Åland seems to be on the point of succeeding, as a result of the current wave of regionalisation rolling across Europe. It stands just a hair's breadth away from being the manifestation of subsidiarity outside the traditional, hierarchical administrative structure. The way forward shown by Åland may, in some ways, act as a precedent for future region-building. Its example might be followed by other European regions in their quest for regional autonomy (Lindström, 1992).

4.3 The Barents region: a functional region

This new region is of an entirely different nature. It is the product of a top-down initiative in which the Norwegian Foreign Ministry has played a major role. The basis for cooperation is entrusted in seven administrative regions: northern Nordland, Troms, Finmark, Swedish Norrboten, Finnish Lappland, and the Russian counties of Murmansk and Archangel. The autonomous Republic of Karelia has also expressed its wish to participate in the work. The aim of the septenary association is to establish a functional region on the basis of horizontal integration (Jervell, 1992).

The Barents Council and the Regional Council are the most important administrative and political bodies. The Barents Council is made up of . representatives from Norway, Sweden, Finland, Iceland, Denmark, and Russia. The Regional Council consists of actors from the seven regions involved. Its task is to promote region-building through mobilising private and public investment, as well as stimulating and sponsoring local actors to play dynamic roles.

The agreement on mutual cooperation was signed in 1993 by the ministerial foreign secretaries of each country with territory incorporated into the Barents region, as well as by representatives for each of the seven county councils. The EC Commission signed as well, thereby expressing an equal interest in cooperating with Russia as part of the regime of the Barents region. Subject to the outcome of current negotiations, the Nordic Council of Ministers may also sign the agreement.

The task of the Regional Council is to make functional the horizontal cooperation, and furthermore give the region a strong identity. It must establish institutions which will take on much administrative responsibility. The newly appointed Secretariat is based in the Norwegian Arctic coastal town of Kirkenes, and the Norwegian government has granted NKr 250 million as a start to the envisaged regional development. The Finnish government has also contributed by being involved in environmental research projects, such as the widespread implications for the Barents region's environment of the highly polluting industrial district of Murmansk.

An expressed aim, integral to the treaty, is that development should adhere, within reason, to EC policy. Progress should be compatible with the concurrent political and economic integration process involving the EC and Norden.

Owing to its particular institutional form and special construction, the Great Barents region is unique in Europe. It will be interesting to see whether other European transnational regions crossing the former Iron Curtain will be born. The main characteristics of the Great Barents region may be defined as follows: a vast territory, a harsh climate, a dispersed low-density population, a coexistence of several indigenous peoples, and a wealth of untapped resources. As the statistics show, the natural resources are truly enormous in this region.

The functional region comprises seven administrative regions: Nordland, Troms, and Finmark in Norway; Norrboten in Sweden; Lappland in Finland; and Murmansk county (including Murmansk city with 1 155 000 inhabitants) and Archangel county in Russia. Out of this 'patchwork quilt' the intention is to establish a functional region on a horizontal-integration basis more than a vertical one because of the large distances separating the widely scattered cities and towns. The higher political organs are the Barents Council and the Regional Council. The aim is to make the horizontal cooperation functional by giving it administrative powers, at the same time establishing a strong regional identity, according to table 1.

The regional task ahead demands effective cooperation between the subregions on the following issues: polar resource utilisation, trade principle formulation, environmental problem-solving, and security assurance in the light of the transition taking place in post-Communist Russia. Beyond the regional development tasks, the Barents region seeks to win recognition as an identity region. For more than 1000 years, the region has been dependent upon its well-established, interregional trade links. An important part of this network was the Pomor trade which operated until approximately the start of this century. However, the former trade links were abruptly severed as a result of the Bolshevik Revolution in Russia, the events following the year 1917, as well as the geographical division of the area because of the encroachment of the Soviet Union and the imposition of a new border during the Finno–Russian dispute during the Second World War. The dissolution of the Soviet Union has been too recent to allow the former cohesion of the whole region to manifest itself yet, therefore the current identity based on homogeneity is very weak today.

Linguistically the region is split into three, radically different, main languages: Russian, Finnish, and Norwegian or Swedish. This hampers interregional communication and network-building. Cultural differences tend to be divisive rather than unifying, particularly when one also considers the conflict between the original nomadic culture of the Lapps and their contrasting fixed or rigid settlement patterns and infrastructure; symbols of modern-day Western society, which has increased in importance during this century in the region.

The Barents region lacks the unifying inspiration necessary to mobilise and act in the same way as Åland. It lacks a common identity. Its future is therefore very dependent on its being able to establish itself as an effective functional region.

In conclusion, it would seem that the most important problems confronting the nascent Barents region will first and foremost concern the exploitation of the natural resources in the polar regions, the establishment of trade principles, the solution of the threatening environmental problems, and the security problem in relation to the unstable political situation in post-Communist, renascent Russia. We must assume that policies will be agreed upon during the ensuing cooperation between the different constituent members of the Barents region in order to guarantee the responsible extraction and processing of the vast wealth of natural resources and at the same time guarantee the protection and preservation of the highly vulnerable Arctic ecosystems and their endangered species of flora and fauna. In addition, future policy should also aim at effectualising the North East Passage trade route to Asia. This will require advanced technological solutions to overcome the pack-ice barrier, allowing commercial shipping to thrive and representing a major historical breakthrough for the Arctic core region.

References
Alemand F R, 1979 *Aufstand der Regionen* (The Regions Recreated) (Piper, Frankfurt am Main)
Amdam J, Veggeland N, 1991 *Teorier om Samfunnsplanlegging* (Theories on Planning) (The Scandinavian University Press, Oslo)
Cappellin R, 1990, "The European internal market and the internationalization of small and medium-sized enterprises" *Built Environment* **16** 69–84

CEC, 1992 *Europe 2000: Outlook for the Development of the European Community's Territory* (Commission of the European Community, Brussels)

Cecchini P, and others, 1988 *The European Challenge* (Gower, Aldershot, Hants)

Christaller W, 1966 *Central Places in Southern Germany* (Prentice-Hall, Englewood Cliffs, NJ)

Dellenbrant J Å, 1991, "The re-emergence of multi-partism in the Baltic states", in *The New Democracies in Eastern Europe: Party Systems and Political Cleavages* Eds S Berglund, J Å Dellenbrant (Gower, Aldershot, Hants) pp 71 – 106

Gerner K, 1990, "Två hundra års europeisk utvekling—karaktäriserat av nationalismen, rasismen och territorialstaten—går mod sit slut" (The march towards doom for the past two hundred years of erroneous European development characterized by nationalism, racism and the territorial national state) *Nord Revy* **5/6** 11 – 16 (NordREFO, Copenhagen)

Godet M, 1987 *Scenarios and Strategic Management* (Butterworth, Sevenoaks, Kent)

Habermas J, 1968 *Erkenntnis und Interesse* (Suhrkamp, Frankfurt am Main) published in English in 1972 as *Knowledge and Human Interest* (Heinemann Educational Books, London)

Harvey D, 1990 *The Condition of Postmodernity* (Basil Blackwell, Oxford)

Hedegaard L, Veggeland N, 1991, "Den inverterte stat-regionalismens neste trinn" (The inverted state—the next step of the new regionalism) *Nord Revy* **3** 9 – 16 (NordREFO, Copenhagen)

Illeris S, 1992, "Urban and regional development in Western Europe in the 1990s—a mosaic rather than the triumph of the 'Blue Banana'" *Scandinavian Housing and Planning Research* **9** 201 – 215

Jacobs J, 1985 *Cities and the Wealth of Nations. Principles of Economic Life* (Vintage Books, New York)

Jervell J, 1992, "A report from Europe's northern periphery—the Baltic Sea area", Europe-programmes, St Olavsplass, 0130 Oslo

Kuhn Th, 1962 *The Structure of Scientific Revolutions* (The University of Chicago Press, Chicago)

Lindström B, 1992, "Åland—Kulturautonomi i Europa Perspektiv" (The society of Åland—cultural autonomy in a European perspective) *Nord Revy* **4/5** 57 – 59 (NordREFO, Copenhagen)

Linzie J, Boman D, 1991 *Mälarregionen i ett Gränslöst Europa* (The Region of Mälaren in a Europe without Borders) (Public Publisher, Stockholm)

Naisbitt J, 1984 *Megatrends* (Futura, London)

Östhol A, 1991 *Regioner inför Europeisk Integrasjon. Politik över Gränser* (Regions Confronting European Integration. Transborder Politics) (Umeå, Sweden)

Porter M, 1990 *The Competitive Advantage of Nations* (The Free Press, New York)

Scott A J, 1990, "Flexible production systems and regional development—the rise of new industrial spaces in North America and Western Europe" *Nord Revy* **1** 59 – 77 (NordREFO, Copenhagen)

Stöhr W B (Ed.), 1990 *Global Challenge and Local Response: Local Initiatives for Economic Regeneration in Contemporary Europe* (Mansell, London)

Veggeland N, 1992a, "The regions of Europe: development on the basis of a concentration model or a mosaic model?" OECD WP 6 (OECD, Paris)

Veggeland N, 1992b *Region-building and Potential Patterns of Regional Development in the Baltic Rim* RSA, Nordic Section, University of Kiel, Kiel

Veggeland N, 1993 *Regionalism or Federalism? Two Visions of a New Europe. Periphery Strategies in European Integration* (Springer, Berlin)

Veggeland N, and others, 1993 *The Impact of the Development of the Nordic Countries on Regional Development and Spatial Organization in the European Community* (DG XVI, Brussels)

Transport and Communication Barriers in Europe

P Rietveld
Free University, Amsterdam

1 Introduction

The ongoing process of economic integration in Europe leads to a reduction in the importance of barriers as a factor discouraging spatial interaction. The impact of borders on spatial interaction is multidimensional. Borders correlate not only with fiscal and institutional differences, but also with cultural and language differences. Therefore it is interesting to investigate more carefully the impact of borders on spatial interaction, and, more specifically, the impact of the changes in the nature of borders now taking place in Europe.

The barrier effects of borders lead to certain disadvantages for border regions because interactions with foreign-neighbour regions are weak. For particular places near to borders and suitably located at infrastructure links, there are opportunities to function as export nodes. For other places in the border regions there may not be such opportunities. This means that in studies of the impacts of borders on regions one should take into account differences among subregions. At the European level there is certainly no reason to equate border regions with problem regions. If one considers the problem regions in the various EC countries, one observes that many of them are not border regions (see Armstrong and Taylor, 1985). In this respect, it is useful to point at a certain bias in the discussions on border regions. If borders are interpreted as semipermeable lines in space which discourage interaction between neighbouring regions, seacoasts can be given a similar description. Coastal regions have a bigger disadvantage compared with regions located at national borders because the communication partners on the other side of the line are virtually absent, whereas with border regions they are not absent, just more difficult to reach. Of course, a location at a seacoast gives certain advantages to a region: it can exploit sea-related resources (such as oil, fish, tourism) and may host seaports. But, especially given the declining economic importance of sea transport relative to other transport modes, coastal regions may be in a less advantaged position compared with border regions (see Rietveld and Boonstra, 1993).

This chapter is organised as follows. In section 2 a typology of border-related barriers will be discussed. In section 3 I will present results on the barrier effects of borders for the structure of road and rail networks. Section 4 will be devoted to the role of barriers in the *use* of the railway network. In section 5 results will be presented for telecommunication interactions. In section 6 I will discuss the consequences of the conclusions about barriers for the analysis of accessibilities of cities in European infrastructure networks.

2 A typology of border-related barriers

A framework to analyse the impact of borders has been developed by Cattan and Grasland (1993). In this framework (see figure 1), two factors have been distinguished which affect places in space: distance and borders. The impacts of distance and borders are specified for two types of variables: state variables, relating to the situation in a certain place; and flow variables, relating to the interaction between different places. Two possible effects of borders are considered. They lead to: (1) nonhomogeneities between places at different sides of the border, and (2) discontinuities in flows between places at different sides of the border. Distance has a similar impact on places and interaction, but its effect is much more gradual.

In research activities, attention is usually focused on the items in the upper part of figure 1. For example, the impact of distance (or travel costs) on transport flows, F_{ij}, has been widely studied in the context of spatial interaction models. Spatial autocorrelation analysis has been a similar tool in the investigation of similarities between places. In this case

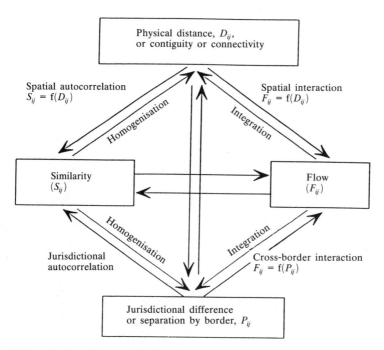

Figure 1. A methodological framework for the analysis of barriers and discontinuities (adapted from Cattan and Grasland, 1993).

the dependent variable is a similarity index, S_{ij}. The role of borders has usually been neglected in this context. For similarity indices it would mean that similarity depends not only on distance, but also on whether or not two places are on the same side of a border. For flows, borders would also have a potential impact that is in addition to that of distance.

The two aspects—similarity of places, and flows between places—are clearly related. For example, places may be different because one place may have adopted an innovation the other did not adopt. An improvement in communications will usually stimulate equal patterns of innovation adoption. Thus a reduction in the barrier effects of borders may lead to an increase in the similarities between places on different sides of the border. Such a parallel development is not guaranteed, however. For example, a reduction in trade barriers will usually stimulate a specialisation in production processes, which will lead to a decrease in the similarity of the economic structure between places or regions.

We note in passing that the concepts of flows and similarity introduced here are closely related to the two basic types of regional concepts commonly used: homogeneous regions and functional regions. A systematic treatment of delimitations for both types of regions at the European level to determine the different roles of borders versus distance (proximity) would be an interesting research project.

In this chapter I will focus on the impacts of borders on flows; that is, on the barrier effects of borders. The impacts on similarities will not be treated here (for an example in the field of fertility indices refer to Decroly and Grasland, 1992).

Border-related barriers can be defined to exist when the intensity of interaction in space suddenly drops at places where a border is crossed. Various reasons for the existence of the barrier effects of borders can be distinguished:
(1) weak or expensive infrastructure services in transport and communication for international links;
(2) preferences of consumers for domestic rather than foreign products and destinations;
(3) government interventions of various types; and
(4) lack of information on foreign countries.

The first type of border-related barrier effect concerns the *supply of transport and communication services*. This effect is expressed in the form of various types of costs. If one were to compute generalised costs, one would observe a discontinuity in these costs when a border is crossed. The generalised costs consist of two main components: monetary expenditures and time-related costs.

An example where there is an extra *monetary* burden related to international transport compared with domestic transport is in the airline sector. The reason is that international regulatory agreements often limit the supply of international services so that tariffs are higher. In international road transport, cabotage and quota systems may lead to inefficiencies and hence to high tariffs. In international rail transport the lack of cooperation between national railway companies leads to relatively high international tariffs. In telecommuniations a similar tendency can be observed: international tariffs are often much higher than are long-distance domestic tariffs, even though the distance between the communication partners may be very much the same.

Most cases of supply-related transport costs concern the *time* component. Take, as an example, the road network. International links are underdeveloped in the road system, as can be seen, for example, in the Alps region. This leads to detour factors which may be somewhat higher in international transport than in domestic transport. In railway infrastructure one observes that countries start investments in high-speed rail for domestic links (France, Germany, Spain). Only at a later stage are international links added. This means that the speeds of services between major links in the same country are faster than those between comparable links in different countries. Another example can be found in the field of telecommunications. There is a lack of supply of telecommunication infrastructure in the former USSR. This leads to high failure rates when one wants to establish international contacts with Russia, for example, and this means that one loses much more time than with calls to other destinations. Another example in the field of telecommunications is found in certain developing countries where international calls are not automatic, which also leads to time losses.

The above examples concern time-related barrier effects due to the absence of a sufficient infrastructure. A somewhat different barrier effect results from the way infrastructure is used. For example, international train services usually have lower frequencies than those between comparable national links. This means that the international traveller faces longer travel times which lead to more waiting or a less efficient use of time abroad. A similar case holds true for international airline services.

Rail transport provides other examples of barrier effects. Technical incompatibility in railway systems as a result of differences in gauge (for example between Spain and France) or voltage (for example between Germany and the Netherlands) leads to time losses when passing the border because one has to change carriages and/or locomotives.

The second group of barrier effects concern a *preference of consumers and producers* for domestic interactions rather than international interactions. Such a preference may be based on taste; for example, in food consumption one can observe clear differences in national habits, leading to a disincentive for the international trade in certain food products. Language, ethnic, and cultural differences can lead to a strong preference for trade or communication partners within a country rather than with other countries. This not only holds true for consumers, but also for firms. As indicated by Hofstede (1980), there are substantial cultural differences between certain groups of countries which makes cooperation between firms in these countries difficult. Another example is found with governments in their role of final consumer; they may give priority to producers from their own country in the procurement of equipment, weapons, business services, and so on.

The third group of border-related barrier effects concerns the *regulations or interventions of national governments*. These interventions can have both a monetary and a time effect. Examples of monetary effects are the costs of getting a visa or the special taxes levied on people crossing the border. An interesting illustration of the second example is found in Indonesia where every Indonesian citizen leaving the country has to pay an amount of some US$100. This tax was imposed in order to discourage cross-border shopping in Singapore. Another well-known example of a monetary effect occurs with fiscal barriers where import duties lead to a disincentive to import products from abroad. A similar effect occurs when excise taxes of particular products are different.

Another example of a regulation leading to higher costs when trade takes place internationally is related to currencies. The introduction of the European ecu has the aim of removing this cost, but as long as this has not yet been realised, banks will continue to charge customers for the change services they provide. In addition, the hedging costs of firms operating in international markets may be substantial.

For the introduction of particular new products in a country, firms have to follow certification procedures. If each country has its own procedure this will lead to additional costs and the possibility of delays. A related problem is that countries often differ in the specification of the requirements certain products must satisfy. This leads to the need to adapt products to particular national standards, which obviously has a cost-increasing effect. A well-known example is the difference between the United Kingdom and the other European countries in the choice of which side of the road is used for driving, leading to differences in automobile design.

Time-related barriers of an institutional nature concern the waste of time in obtaining a visa, waiting at customs offices, waiting at borders, and so on. Avoiding border delays is very important for firms working within a just-in-time concept. It may induce the selection of domestic rather than international suppliers. To these time losses must be added the time needed for extra paperwork in the case of international trade.

The fourth reason for the existence of barriers relates to the *lack of information on foreign destinations*. A lack of information always plays a role in the intensity of spatial interaction, but in border-crossing interactions it is more severe. For example, many newpapers, data banks, and information systems have a clear national orientation. Acquiring additional information is possible, but it gives rise to costs in terms of money and time. Personal information networks also often have a domestic bias.

The information people have is strongly influenced by interaction patterns in the past. Thus information-related barriers to international interactions depend on the other types of barriers mentioned above. They can be said to reinforce them. Because the stock of information is built gradually, the historical component of barrier effects may be expected to be substantial.

In the above list of the factors leading to barrier effects of borders we find both symmetric and asymmetric effects. Symmetry occurs when spatial interaction is reduced in both directions to the same extent. There are also examples where the effect is asymmetric: the reduction takes place in both directions, but not to the same extent. Yet another possibility is that borders lead to a decrease in interaction in one direction and an increase in the other direction. In this case one might speak of an adverse border effect. Cross-border shopping is an example. Another example can be found in tourism, where certain tourists prefer foreign locations over otherwise identical domestic locations because they are more interesting. In the context of figure 1 this means that spatial heterogeneity stimulates international flows.

Border-related barriers are not the only barriers which may exist in space, however. For example, migration flows in a country with several ethnic or language groups, each having their own home region, will be biased towards the home region (see Cattan and Grasland, 1992, for an example in former Czechoslovakia). Also, telecommunication flows may be biased within countries towards regions with the same language, as found, for example, by Klaassen et al (1972) for Belgium, and Rossera (1990) and Donzé (1993) for Switzerland. In this chapter, however, I will focus on border-related barriers.

3 Barrier effects of borders in the railway and highway network
Despite the relatively small size of most European countries and the emphasis on economic integration, the planning and operation of infrastructure is predominantly done by individual countries using a narrow national perspective. Only quite recently has the international dimension grown in importance, as can be seen from initiatives such as the Channel Tunnel, a bridge between Sweden and Denmark, and a high-speed railway connection between France, Belgium, Germany, and the Netherlands. The existing networks clearly display a national orientation.

One way to investigate the role of borders in infrastructure networks is to use a density indicator. Highway density is measured as the length (in km) of the highway network divided by the area (in km^2) of the country. In a densely populated country such as The Netherlands the highway density is as high as 0.05 km per km^2. This means that the average length of the highways in an arbitary area of 100 km^2 is equal to 5 km. In border areas this density is usually lower than the national average which is partly a consequence of the low population densities which may occur in border areas, and partly because borders exert a barrier effect.

In table 1, the densities of railways and highways are presented for a number of borderlines in Europe. The numbers are computed relative to the density in the border region. For example, the number of 0.25 for the German–Belgian border means that the railway density on this border is only 25% of the density in the German and Belgian border regions. The table shows very clearly that substantial barrier effects exist for national borders. In all cases the border-crossing densities are much lower than the average densities in border areas. The average reduction factor is 0.18 for rail and 0.22 for highways. The balance between the two varies from country to country. For example, in the Netherlands, Belgium, and Germany the border effect is most clearly visible for rail, whereas for Switzerland it is the highway system which tends to be most clearly affected by borders. For a more detailed account of the empirical results, refer to the work of Bruinsma and Rietveld (1992).

The barrier effects of borders give rise to relatively large detours when one wants to cross a border. The detour factors will be largest for short-distance trips across the border for example from C to D in figure 2.

Table 1. Network densities for rail and road on borderlines (1989).

Border between countries	Network density on borderline relative to border area	
	railway	highway
Belgium – the Netherlands	0.10	0.21
Belgium – France	0.20	0.29
Germany – the Netherlands	0.12	0.31
Germany – Belgium	0.25	0.36
Germany – France	0.18	0.22
Switzerland – Austria	0.20	0.00
Switzerland – France	0.23	0.31
Italy – France	0.12	0.16
Italy – Switzerland	0.16	0.11

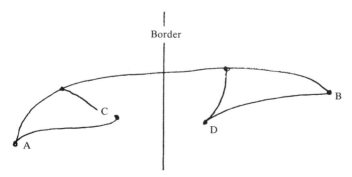

Figure 2. Network with border effects.

For trips originating and ending in nonborder regions (A and B in figure 2) these detour factors will be smaller. Thus it will be border regions themselves which are most strongly affected by the lack of border-crossing network infrastructure.

4 Barriers effects of borders in the use of the railway network

Consider two cities at a certain distance from each other and connected by a railway line. The frequencies of the train services between these cities tend to be higher when they cities are located in the same country compared with the situation where the two cities are in different countries. In this section I give a numerical estimate of the extent to which this effect occurs. The method used is the quasi-experimental approach. In this approach (see Isserman, 1989), one compares a pair of cities (A and B) with another pair (A and C). The cities B and C have been chosen to be identical in all relevant economic characteristics. In addition, the distance between A and B is equal to that between A and C. The only difference is that A and B are located in the same country, which is not the case with A and C. By comparing the frequency of train services between A and B with that between A and C one can isolate the impact of borders.

The advantage of the quasi-experimental approach is that one does not need to formulate and estimate a model to isolate the border effect. An obvious disadvantage of this approach is that one will never find cities which are entirely identical in to all relevant features. One is forced therefore to use cities which are only approximately identical, which produces noise in the outcomes.

In table 2 we present results for train-service frequencies for a number of approximately identical pairs of cities in Europe. Two pairs of cities are called identical in this context when: (a) the travel time between the two cities in each pair is equal; and (b) the sizes of the cities (measured as the number of trains coming from all directions that make a stop in each city) are equal for each pair.

The reduction factor for international services on average is smaller than 1; that is, international services are on average less frequent than domestic services. From a comparison of about forty city pairs, Boonstra (1992) finds that the average reduction factor is equal to 0.44. This means that against ten trains a day on a certain domestic connection there are about four or five international trains to a similar destination at a similar travel time away. Table 2 shows that there are substantial variations among city pairs: in some cases (for example, Nürnberg–Linz) one does not observe a border effect, in other cases the difference in frequency is quite large.

In most cases, crossing a border in Europe means that one also crosses a linguistic frontier, but in other cases national borders do not have this property. A further analysis of the data reveals that the reduction factor is indeed different for countries where the same language is spoken (average value 0.57) compared with countries with different languages (average 0.38) (compare Boonstra, 1992).

It is interesting to compare these results with those found for the airline network (see Rietveld, 1992). For the airline network the reduction factor of borders on flights is equal to 0.32. Thus, borders seem to have a stronger impact on the airline system than on the railway system. This can most probably be explained by the combination of hub-and-spoke networks in the airline system and the high degree of regulation of international flights in Europe. Those factors have induced the formation of hubs in the capitals of almost all European countries. Other cities in these countries are mainly served by the domestic airline and their international links usually take place via the national hub. In the airline system one again observes that language plays an important role. The reduction factor is 0.36 between countries with the same language, whereas it is 0.28 between countries with a different language.

Table 2. Frequencies of railway connections between equivalent pairs of cities (1991) (Thomas Cook, 1992).

Railway station pair	Country pair	Frequency per day	Reduction factor
Amsterdam – Groningen	The Netherlands – the Netherlands	20	
Amsterdam – Oberhausen	The Netherlands – Germany	14	0.70
Hamburg – Essen	Germany – Germany	14	
Hamburg – Århus	Germany – Denmark	14	1.00
Essen – Hannover	Germany – Germany	19	
Essen – Amsterdam	Germany – the Netherlands	12	0.63
Innsbruck – Salzburg	Austria – Austria	25	
Innsbruck – Augsburg	Austria – Germany	6	0.24
Saarbrücken – Köln	Germany – Germany	17	
Saarbrücken – Paris	Germany – France	6	0.35
Köln – Mannheim	Germany – Germany	33	
Köln – Utrecht	Germany – the Netherlands	12	0.36
Nürnberg – Heidelberg	Germany – Germany	9	
Nürnberg – Linz	Germany – Austria	9	1.00
Paris – Metz	France – France	23	
Paris – Courtrai	France – Belgium	6	0.26
Paris – Nancy	France – France	14	
Paris – Courtrai	France – Belgium	6	0.43
Lyon – Nancy	France – France	6	
Lyon – Torino	France – Italy	4	0.67
Würzburg – Erfurt	Germany – Germany	8	
Bremen – Groningen	Germany – the Netherlands	3	0.38

5 Barrier effects of borders in telecommunications

In this section I study the extent to which borders lead to a reduction of telecommunication flows. I will use a gravity-type model for this purpose. The telecommunication flow X_{rs} between regions r and s depends on a number of factors including the distance d_{rs}. This dependence is reflected by a distance decay function $\exp(-ad_{rs})$ or d_{rs}^{-b}. A border effect can be introduced by adding an extra reduction factor δ_{ij} where i and j denote the countries in which the regions r and s are located. When r and s are located in the same country δ_{ij} is set equal to 1, so that a reduction effect does not occur. On the other hand, when r and s are not in the same country, the decay factor becomes equal to $\exp(-ac_{rs})\delta_{ij}$ where δ_{ij} is smaller than 1.

The barrier factor found for EC and EFTA (Greece was a member of the European Free Trade Association) countries is about 0.30 to 0.40 for both countries in table 3. This means that crossing a border from these countries leads to a reduction in telecommunication flows which makes them only 30% to 40% of the volume one would expect if no borders existed. The relatively high outcome for the Dutch–Belgian border suggests that language is an important factor. This is also suggested by the high outcome for communication between Greece and Cyprus (although it is difficult to believe that in this case the barrier effect is so much higher than 1).

Telecommunication interactions with Eastern Europe are very low for both countries. Telecommunication interaction is also low with developing countries for the Netherlands and Greece. An exception is telecommunication

Table 3. Barrier effects of national borders for the Netherlands (1983) and Greece (1988) (sources: Giaoutzi and Strategea, 1992; Rietveld and Janssen, 1990).

The Netherlands		Greece	
country	reduction factor	country	reduction factor
Belgium	0.40*	EC	0.31*
Germany	0.36*	EFTA	0.28*
Rest of EC	0.31*	Eastern Europe	0.04*
Scandinavia	0.31*	USA, Canada, Japan	0.22*
Central Europe	0.36*	Africa	0.13*
Eastern Europe	0.05*	South America	0.06*
USA, Canada, Japan	0.34*	China, India, Hong Kong	0.05*
Developing countries	0.08*	Middle East	0.30*
Indonesia	0.88	Turkey, Yugoslavia	0.22*
		Australia/New Zealand	1.05
		Cyprus	9.84*
$R^2 = 0.812$		$R^2 = 0.613$	

* Significantly different from 1.00 at the 5% level.

interaction between Indonesia and the Netherlands which suggests that former colonial relationships play an important role.

6 National borders and the accessibility of European cities

In this section I discuss the consequences of barrier effects of borders on the accessibility of European cities. It is generally recognised that the unification of the European market will lead to an intensification of the competition between European cities. The accessibility of these cities in a European context is an important factor determining the competitive position of the cities. The improvement of infrastructure links (for example by extending the network of high-speed rail connections) is an important strategy followed by many governments. The impact of nonphysical factors such as the border effects on the accessibility of cities has received much less attention, however. In this chapter I discuss some results of a broader study of accessibility of cities (compare Bruinsma and Rietveld, 1993).

In this study, accessibility is measured by means of a gravity-type formula of spatial interaction based on the mass (population size) of cities and travel times according to various types of transport modes. I will only discuss the road network. Forty cities are taken into account (see figure 3). When border effects are ignored, one finds accessibilities of cities as presented in column 1 of table 4. Paris and London have dominant positions

90 – 100
80 – 89
70 – 79
60 – 69
50 – 59
40 – 49
<40

Figure 3. Accessibility (weighted by population size) for road traffic.

(mainly because of their own mass). Smaller cities located near other cities (for example, in the Ruhr area and the English Midlands) may also achieve relatively high positions. In order to investigate the effect of borders I have imposed reduction factors, the values of which were inspired by the earlier sections of this work (see table 5). The resulting values of the accessibility index are presented in the column 2 of table 4. It appears that especially medium-sized cities in smaller countries, such as Belgium, the Netherlands, Austria, and Switzerland, suffer from the existence of barrier effects of borders. It is these cities which will experience the largest increase in accessibility when the border effects are reduced.

Table 4. Impact of borders as barriers in the road network on the accessibility of European cities.

City	1	2	City	1	2
Paris	100	97	Budapest	61	48
London	94	100	Turin	61	49
Düsseldorf	78	69	Newcastle	60	61
Essen	77	68	Vienna	60	43
Köln	75	64	Genoa	59	50
Berlin	74	71	Madrid	58	59
Leeds	74	77	Prague	58	38
Manchester	71	73	Marseille	56	47
Brussels	70	41	Barcelona	54	48
Birmingham	70	70	Zagreb	54	39
Frankfurt	70	59	Copenhagen	52	42
Rotterdam	69	49	Athens	52	55
Liverpool	68	69	Belgrade	52	41
Istanbul	67	73	Warsaw	51	44
Amsterdam	67	47	Bucharest	50	45
Hamburg	66	60	Naples	49	46
Milan	65	54	Lodz	49	39
Rome	63	62	Lisbon	48	48
Munich	63	62	Sofia	45	35
Zurich	63	40	Stockholm	45	41
Lyon	62	51	Dublin	43	36

Note: 1 Border effects ignored; 2 with border effects.

Table 5. Border-related reduction factors for road transport.

	EC country	EFTA country	Eastern European country
EC country	0.250	0.167	0.125
EFTA country	0.167	0.167	0.125
Eastern European country	0.125	0.125	0.167

7 Conclusions

National borders exert a strong influence on the shape of railway and highway networks, on the service levels of the railway system, and on telecommunication flows. In Western Europe the border-related reduction factor found for spatial interaction usually varies between 0.20 and 0.50. With Eastern Europe, even larger reductions can be found. Language can be shown to be an important barrier component. The absence of linguistic differences at both sides of a border dampens the barrier effects of the border. Barrier effects of borders have a substantial impact on the accessibility of cities in international networks. It is the medium-sized cities of smaller countries which may expect the largest gains in accessibility when the barrier effects of borders are removed.

References

Armstrong H, Taylor J, 1985 *Regional Economics and Policy* (Philip Allan, Oxford)
Boonstra J, 1992, "Barrieres in verkeer en infrastructuur; een internationaal perspectief" (Barriers in transport and infrastructure, an international perspective), Faculty of Economics, Vrije Universiteit, Amsterdam
Bruinsma F, Rietveld P, 1992, "De structurerende werking van infrastructuur", Economische faculteit, Vrije Universiteit, Amsterdam
Bruinsma F, Rietveld P, 1993, "Urban agglomerations in European infrastructure networks" *Urban Studies* **30** 919–934
Cattan N, Grasland C, 1993, "Migratisons of population in Czechoslovakia; a comparison of political and spatial determinants of migration and the measurement of barriers" *Trinity Papers in Geography* forthcoming
Decroly J M, Grasland C, 1992, "Frontières, systèmes politiques et fécondité en Europe" (Borders, political systems and fertility in Europe) *Espace, Populations, Sociétés* **2** 81–118
Donzé L, 1993, "Barriers to communication in Swiss telephone flows" *Sisteme Urbani* forthcoming
Giaoutzi M, Strategea A, 1992, "Telephone calls and communication barriers in Greece" National Technical University, Athens, Greece
Hofstede G, 1980 *Cultures Consequences; International Differences in Work Related Values* (Sage, Beverly Hills, CA)
Isserman A, 1989 *Research Designs for Quasi Experimental Control Group Analysis in Regional Science* West Virginia University, Morgantown
Klaassen L H, Wagenaar S, Van der Weg A, 1972, "Measuring psychological distance between the Flemings and the Walloons" *Papers of the Regional Science Association* **29** 45–62
Rietveld P, 1992, "International transportation and communication networks in Europe, the role of barrier effects", paper presented at the 6th World Conference for Transportation Research, Lyon; copy available from this author
Rietveld P, Boonstra J, 1993, "On the supply of network infrastructure" *Nieuwe Ideeen in Nederlands Ruimtelijk Onderzoek* **3** forthcoming
Rietveld P, Janssen L, 1990, "Telephone calls and communication barriers; the case of the Netherlands" *Annals of Regional Science* **24** 307–318
Rossera F, 1990, "Discontinuities and barriers in communications, the case of Swiss communities of different language" *Annals of Regional Science* **24** 319–336
Thomas Cook, 1992 *European Timetable* (Thomas Cook Publishing, London)

How can Existing Barriers and Border Effects be Overcome? A Theoretical Approach

R Ratti
Institute of Economic Research, Bellinzona

1 Introduction

In the recent debate on European integration two main topics have been discussed: 'a Europe without frontiers' and 'a Europe of regions'. The first emphasises common policies to diminish a certain type of (institutional) frontier, on policies to implement the four freedoms, which will certainly transform the general nature of the frontier itself. The second is more global and complex; as well as stressing the reduction of certain frontiers, it will tolerate other geographical, social, cultural, and structural limits (Nijkamp et al, 1990). Thus, the most important difference between the Europe of the late 20th century and the 'old' Europe of countries will lie not just in the abolition of barriers and frontiers, but also, in a more general sense, in the transformation that the frontier will undergo, from a barrier into a contact line.

In this context we have to formulate the theoretical hypothesis that emphasises the overcoming of barriers through the constitution of contact areas allowing interregional cooperation (Ratti and Reichman, 1993). After some necessary specifications about the nature and the typology of frontier and border effects (see Ratti, 1988; 1990), I develop two different approaches to overcome existing barriers and border effects. The first, a microeconomic approach, examines the frontier through the analysis of the economic actor's strategic behaviour, and is based on the theory of industrial organisation (Ratti, 1992); the second approach has a meso-economic character and considers the role of 'frontier' within a specific supporting space or milieu.

2 The specific nature of frontier and border effects
2.1 The ambiguity of the frontier concept

An examination of the socioeconomic literature (Button and Rossera, 1990) has led me to distinguish between two different views or frameworks of analysis. 'Frontier' is an ambiguous concept (Reichman, 1993), generally representing either a border of a region lying astride the boundary (a line representing the legal limit of a state), or referring to a concept of a marginal or peripheral zone. To every framework of analysis corresponds a specific perspective and also a number of diverse and complementary political objectives.

Thus, two diverse views can be distinguished (Ratti, 1990):
(1) the traditional view, that is, the one of the 'border area', defined as the territory next to a fixed frontier line (in most cases institutional) inside

which significant socioeconomic effects due to the existence of a border are felt (Hansen, 1977);

(2) the view of the 'frontier limit', in which the border is seen less as a demarcation line but, instead, as an external limit, which may be mobile over time (Turner, 1921). In economic terms the border is the place where the marginal costs are equal to the marginal prices (Di Tella, 1982). Every resistance or removal of obstacles to communication will have an influence, beyond that of distance, over the diffusion processes of tangible or intangible goods.

2.2 The duality of the frontier – border effect

Having discussed the ambiguity of the frontier concept and having chosen a border approach which is within an institutional framework of analysis, it is very important to consider the duality of the function of a frontier: as a dividing line or as a contact zone. Both these functions determine the specific nature of the development of border regions.

As a starting point, the border can be viewed as a separation factor: a demarcation line between different political – institutional systems. In this case, the border effect manifests itself in the following three functions (Guichonnet and Raffestin, 1974):

(a) a legal function, where the border line exactly delimits the territories subject to juridical standards and to the country's legislation;

(b) a control function, where every crossing of the border line is submitted, in principle, to a state control;

(c) a fiscal function, where the control function is accompanied by a perception of custom rights assuring the adaptation of the fiscal rights in force in the country of entry.

The nature of these functions, which all depend on the central government, thus have important consequences for the power of the region to govern its internal and external relations (House, 1980). In fact, the concept of a border, seen as a separation line is essentially the result of a preoccupation with national order and international politics. At the limit, this justifies the peripheral and dependency character of the border region. In the sense of this definition, this operation consists of an evaluation, or even a cancellation, of some constituent characteristics of the region. Therefore, the term border area appears more adequate to define those territories marked by the 'line-border'.

Moreover, the border can be seen as a contact factor. In this sense it is no longer a line, but a functional space as an intermediate element between different societies and collectivities. Then, by this definition, it is convenient to talk about transborder regions (Biucchi and Gaudard, 1981). This second approach puts stress on the organisation of space and the global administration, accounting for the sociocultural and identity factors. In this case, the chief concerns contrast sharply with the more strictly functional approach of the 'line-border demarcation'.

Thus, it is possible to draw three main conclusions:
(1) the twin notions of border, namely line and contact, arc in reality most often mixed up and their respective degrees of importance vary as a function of historical contingencies (for example, the notion of a barrier-border has been historically bound, since the 18th century, to the construction of the nation-states);
(2) the effects of one or other of the concepts determine specific and original consequences in the spatial organisation of border territories (for example, in the case of the establishment of a regionalistic process, the barrier-border is a hindrance whereas the contact-border may serve to promote development);
(3) the analysis and interpretation of the development dynamics of the border regions requires a multidisciplinary and systematic approach.

2.3 Three types of border effect

In an analytical and historical approach, the evolution of the concept of border is outlined in the three following phases. First, a traditional approach sees the boundary as a dividing line, the source of a long series of discriminating effects. This is the approach of *a border as a barrier* linked to a defined period in history. Indeed, at the time of the construction of nation-states, rulers were more concerned with central effects than with peripheral ones.

The basic thesis surely is that of Hansen (1977), according to which border regions were traditionally fettered and retarded in their development. This was because of, first, their peripheral situation relative to economic centres in the country, and second the *principle of separation*, under which higher priority is given by government to sectoral policies than to social and economic links, within or between regions (Loesch, 1940).

The second approach sees the border as a *filter* mediating discrimination between a number of political and economic systems, bringing in the key concept of differential revenue (Ratti, 1990; 1993). In other words, economics in the border areas may make situations of rents, positive or negative, on both sides of the landmark, the net effect of such annuity not necessarily being zero. Smuggling is a vivid historical instance of the phenomenon, but this is also a good explanation of the flow of foreign, in general, and border, in particular, workers.

The third approach is the *open border*, with a characteristic functional dominance of connection, and not of separation, between a number of political and institutional systems; this is the model implied in the project of Europe without boundaries. The economic, cultural, and political development of the two territories limited by the boundary will not be determined by the sole development of one or other of the territories but by that of both together. The open border implies a change from the concepts of border economics to that of economics across boundaries. In this situation, which might lead to quick and basic adjustments, the strategic behaviour of actors is crucial (Faludi, 1986; Covin and Slevin, 1989). A strategy shaped as a cooperation network is shown by theory as the most efficient in overcoming hindrances and uncertain situations typical of border environments (Camagni, 1991).

3 Overcoming the 'obstacle-border' by means of the operators' strategic behaviour

The study of the behaviour of actors in facing barriers or other effects can be theoretically analysed through the modern theory of industrial organisation. In fact, the hypothesis of a situation of uncertainty, bounded rationality, and market failure, connected with the existence of a frontier, corresponds to the thesis of a solution in terms of organisation.

The capacity and difficulty or impossibility of providing a strategical answer to barrier and border obstacles will explain the three barrier effects, filter effects, or polarizing effects previously described and, above all, their dynamics. This seems very important in an era of 'boundaryless Europe', which will create other rapid changes (in terms of decline or emergence) in border regions. Let us summarise some necessary theoretical elements.

3.1 Postulates

(1) Beside the 'firm' and the 'market', there exists a third form of organisation and regulation of production: the cooperation between enterprises.

"The dichotomy between firm and market, between direct and spontaneous coordination, is misleading; it ignores the institutional fact of interfirm cooperation and assumes away the distinct method of coordination that this can provide" (Richardson, 1972, page 895).

(2) The existence of 'uncertainty' requires new functions, particularly of coordination.

"The presence of inescapable static and dynamic uncertainty in the real world implies the presence of extra costs and therefore new functions to cope with these costs and new "operators or institutions" organizing these functions and shaping factual behavior" (Camagni, 1991, page 130).

(3) The concept of 'transaction cost' constitutes the discriminating instrument between the functions assumed by the firm, the market, or the cooperation.

"A firm will expand until the cost of organizing an extra transaction within the firm becomes equal to the cost of carrying out the same transaction by means of an exchange on the open market or the cost of organizing within another firm" (Coase, 1937, page 395).

3.2 Thesis

The existence of market distortions and transaction costs constrains the enterprise to adopt two types of strategic behaviour:

(a) vertical integration, following classical reasoning (Williamson, 1975; 1985; 1986);

(b) horizontal integration, as an intermediate organisation form that is more flexible and based upon a logic of dialogue (Porter, 1980; 1986); this is particularly attractive for small and medium-sized enterprises (SMEs) searching for 'synergies' (Kamann and Strijker, 1991).

There is a good probability that these intermediate forms of cooperation will be territory dependent, because of the need to conform to a common code of behaviour.

"The distance of dialogue is restricted by the need for a common code and the need for face-to-face contacts ... This need for proximity is based on the assumption that common code is embedded in a contextual framework characterized by common language, law, value, social background and joint ability of orientation" (Christensen, 1988, page 11).

3.3 Corollaries

The existence of a 'border' or any other form of 'barrier to communication' immediately constitutes a determinant factor of uncertainty and costs of transaction. The study of these borders or barriers then becomes a crucial element in the constitution and dynamic explanation of an intermediate organisation of the *reseau* (network) type (see figure 1).

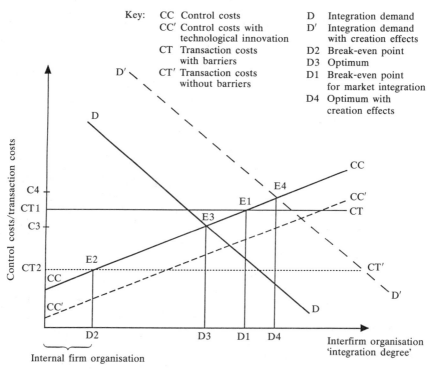

Figure 1. The degrees of integration of a firm (transaction costs, control costs and preference to the integration) (source: Ratti, 1990).

(1) The degree of integration of a firm, constituted by the agreement with other enterprises (from the simple licence agreement, to the joint venture, to a branch) is a function of the transaction costs or the market access costs (CT-CT or CT'-CT'), or of the control costs of the developed inter-firm organisation (CC-CC or CC'-CC'), and also of a preference curve to the integration, corresponding to the demand curve (D-D or D'-D').

(2) The transaction costs are a exogenous constraining data. Below a certain level (CT'-CT'), the firm will have the interest to develop further its internal organisation. Beyond that point, an interenterprise cooperation would constitute a less-expensive option in relation to the market solution.

(3) The control costs are represented by a growing function of the 'integration quantity'. The points E1 and E2 on figure 1 are situations where there are equivalences between the possibility of referring to the market and that of organising certain functions of production with other enterprises.

(4) The optimum is established by considering the demand curve; that is, the preference curve of the integration. The point E3 is lower than E1 because it is possible to account for a certain fear due to the risks of all external cooperation formulae.

(5) The presence of a border or a barrier signifies a line of high trans-action costs (CT'-CT'). It will then allow some intermediate solutions with an integration as high as the market distortion. All uncertainty reductions resulting from the barrier-border would approach market solutions. This would indicate that the cooperation solutions are not necessarily stable nor better.

(6) The opportunity of the firm to take advantage of a planned solution with other enterprises shows in the lowering of the curve CC-CC toward CC'-CC', by means of technological innovation and management. This shows the innovative character of the network, but does not necessarily guarantee that it will be advantageous to the firm in absolute terms.

(7) The reasoning has been conducted in terms of minimised costs. To the objection that the resilient integration also requires a creation effect, it is possible to answer, in this case, that the preference curve can be displaced upward (from D-D toward D'-D'). It also will determine an optimum (E4), which will be even higher than the transaction costs, having as a consequence a particularly high degree of integration.

Finally, even supposing that the trend of some transaction costs is inclined downwards, following the Europe-without-borders postulates, the rele-vance and the continuity of an organisation in a network depends on its capacity to innovate, both in terms of minimising control costs and in terms of value creation.

   In conclusion, for the new context of an open border, the theoretical analysis advocates that economic development of the border areas will not be determined by the political-institutional differential and therefore by the differentiated position of profits, positive and negative, from the effect of belonging to one or the other nation, but rather by the comparatively real advantages of both border areas. The 'open border' implies the passage from the concept of a border-areas economy to that of a transborder economy. This situation can imply some quick and fundamental adjustments. The strategic behaviour of the partners is particularly crucial.

A strategy in terms of a cooperation network is the most efficient approach to overcome persistent or residual obstacles and uncertainty situations typical of a border context. But, all this needs to be supported by a strategy of functional synergies, capable of being realised at a level covering the whole transborder area in a timely manner, such as in the case of the filter-border.

4 Overcoming the 'obstacle-border' by functional space analysis: the supporting space

Beside the microeconomic point of view, analysed through the strategic behaviour of the parties, a second theoretical possibility for interpreting the border function, particularly as a contact area, is represented in terms of spatial analysis. This is the study of the strategic spaces of enterprises, and, particularly, what has been called the supporting space, that is, the ensemble of the factor-frames and of the relations 'preceding the market'.

4.1 Postulates

The 'strategic' or 'life' spaces of an enterprise are determined by three functional spaces (Ratti, 1971; 1992; 1993).

(a) The 'production space' of the firm is determined by the spatial division of work, following the model of the segmentation theory. An enterprise buying outside will define and delocalise its production, following the technological, economic, and sociocultural characteristics specific to each segment and to each production region.

(b) The 'market space' is determined by the relations that the enterprise has with its different markets. These spatial relations are characterised by the number, intensity, and structure, and by the evolution process, of these markets relative to their environment.

This definition, in the spatial-functional terms of the offer and demand, already constitutes a significant step in the dynamic approach of the enterprise development. However, it still seems insufficient to deal with the interior and exterior strategic aspects of the enterprise. A third functional space of the enterprise is therefore proposed.

(c) The 'supporting space' describes three types of precompetitive relation: the qualified or privileged relations at the organisational level of the production factors (capital origin, information source, technological ability, particular ties at the human capital level, and so on); the strategic relations of the enterprise with its partners, suppliers, or clients (privileged information exchange, cooperation, partnership, alliance, partial integration); the strategic relations with the territorial environment parties (public institutions, private or semipublic associations).

It is possible to represent (figure 2) the characteristic traits of the spatial-functional relations of an enterprise following the traditional nonspatial model. From this model, the strategic space of the enterprise is defined.

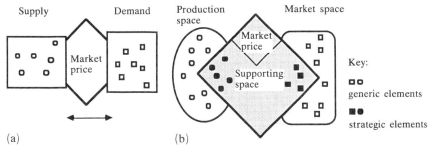

Figure 2. The economic-functional strategic spaces of a firm. (a) Traditional model (open price—dominated market); (b) economic functional spatial model with precompetitive alliances.

4.2 Thesis
Among the three functional spaces of the enterprise, the supporting space appears to be particularly crucial to its strategic orientation. Specifically it allows the so-called factor-frames, and also some important relations of precompetition character, to be taken into account.

The aggregation of the functional spaces of the different enterprises can, in some circumstances (Christensen, 1988), give way to some spatial functional relations. Territorially, in terms of polarised space or of functional space 'force fields', the supporting space dynamics pushes the enterprises to look for common interests and to cooperate with the territorial institutions for the creation of a favourable environment.

This relative coincidence between a strong node of functional spaces and territorial spaces allows 'local synergies'. This is defined as the result of a territorial materialisation of an ensemble of functional relations structured in terms of a pole or force field. This logic leads to the other notions applied in recent regional research literature: local industrial network, localised ecosystem, industrial district, localised industrial system, and toward the notion of milieu developed by the GREMI (Groupe de Recherche Européen sur les Milieux Innovateurs: see Aydalot and Keeble, 1988; Camagni, 1991).

4.3 Corollaries
(1) The two border characteristics (barrier or contact) influence, in a determinant manner, the strategy spaces of the enterprises, particularly their supporting spaces.
(2) Where the separation factors are dominant, the possibility that the border area is the origin of the creation of a real supporting space is insignificant. Often, the existence of this type of space is strongly dependent on the politics of the nation-states and entry port. The eventual

Interregional Cooperation and the Design of a Regional Foreign Policy

R Cappellin
University of Calabria and Bocconi University

1 Introduction

The purpose in this study is to analyse the potential for a more active role of regional governments in international relations. In fact, a tighter integration between neighbouring regions of different countries is required for them to attain that critical mass needed to become real actors within an international economy that is too large for an individual region to compete successfully. This may be of extreme importance for some border regions, such as those on the borders between the European Community and the countries of Eastern Europe, which may be considered peripheral within the national context but which are central within a larger European perspective and may act as a gateway or interface in the relations between the different countries.

First of all, therefore, the theoretical factors justifying international initiatives by regional governments will be analysed. Then, based on the results of an empirical study of the cooperation schemes between the public institutions and collective organisations of the regions of the Alpine area, some operational problems in the creation and development of an interregional alliance will be discussed.

2 The theoretical bases for interregional cooperation

The growing importance of international and interregional relations and their impact on regional and national economies have obliged individual regional authorities to strengthen their contacts with other regional administrations in order to develop specific schemes of interregional cooperation. The capability of regional governments to undertake specific projects of interregional cooperation is more important in the case of the development of transnational cooperation schemes, because, unlike initiatives within a single country, the coordination of various regional programmes at an international scale cannot be imposed by a national government.

A cooperative approach to relations between regions of different countries constitutes an alternative to the competitive and conflictual approach which in the past has been typical of the relations between border regions (Maillat, 1990). These new relations may help toward overcoming those frequent, but often objectively less important, reasons for bilateral conflicts, which often in the past have characterised the bilateral relations between border regions. Moreover, although border regions are usually peripheral in a national perspective, closer cooperation between regions of different countries has often enabled border regions to rediscover for themselves a central geographical position within the greater European context.

Interregional cooperation may also lead regional governments to overcome a purely competitive and conflictual relation with the central areas of their respective countries, by diversifying the scope of their external relations. This may be especially important not only for regions at the internal borders of the EC but also for many Southern European regions which are peripheral in a EC framework. Only through a more committed cooperation with other non-EC countries in the Mediterranean area are they likely to escape from a situation of comparative isolation.

Interregional cooperation can be justified from a theoretical point of view for a variety of reasons similar to those which, according to recent studies of industrial organisation, justify the growth of agreements and other forms of cooperation among firms, particularly at an international level. In particular the following eight cooperation factors may be identified. These can function individually, but more often they act in simultaneous combination.

First, a precondition essential to the implementation of any interregional cooperation scheme is the existence of common cultural values in the regions concerned, given that any form of cooperation can develop only when built on a foundation of mutual knowledge and trust.

Second, the development of interregional alliances is allowed where network economies exist (Cappellin, 1988; Cappellin and Nijkamp, 1990; Teece, 1982), in terms of the exchange of information and know-how in policy areas common between the regions concerned. In fact, the incentive to cooperate increases with the number of regions involved, because this allows access to a greater pool of knowledge and expertise than would have been available within the individual regions. This type of cooperation demands that the information exchanged is a kind of 'public good', as its transfer to other regions does not imply that the original owner will lose it. Obviously, it is also essential that the transfer of such information does not substantially modify the competitive advantage of one region over others. Therefore, this factor of cooperation is particularly important in the areas of culture and of precompetitive basic research.

Third, interregional cooperation may be justified by the objective of using common resources jointly and in a coordinated manner. The purpose of this is to avoid the creation of external diseconomies deriving from a one-sided use of these resources. Typical here is the utilisation and management of common natural resources such as common seas and rivers. Another example could be the case of joint ventures in the development of common services such as specific transport infrastructures, where interregional cooperation helps to avoid the problem of 'free riding' or the free use by some other regions of services set up by particular regions.

A fourth factor, closely connected with that above, is the need to overcome specific size thresholds or to exploit specific economies of scale in the creation of certain public services such as airports, universities and research centres, international fairs, advertising campaigns, and so on (Cappellin, 1989b; 1991). Clearly, as in the case of the previous factor, in order for this factor to be relevant, the regions considered must be geographic neighbours, given that 'common services' implies the need for easy mobility on the part of the potential consumers between the particular regions considered.

A fifth consideration is that interregional cooperation may be necessary because the various regions represent an organic geoeconomic basin and this allows economies of scope to be exploited in the use of various instruments in different policy areas. The existence of economies of scope in a territorial context may be seen in the fact that the management of different services implies significantly complementary relations, thus requiring an integrated approach and a larger planning area than does an individual region. This fact is even more important within the context of socio-economic planning and industrial policy, where the effectiveness of the particular measures demands that the area concerned has a high level of internal interconnection, or in any case it is more important than the particular area's relations with other external areas. Thus, in these cases, a variety of economic policy instruments can be used in order to achieve a series of different but interrelated objectives, and spill-over effects may be avoided; effects which would weaken the efficiency of these instruments.

A sixth factor for interregional cooperation is the aim to reduce the various 'transaction costs', whether material or immaterial, which constitute an obstacle to economic relations between the private firms of the various regions, and to promote greater economic integration between them (Cappellin, 1988). Therefore, another aim of cooperation between regional governments is to create appropriate interfaces between the various regional economies; for example, to provide information regarding the legal systems within the various countries and regions, to remove various artificial barriers, to implement programmes which may stimulate cooperation between the private organisations and firms of the various regions, and to create the transport and communication infrastructures so essential in order to link the economies of the individual regions.

Seventh, interregional cooperation is vital in order to limit or regulate the level of competition between the regions, thereby avoiding economic conflicts and retaliatory measures. Examples of this are competitive incentive schemes designed to attract outside investments, or competition between different regions to obtain important national public works or to be selected as the site of major events, such as international exhibitions and sporting events decided by the national governments or even at the international level.

Interregional cooperation is essential if the regions wish to protect and expand their areas of active autonomy, free of interference from national governments or EC institutions, or if the regions seek to influence decisions taken at these levels. Therefore, an eighth factor which justifies interregional cooperation is the aim to increase the joint bargaining power of the individual regions in their relations with outside organisations (or any 'common external enemy'). Thus, cooperation strengthens the competitive capability of individual regions with respect to other regions or with other regional alliances created on a European scale.

The interdependence between the various factors making up a process of interregional cooperation can be described as in figure 1. First and foremost, the purpose of interregional cooperation is to achieve a kind of synergy whereby the output generated by cooperation is greater than that which the individual regions could achieve on the basis of their own resources alone. Through cooperation each region can have access more or less freely to the resources of other regions, creating positive synergies from the combined effect of these and its own endogenous resources.

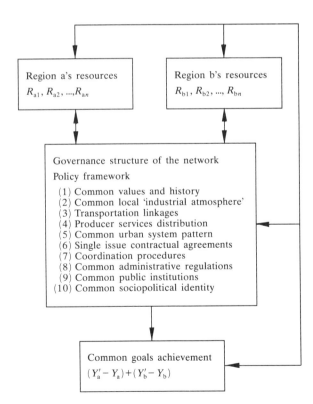

Figure 1. The factors of an interregional cooperation.

These resources are essentially the labour force, technological and organisational know-how, specific production capabilities, privileged access to specific information circuits or special networks, and other factors.

Interregional alliances have a specific time and geographical dimension. They are influenced by the distance between the actual regions considered, in that sociocultural and economic characteristics tend to be more similar between neighbouring regions. This distance factor hampers the accessibility of one region's resources to those of another region. However, distance can be modified by mutual decisions aimed at reducing transaction, transport, communication, and coordination costs between the individual regions that belong to a particular alliance.

Also, interregional cooperation is a circular cumulative process. The longer an alliance lasts, the greater will be the scope of common resources made available to the regions concerned, and consequently the wider the range of objectives the regions may jointly agree to attain. Alliances tend to become more stable with the passage of time because the growing reciprocal knowledge and trust between the regions induce them to direct the development of their own resources towards the achievement of jointly agreed objectives. Consequently, regions become more closely bound together in a kind of 'idiosyncratic relationship' (Williamson, 1981).

Every alliance demands a common decisionmaking process or a common governance structure, made by common procedures and institutions which will continue to identify new common objectives and make decisions on how these are to be achieved. So the capabilities and resources of the individual regions determine the characteristics of the interregional alliance's decisionmaking structure. However, the jointly made decisions affect, over the medium term, the allocation of regional resources and encourage a specialisation in complementary areas.

The effectiveness and efficiency of a common policymaking structure in an interregional alliance depend on the existence of a common social and political identity or the existence of common values and historical traditions, of a common productive know-how or of a similar industrial environment, of favourable transport and communication links, and of close relations among the various urban centres, where headquarter functions are concentrated together with services which facilitate the circulation of technological and economic information. The governance structure in an interregional alliance may be more or less institutionalised and binding in type, ranging from sporadic agreements on specific topics to a permanent coordination, through to the harmonisation of respective administrative procedures, or even to the creation of very binding forms such as common public institutions.

An alliance between regions can be compared to a kind of joint investment, or to the setting up of a company or of a joint venture. Regional governments should be capable of diverting the available resources toward new objectives, which implies a certain margin of risk. As opposed to the case in a commercial exchange, the individual regions are not aware of what will be the future return on the resources they make accessible to the other regions. They can only make predictions, by nature uncertain, of the benefits they will derive in their future together with the other regions, and they can only decide the rules to be followed in allocating those anticipated benefits. Therefore, the creation of interregional alliances requires regional public authorities to adopt an entrepreneurial approach and demands the development of a project design capability.

There are a variety of measures regional authorities may take in order to develop international relations. However, often these measures are incoherent as a whole, both because they apply to widely differing sectors and because they are oriented towards widely differing countries and regions. This indicates the need for a strategic coordination, the targeting of more clearly defined objectives, and the integration of different types of resources.

In cases where the various aspects of international relations within a single region were coordinated, a form of regional 'foreign policy' could develop (Cappellin, 1990b; CNEL, 1990). In brief, a regional foreign policy could cover the following policy areas which correspond to the list of reasons described above whereby interregional cooperation at a transnational level is justified on a purely economic basis.

(1) Information exchange between local and regional authorities on: sectoral policies; technologies applied to specific public services; scientific collaboration between local universities; common training courses for public employees, private sector managers, and personnel; and cultural and scientific exchange schemes.

(2) Joint financing of services and infrastructures: transport infrastructures; communication infrastructures; environmental protection of common watercourses and marine areas; and economic investment in and environmental improvement of urban centres which represent nodes in international transport networks.

(3) Interface activities with the private sector: bilateral business centres; cooperation for regional trade fairs and exhibitions; joint business centres with other regions in outside countries; and common programmes to encourage tourism and investment from other areas of the world.

(4) Joint action with national and EC institutions: planning of regional policy measures by national government and the EC; implementation of international cooperation schemes promoted by national governments; implementation of international cooperation schemes between the EC and other countries; and pressure on national governments to coordinate legislation or integrate their respective measures which may affect border regions.

(5) Regulation of competition between local and regional institutions in: the transport sector; international trade fairs; and localisation incentives.

From the above it is clear that a regional foreign policy does not merely imply twinning with similar institutions in other countries, nor does it mean an undue expansion into the field of national government prerogatives. It concerns fields of policymaking which typically are confined to local and regional governments. However, regional foreign policy demands that a strategic approach be used in these policy fields, implying the following prerequisites (Cappellin, 1992):

(a) identification of specific priority objectives,

(b) collaboration at a regional level between the various public and private institutions in a particular region,

(c) concentration of available resources in a restricted number of programmes at an international level, and

(d) gradual yet continuous effort.

To date, the foreign policy of regional governments has usually been restricted to the field of information. Results attained in this field may on the surface appear negligible in 'operative' terms, but nevertheless they represent a development of crucial importance. This is because the gradual development of mutual knowledge and trust between the administrative bodies in the various regions is by nature a slow process. However, it is the fundamental basis for further development because without this essential element, it would be pointless even to consider more ambitious objectives. Furthermore, the operative effects of projects undertaken to date cannot be measured immediately, because the exchange of information and expertise has unquestionably led each administration to take a more modern approach in their policies than if they had remained enclosed in an arrogant parochialism.

The problem to be considered now is how to progress toward more demanding international relations, such as the joint financing of infrastructure programmes and common services or the reciprocal coordination in a joint bargaining process with national and EC authorities. As indicated above, regional foreign policy need not necessarily conflict with the foreign policy of national authorities except where national authorities explicitly aim to prevent regional institutions establishing their own relations with other foreign regional institutions and with the European Community itself.

Regional foreign policy must be based on the principle that there is no longer any aspect of the economic and social structure of a region which is not affected by constraints or opportunities deriving from an economic system considerably more integrated at the international level. Therefore, the regional institutions, within the context of the policy areas which belong to them, must necessarily take into consideration these international constraints and opportunities.

From an economic point of view, it seems that the specific areas of the actions of the regional institutions should be defined by stating specific objectives and economic policy tools and by reserving other objectives and tools for the national authorities (Molle and Cappellin, 1988). There seems instead no economic justification, although there may be one from a strictly political point of view, for constraining regional initiatives of interregional cooperation to a specific geographical area.

In fact, there appears to be no reason why regional institutions should have the power to make agreements with other regions of the same country and not with similar institutions in other countries, especially if the latter belong to the European Community. It is an anachronism that at a time when people and firms have greater freedom of movement internationally than ever before and act according to the concept of free competition and cooperation with people and firms in other countries, local and regional institutions are artificially prevented from establishing a basis of cooperation to resolve mutual problems with similar institutions in other countries which are part of the Single European Market. The lack of coordination between local authorities in neighbouring countries inevitably entails conflicts and obstacles or a lack of efficiency in the use of resources. This represents a solid case of 'costs of non-Europe'; that is, costs arising out of a lack of European integration.

In conclusion, it may be said that regional foreign policy has the same general aim as national foreign policy—to promote economic and political integration—but it differs in terms of its specific areas of action, objectives, and tools. Given that it is only applicable in those policy areas, it should target those specific objectives and it may only use those tools that are the specific prerogative of regional authorities within the context of the legal constituency of a particular country.

3 Conditions for creating interregional agreements

In order to identify the factors leading to the creation and development of interregional agreements a series of interviews have been conducted with over fifty public institutions, private organisations, and interest groups in four regions: Lombardy, Friuli Venezia Giulia, Bavaria, and Carinthia (Cappellin, 1990; Fisher et al, 1990; Funck and Kowalski, 1990; Grandinetti and Rullani, 1990). For more than fourteen years these regions have cooperated in the framework of the Alpe Adria Working Community (Cappellin, 1989c; CNEL, 1990; ISPI, 1988).

Although the empirical findings of this study certainly confirm the existence of intense historical relationships between the regions of the so-called Mitteleuropa (Central Europe), they may also be instrumental in identifying more general problems, which may be relevant for any scheme of interregional cooperation. First the factors which seem crucial in creating interregional and international agreements will be analysed.

3.1 Regional capabilities

An interregional agreement implies the existence and exploitation of specific complementary resources, material and immaterial, typical of the individual regions concerned. Interregional cooperation is based on the fact that regions have different endowments of resources and different characteristics. Therefore, the internationalisation of regional economies and the development of various forms of cooperation on an interregional and international scale does not necessarily exclude a policy of regional 'endogenous development' (Bianchi, 1990; Cappellin, 1983; 1990a; Konsolas, 1990), which is based on the exploitation of regional resources.

In fact, the expansion of international relations between regional public and private organisations may ensure that specific factors (technological, productive, commercial, and also infrastructural, social, and environmental factors) of the competitive edge inherent to a particular region are fully utilised through the exchange with other resources of other regions. Moreover, as in an endogenous development strategy, regional culture and identity constitute a unique resource, they form the basis of a common social identity, create a sense of mutual belonging, and therefore are a source of inspiration, which stimulates the capability of a region to adopt initiatives in an international framework.

The strong trends toward a cultural uniformity between various countries and regions, as the 'global village' image would imply, must not lead us to forget that the real word is, has always been, and most probably will always be, characterised by historical differences, and variations in culture, terms of reference, and patterns of industrial development. The individual regions and countries will always be separated by a geographic and social distance. International cooperation schemes between different regional and national governments have the task of overcoming these unavoidable obstacles and of fostering the special or unique role that each region and country can play within an interregional and international context.

The different endowment of resources between the various regions, represented by their respective production know-how, whether technological or commercial and organisational, is embodied in the capacity and ability of the local labour force and represents the result of the knowledge and expertise that has been accumulated in that region. Therefore, it justifies the implementation of different strategies of industrial and international policy on the part of the various institutions. These strategies must be appropriate with respect to the specific characteristics of the particular regions concerned, and those of the other regions or countries with which they seek to promote cooperative relationships.

3.2 Common objectives
An interregional agreement implies the existence of, the constant renegotiation of, and the operative identification of common objectives. To a large extent, these must entail the use of those economic and territorial factors described above which justify interregional cooperation, such as: economies of scale, complementary individual resources, common natural resources, close integration between different socioeconomic systems,

network economies in the circulation of information, and checks of uncertainties and reciprocal competition.

According to a neo-mercantilistic approach, regional policies aimed at the internationalisation of the regional economy should endeavour only to reinforce their own trade balance or foreign investments of local firms. On the contrary, a greater integration of a regional economy in the European economy requires not only greater exports but also greater imports and should also reinforce foreign investments to the region in question.

Interregional agreements often have their origins in the necessity to resolve specific conflicts between regions of different countries, whereas formal agreements usually do not exist between regions that normally cooperate, such as those belonging to the same country. In particular, the existence of linguistic minority groups has been an important factor in the development of interregional agreements.

The experience of various regional 'working communities' has demonstrated that favourable attitudes towards interregional cooperation will increase if the focus shifts from bilateral relationships, or the harmonisation of existing respective policies, to common external relationships such as cooperation in tackling the new commercial, technological, and political challenges originating from outside the EC. External challenges and opportunities increase the bilateral cohesion within interregional cooperation.

Interregional cooperation may aim to ensure that the individual regions have greater international 'visibility', to improve their image as perceived by the outside world and to strengthen their reputation. It also reinforces their contractual 'bargaining power' in their relations with other regions or national and EC institutions.

Cooperation means that specific objectives may be attained more efficiently by a joint use of local resources. It also means that these objectives may be attained more rapidly, thus allowing the regions involved in cooperation schemes a lead time over their competitors.

3.3 Obstacles to interregional agreements

Interregional relations are hindered by the existence of specific transaction costs. Measures must therefore be taken to reduce the physical, social, or technological distances impeding a greater synergy between the regions and to create communication channels, infrastructure, and specific legislative procedures to govern the agreement and to regulate the relations between the partners of the agreement.

Lack of information regarding potential partners may clearly be an obstacle towards the establishment of agreements, although its importance is certainly lower in the case of public institutions and collective organisations, which are more visible than individual small and medium firms. A more frequent obstacle seems to be an insufficient knowledge of respective strategies and capabilities, as this often requires a long period of preliminary contacts.

A significant obstacle is the fact that many regional public institutions and collective organisations seem to be concerned only with local problems and not to be aware of the need for a strategy in external relations. This attitude is particularly frequent in countries, such as Italy, where national legislation has always sought to restrict the regions' and local authorities' political autonomy and in particular the power to represent abroad their inhabitants' interests, whereby it has restricted their role to a purely administrative function and to the implementation of centrally decided policies.

Here it may be observed that the internationalisation of public institutions, as in the case of private firms, is not only driven by the potential for gaining an advantage (pull factors), which may be only probable and not effective, but is stimulated also by the existence of an urgent need (push factors) to leave a too localistic approach. Perhaps only the fear of losing the consent of public opinion, which is increasingly perceiving the importance of international relations, will persuade some regional governments to pay greater attention to initiatives aimed at supporting their respective regional production systems in the face of international competition.

In some instances, above all in the case of larger and more economically developed regions, one has the impression that although regional institutions and collective organisations acknowledge the importance of international relations, they are insufficiently committed to developing international relations with other neighbouring regions because they are convinced that they are powerful enough to act autonomously and do not perceive the usefulness of alliances with other smaller and less developed regions. This belief in the capability of facing alone all comers seems a rather myopic view in an increasingly integrated international context where an individual region, however large, could never be competitive or play an effective role outside a specific system of alliances.

In some cases, the lack of commitment to the creation of new international alliances or to the progress of existing interregional alliances derives from a kind of jealousy in guarding the own autonomy in international relations or from the fear of having to share these with other far weaker regions. This is partially justified by the fact that each alliance, although on the surface based on total equality between its partners, always has an internal structure that may be more or less hierarchical. Thus, the participation in an alliance is not the automatic outcome of demand by the region concerned, as an obstacle may lie in the lack of interest by potential partners, reflecting the low esteem they have of this region's capability to offer some original contribution.

4 Continuity and success of an agreement

Many recent analyses of international agreements seem to attribute excessive importance to those factors encouraging or preventing the creation of an agreement. In reality, the creation of an agreement is not a sudden occurrence and it may instead be compared to a gradual learning process, which implies numerous phases or temporal stages. Thus, it seems reductive to distinguish two extreme situations—the lack of any agreement and the existence of an agreement—given that various forms of interregional cooperation, though informal in type, may be more effective in practical terms than are fully institutionalised forms that have no internal dynamism.

In some instances, it seems almost as though there were an inverse correlation between an alliance's level of formalisation and its true effectiveness, because some agreements appear to have been made only in order to identify officially the partner concerned, as in the case of many Eastern European countries, whereas the design of specific operative programmes is deferred to some future date. On the contrary, no formal agreements normally exist between neighbouring regions that have close contacts in many important fields, such as between regions of the same country. Moreover, there may be a long period of time between an intense mutual exchange of information, enabling the growth of reciprocal knowledge and trust, and the identification and implementation of an actual cooperation programme. Thus the success and continuity of an agreement depends on many factors.

4.1 Delays in the effectiveness of an agreement

Even once an agreement has been signed, it takes a rather long period of time before it becomes effective. There is an inevitable delay between the passive acquisition by a region of technological information, services, and financial and productive resources and the time when these external inputs are incorporated into the region's own productive system and the development of synergies with its endogenous resources. The transfer of technologies or organisational methods from one region to another may indeed be a long and complex process. This appears even more true in the instance of cooperation with the regions of Eastern Europe, whose economic and institutional structures differ extensively from that of the EC regions.

Here, the above mentioned distance between the partners in an agreement is of crucial importance, because the further the cultural or economic structures of the regions are from each other, the greater the chance that no proper transfer of expertise will occur or that there will be no capability to put the transferred knowledge into effective use in the process of development of the regional economy concerned.

4.2 Development of an agreement into new areas

It is difficult to quantify the success of an agreement because of the dynamic features which characterise each individual form of cooperation. An ex ante evaluation of the costs and benefits will certainly differ from an ex post assessment because of the existence of numerous unexpected positive and negative factors. An agreement may initially have one specific objective that during the process may prove of less importance compared with new directions in which the relationship can develop. The interregional agreements between firms and institutions examined in this study of the Alpe–Adria regions reveal that for many institutions and collective organisations the initial motivations behind the will to cooperate become almost irrelevant as justification of the particular operative agreements being developed, whereas the true basis of these latter relies on the positive development of bilateral relations over a long period of time.

Consequently, the success of an agreement is not simply defined as the occurrence of the initially concerted initiatives. Clearly, an agreement capable of expanding into new fields over a fairly short term and which is superseded by more complex and extensive agreements is more successful than one which lasts over a long time without undergoing substantial alterations.

Allied to these factors justifying the creation of an agreement and the ways in which it develops, are the reasons for which an agreement cannot accomplish its aims or may even be interrupted. The fact that there are clear benefits to be gained from creating an agreement does not represent sufficient reason for the agreement to be implemented, continued, and developed. Often, existing opportunities are not exploited because certain obstacles stand in the way.

4.3 Internal organisational capabilities

An alliance may fail and be broken. This may occur because of well-defined objective and subjective circumstances, whereby there is no point in continuing the alliance. In fact, where institutions and organisations have an insufficient internal organisation, an agreement may be broken because there is no capability to manage the continuity of the cooperative relationship and to invest in it. The dynamic nature of every cooperative relationship demands continuous effort in exchanging information and agreeing on new measures to resolve new problems and adapt its objectives. Inevitably, an agreement will cease if its inherent capacity to adjust is insufficient in relation to the dynamism of each partner's internal and external relations.

Even though agreements between public institutions and collective organisations are broken less frequently than those between private firms, many international cooperation agreements are basically ineffective for a long period of time because the efforts made to establish the initial contact are not backed up by any specific more-continuous action. Therefore, regions seeking to develop an effective regional foreign policy have to adapt their own internal organisational structure so that they can initiate new contacts and also gradually cultivate and develop those already in existence. In particular, smaller and more peripheral regions have not identified external relations as a field requiring a continuous effort and a stable organisational structure.

4.4 Rules and procedures for collaboration

In some cases, the interruption or the ineffectiveness of an interregional alliance may be the result of a conflict between partners in sharing the monetary and nonmonetary benefits deriving from the alliance. In this instance, the crucial factor is often the lack of clear rules, periodically reviewed, which define precisely each partner's area of responsibility and their rights. Where no clear rules or procedures for collaboration exist, the probability that one partner will seek to take advantage of the other will be greater.

All alliances embody the risk that one of the partners will behave opportunistically, depriving the other partner of some competitive edge or using the alliance instrumentally in order to obtain some particular advantage in areas different from those officially concerned. Basically, the problem seems to derive from the inability of one partner to organise its own international relations systematically or to agree with the other partner on appropriate changes in the rules of the alliance. An alliance will last only if it guarantees a *Pareto optimum* or a position where all partners are ensured an advantage, although this may differ for each partner, compared with the alternative situation of mutual competiton.

4.5 Changes in the temporal and geographic perspective

Often, the failure or ineffectiveness of an alliance may be due to the fact that each partner assigns to it a different level of importance or a different time horizon. Some may consider the alliance as a purely tactical initiative, whereas others may see it as strategic. Moreover, as time passes, the importance each partner assigns to the alliance may also change. Consequently, the level of commitment by each side may differ substantially.

An alliance inevitably implies some restriction on each party's freedom of action. Although, unlike commercial agreements, an alliance between public institutions and collective organisations can usually not contain exclusivity clauses, in this case the partners have the problem of whether the alliance could be compatible with other alliances to which they belong and intend to belong in the future. Therefore, one of the reasons why interregional alliances fail or are ineffective is that one of the partners at a certain stage feels the need for greater freedom of action with other potential actors and a wish to establish new strategic alliances.

In fact, it seems that once an external relation strategy based on multiple alliances (global strategic partnerships) is adopted, it is unlikely that individual regional or local institutions will return to a condition of 'splendid isolation'.

5 A typology of interregional agreements

Clearly, a regional foreign policy based on a strategy aimed at the development of interregional cooperation, must adequately choose the type of agreements to be promoted, thus defining the participating regions and the objects of the agreements themselves.

5.1 Bilateral or multilateral agreements

Often, large schemes for interregional cooperation, such as the three Alpine working communities (Alpe-Adria, Arge-Alp, and COTRAO), are criticised for their low operative capacity, which is attributed to a supposedly too large number of participating regions (more than fifteen regions), and someone advocates the necessity for more specific agreements of a bilateral nature. Nevertheless, it may be recognised that these two approaches are complementary, given that an interregional working community can represent the political forum for agreement on general lines and programmes of action, which may then translate into specific projects based on cooperation between a more limited number of regions.

In particular, it seems opportune to point out that the emphasis on a bilateral approach may perhaps suit the efficient operative image sought by certain regional administrators, but it probably would contribute very little in facing the specific problems of a greater integration within a large European framework. Interregional cooperation in the case of Mitteleuropa, of the Mediterranean basin, or also of the Baltic area clearly requires a multilateral approach.

In particular, a multilateral approach is crucial in order to tackle problems such as those in the fields of environment, transport, economic development, and culture, and in order to define the role of these large regions in the European perspective. Clearly, interregional cooperation should not be limited to the problems strictly related to border areas; for instance, those of border crossing or that of specific linguistic minorities. It should instead confront the problems of a more fundamental and strategic nature of the individual regions, such as the location of major international transport nodes or programs promoting culture and technology. Therefore, it is necessary to adopt a less parochial approach and a broader and more explicitly interregional and international framework.

5.2 Exclusive or multiple agreements

Regions may choose to participate in one or a limited number of completely different interregional agreements or they may participate in a wide range of agreements adopting a flexible geometry strategy. Clearly there will be an inevitable competitive relationship between the various agreements and the respective interregional groupings of regions. However, as indicated above, it seems impossible in the case of public institutions such as regional governments to demand compliance with exclusive clauses.

For example, in the case of the regions of Mitteleuropa there is a degree of geographical overlap between two old established working communities, such as the Alpe-Adria and the Arge-Alp communities and the recent working community of the Danube regions, or the interregional group of the Four Motors of Europe (Baden-Württemberg, Lombardia, Rhône-Alpes, and Catalunia) and other more limited cooperation accords existing among particular Italian regions. However, it would be unrealistic to try to merge all these interregional associations within a single association or to expect that a region should choose to belong only to a single association. On the other hand, it is clear that the international role and the competitive advantage of an individual region should depend not only on its availability of material and immaterial resources but also on the networks of agreements that it may have established with other regions.

5.3 Sectoral or territorial agreements

Interregional alliances can be described on the basis of two different approaches: a functional approach and a territorial approach. A characteristic aspect of the territorial approach is that the scope of an alliance is multisectoral and normally involves a limited number of geographically adjacent regions. In a functional alliance the number of regions involved is far larger and the objectives are more restricted, and the time scale tends also to be shorter.

Functional-type alliances usually aim to promote cooperation in specific areas between firms of the various regions: such as marketing, finance, management training, and research and development. Therefore, their purpose is to underpin a process which is already occurring spontaneously among private firms, as is demonstrated by the daily news about acquisitions, mergers, joint ventures, and other forms of agreements between various firms. Territorial alliances are more ambitious in scope and their purpose is to create new forms of cooperation which are intersectoral in nature and are aimed at involving all actors of a regional economy, including those not normally exposed to international competition. These alliances are aimed at integrating not merely the various industrial firms, but the entire socioeconomic system of the regions involved, and even their administrative institutions.

The direct target of a functional approach is to create new relationships between firms or to modify the existing links and to promote greater flows of material and immaterial types between them. The territorial approach seeks instead to achieve the same aim in an indirect way: that is to increase the ability of the various regions to establish international relations by helping them to reach, together with other regions, that critical mass needed to play a role at an international level and through the joint development of their respective endogenous resources.

This can be achieved by means of common integrated programmes among the various regions, aimed at strategic local policy areas such as environmental protection programmes, training, development of technological know-how, or cooperation between regional financial institutions. Territorial alliances may also aim at promoting a closer integration of regional economies by reinforcing the supply of services to firms, as services represent infrastructural networks regulating material and immaterial flows between the various regions.

As opposed to functional alliances, territorial alliances require a geographic vicinity of the various regions, given that it is necessary that the various private and public actors recognise their common identity or their belonging to an area that is supraregional and even transnational, sharing the same values, traditions, culture, and languages. Therefore, territorial alliances have a more solid base than do functional alliances and can more easily adapt to even radical changes either within or outside the regions involved. They tend to be more stable than do functional alliances, which do not normally outlive the attainment of their specific objective.

Although sectoral alliances promote direct interventions for the creation of specific services and productive activities, thus increasing the degree of intervention of the public institutions involved, territorial alliances between regional governments and collective organisations promote 'indirect' interventions aimed at establishing a network of communication channels that could favour the interaction between individuals and private firms, leaving the private firms free to define the specific objects of programmes of cooperation.

The real question seems to be that of acting upon those transaction costs which create obstacles to relations on an interregional scale, starting with transport and communication infrastructures, the knowledge of foreign languages and of the respective regulations, and the creation of interface centres between the individual economic actors. From this point of view interregional cooperation schemes could make an important contribution toward the completion of the European Single Market, by removing some of the costs of non-Europe that have up to now impeded the development of trade, technological, and cultural relations between the EC regions and between these regions and those of non-European countries.

Therefore, territorial-type alliances seem to be more appropriate than do functional alliances in the case of border regions, as in the case of the various working communities of the Alpine area, but they could also concern the regions of Southern Europe such as in 'Objective 1' of the EC regional policy. In reality, the fact that various regions have already developed effective joint cooperation schemes constitutes a significant impetus for other regions in the European Community to develop similar interregional cooperation schemes, to avoid remaining isolated.

6 Conclusions

Contrary to general belief, the globalisation of economies does not necessarily involve an unavoidable omologation process of consumer preferences and firm technologies within the framework of a supposed global village. Instead, it is more likely to lead to the exploitation of differences and encourage firms and regional and national economies to specialise in the production in which they have a comparative advantage (Cappellin, 1990a).

As each financial operator, private or public organisation, and even each regional administration should adapt its strategy in order to become more internationalised, the internationalisation process is basically a bottom-up process of the transformation of the regional economic and social systems. Therefore, the process of internationalisation of regional economies cannot be controlled by some central national authority, but must take into account the varying potential and different strategies of the individual local private and public operators of each region.

The changes in firm organisation and the creation of networks made by agreements and alliances on an interregional and international scale are stimulating a similar integrated system of flows of goods, services, people, and capital (Cappellin, 1989b; 1991). Therefore, regional governments should cooperate in creating important interregional and international infrastructure networks, which could allow these flows to develop, and they should coordinate their own policies with those of other regions belonging to the same country as well as those belonging to foreign countries.

Therefore, the objective of greater economic integration means that the development of transport and communications networks and of other material and immaterial infrastructures is of vital importance. These modern services will be crucial in the design of the structure of the European space.

In conclusion, regions should extend the scope of their cooperation toward the elaboration of common policy proposals at the various national and international institutions. In particular, the experience gained in the field of interregional cooperation by the various regions calls for more demanding programmes than just the exchange of information and know-how, and for the setting up of a regional 'foreign policy' based on specific operative joint projects.

This study had the aim of examining the potential for, and obstacles to, the development of interregional cooperation. Cooperation between regional authorities must be promoted alongside the growth of an increasingly sharp interregional competition within the great European economic space. Moreover, cooperation represents the only effective alternative to the bureaucratic or vertical coordination of individual regional governments by national and EC authorities. In fact, interregional cooperation illustrates that increasing European integration should lead not only to more powerful European institutions, but also to the growth of a federal institutional system, which seems the only one which could allow an effective political autonomy of regional governments.

References
Bianchi P, 1990, "Industrial districts and industrial policy interventions", in *Local Development: Regional Science Studies in Southern Europe* Ed. N Konsolas; Regional Development Institute, Athens, Greece
Cappellin R, 1983, "Productivity growth and technological change in a regional perspective" *Giornale degli Economisti e Annali di Economia* **7 - 8** 459 - 482

Cappellin R, 1988, "Transaction costs and urban agglomeration" *Revue d'Économie Régionale et Urbaine* **2** 261–278

Cappellin R, 1989a, "The diffusion of producer services in the urban system" *Revue d'Économie Régionale et Urbaine* **4** 641–661

Cappellin R, 1989b, "Networks nelle città e networks tra le città" (Inner-city networks and networks between cities), in *Gerarchie e Reti di Città: Tendenze e Politiche* Eds F Curti, L Diappi (F Angeli, Milano) pp 71–97

Cappellin R, 1989c, "Alpe Adria: possibilities and prospects" *Relazione Internazionali* **6** 60–67

Cappellin R, 1990a, "The European internal market and the internationalisation of small and medium size enterprises" *Built Environment* **1** 69–84

Cappellin R (Ed.), 1990b *Interregional Cooperation in the Alpe Adria Area and Changes in the European Economies* (ISPI, Milano)

Cappellin R, 1991, "International networks of cities", in *Innovation Networks: Spatial Perspectives* Ed. R Camagni (Belhaven Press, London) pp 230–244

Cappellin R, 1992, "Theories of local endogenous development and international co-operation", in *Development Issues and Strategies in the New Europe* Ed. M Tykkylainen (Avebury, Aldershot, Hants) pp 1–19

Cappellin R, Nijkamp P (Eds), 1990 *The Spatial Context of Technological Development* (Avebury, Aldershot, Hants)

CNEL, 1990 *Alpe Adria—Documento di Base* (Alpe–Adria: A Primer), Commissione per i Rapporti Internazionali, Relatore Cons. Alfredo Solustri, Session 19, April 1990

Fisher M, Rammer C, Schuch K, Staufer P, 1990, "The regional economy of Carinthia. Structure and aspects of interregional cooperation", in *Interregional Cooperation in the Alpe Adria Area and Changes in the European Economies, Section 4* Ed. R Cappellin (ISPI, Milano) pp 166–207

Funck R, Kowalski J, 1990, "The regional economy of Bavaria. Structure and aspects of interregional cooperation", in *Interregional Cooperation in the Alpe Adria Area and Changes in the European Economies, Section 3* Ed. R Cappellin (ISPI, Milano) pp 126–165

Grandinetti R, Rullani E, 1990, "L'economia regionale del Friuli–Venezia Giulia. Struttura ed aspetti della cooperazione interregionale" (The regional economy of Friuli–Venezia Giulia—structure and aspects of interregional cooperation), in *Interregional Cooperation in the Alpe Adria Area and Changes in the European Economies, Section 5* Ed. R Cappellin (ISPI, Milano) pp 208–276

Konsolas N (Ed.), 1990 *Local Development: Regional Science Studies in Southern Europe* (Regional Development Institute, Athens)

ISPI (Ed.), 1988 *Alpe-Adria: Une Regione Europea. Rapporto per il Decimo Anniversario della Comunità di Lavoro Alpe-Adria* (Alpe–Adria: a European Region. Tenth Anniversary Report on the Work Community of Alpe–Adria), (ISPI, Milano)

Maillat D, 1990, "Transborder regions between members of the EC and non-member countries" *Built Environment* **1** 38–51

Molle W, Cappellin R (Eds), 1988 *Regional Impact of Community Policies in Europe* (Gower, Aldershot, Hants)

Teece D J, 1982, "Toward an economic theory of the multiproduct firm" *Journal of Economic Behaviour and Organisation* **3** 39–63

Williamson O E, 1981, "The modern corporation: origin, evolution, attributes" *Journal of Economic Literature* **19** 1537–1568

Theory and Practice of Cross-border Cooperation of Local Governments: The Case of the EUREGIO Between Germany and the Netherlands

A van der Veen
University of Twente

1 Introduction

In cooperating across borders, (local) governments produce cross-border public goods. In this chapter the theory of fiscal federalism is applied to the behaviour of local governments along the borders in Europe. Special attention will be given to spatial external effects on the core regions in Europe. Consequently, the equity and efficiency aspects of regional policy will be reexamined. As a special case I highlight the first cross-border cooperation in Europe, the EUREGIO. In section 2 I present the theory of cross-border cooperation between local governments. In section 3 I give the example of the EUREGIO, discussing some major fields of activities. Section 4 shows the surplus value of cross-border cooperation in general, whereas in section 5 I present an application to the EUREGIO.

2 Theory of cross-border cooperation between local governments

The theory on cooperation between local governments can be found in the literature on fiscal federalism (Oates, 1972). In the allocative role of local governments, the tastes of the group to whom the benefits of a certain public good accrue determine the level of decentralisation. This allows the provision of different quantities of local goods. Therefore, at first sight, there is something to be said for matching the provision of local public goods with a level of government whose jurisdiction includes only those who benefit from the particular good (Broadway and Wildasin, 1984). In practice there will arise a patchwork pattern of geographically overlapping jurisdictions. Fortunately, however, there are some centralising factors as well. First there is the cost of decisionmaking, where economies of scale force local governments to limit the number of jurisdictions. Second, spatial external effects cause spillovers to beneficiaries in other regions.

Within nations the problem is the appropriate level of government for the provision of public goods is the trade-off between local tastes, economies of scale, and the size of spatial external effects. And each country has its own solution. For instance in the Netherlands the production of public goods is highly centralised, whereas in Germany the Bund has a much lower weight than the Länder.

Given a certain (de)central national organisation in the production of public goods, *cooperation between local governments* may still arise. This is because in providing public goods such as police, infrastructure, theatres, and so on, cooperation may be efficient. The outcome of this process, however, is very uncertain (Olson, 1971). Spatial external effects may thwart local initiatives for cooperation. But of course, economies of scale will ease the process of negotiation.

   Cross-border cooperation in principle has the same type of theoretical foundation as cooperation within nations. As a result of the opening of the borders of the EC, cooperation between (local) governments has a high priority. Along the borders of all European countries (local) governments try to collaborate on common goals. The interesting feature is that the already mentioned patchwork pattern of Oates, of geographically over-lapping jurisdictions of local cooperation networks, is clearly perceptible. Along the border of Germany and the Netherlands, for instance, scores of initiatives for cooperation between (local) governments are arising. Positively stated, this means that the first phase in international coop-eration of local governments is now operational. As in intranational cooperation, the important question now is: how will economies of scale and spatial external effects influence this process? To answer this question we have to assess the roots of cross-border cooperation.

2.1 Why do governments cooperate across borders?
Basically there are two answers to the question of why (local) governments cooperate across borders:
(A) There is a need to solve practical problems, such as organising ambulance transport, physical planning, environmental issues, and so on. It is the search for an optimal spatial jurisdiction in producing certain local (cross-border) public goods, incorporating economies of scale and spatial external effects.
(B) The European internal market creates new relations within Europe. Trade and industry will seek networks of cooperation on an international scale (Cappellin, 1990). Border regions may thus receive, or take, new tasks in channelling transport between urban networks. The spatial trans-lation of these processes will depend upon:
(1) gateways between the national infrastructure systems;
(2) the location of nodal points;
(3) alliances between regions, resulting in clear-cut government policy regarding physical planning, environmental policy, and regional planning.
   The reason for cooperation under (B) is, of course, not basically different from the practical problems under (A). But the spatial external effects of local cross-border cooperation may thus extend to the core regions of nations. Otherwise stated, the core regions also have reasons in stimulating cross-border cooperation. Therefore, national governments will also be involved in the process of cooperation.
   The difference between (A) and (B) is thus a distinction in the *size of spatial external effects*. This characterisation is important because it determines the position of peripheral regions in the national competition

between regions (see Vickerman, 1992, page 147). Border regions under (A) make up arrears in their relation with cross-border counterparts. Regions under (B) do the same but additionally, in the internal market of the EC, have the advantage of supplying the infrastructure for international networks to core regions.

I will return to this subject at the end of the chapter. In the next section the practice of local cooperation in the EUREGIO will be discussed.

3 Practice of cooperation of local governments: the case of the EUREGIO

The EUREGIO is one of the oldest border regions in Europe. It is the product of consultations between Dutch and German municipalities, since 1958, to overcome structural problems on both sides of the border. The peripheral regions along this border had to solve the problem of declining employment in the textile and ready-made clothing industry and in agriculture. Because other industries were highly dependent on these sectors, unemployment in the Dutch part of the EUREGIO increased to 18.0% and in the German part to 19.2%. At present, in the EUREGIO, 106 municipalities cooperate in an area with 1.9 million inhabitants. The cross-border consultations on common problems led to the establishment of the so-called EUREGIO council in 1978, which founded the *first cross-border parliamentary assembly* in Europe. This kind of cooperation on a level of a parliament is a main feature of the EUREGIO.

In figure 1 I highlight the organisation scheme of the EUREGIO. This shows that all municipalities are organised via Regional Associations in the EUREGIO. The EUREGIO Council, a parliamentary assembly, is of course *not* elected by citizens, but is elected by the representatives of the municipalities in the Regional Associations.

I will not discuss the juridicial aspects of this cooperation in detail (see EUREGIO, 1991, where attention is paid to the institutional aspects of cross-border cooperation). It suffices to say that the cooperation is governed by public law and is based on cooperation between local authorities. For Germany and the Netherlands it is important to note that the national governments of both countries concluded a treaty, in 1992, which makes this kind of cross-border cooperation between local authorities possible.

With respect to the administration of the EUREGIO it can be observed that all municipalities have to contribute a certain amount of money per inhabitant. Moreover, to finance prolonged projects, the EC, in the period 1991 – 93, paid Dfl 80 million.

3.1 Fields of activities of the EUREGIO

Within the scope of this chapter it is impossible to discuss all aspects of the activities of the EUREGIO (see figure 1). I will focus on social affairs, especially labour markets, on economics, and on transport and infrastructure.

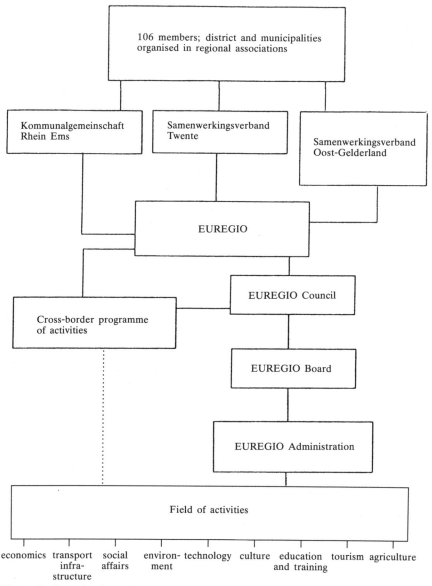

Figure 1. Organisation scheme of the EUREGIO.

3.1.1 *Cross-border labour markets*

As discussed above, one of the main reasons to start cross-border cooperation in the EUREGIO was a high unemployment rate. Therefore, in the cross-border programme of activities, much attention has been given to labour-market issues. Here I will concentrate on commuting, education and training, and employment policy.

In the EUREGIO, with a population of 2 million inhabitants, the number of *commuters* from Holland to Germany is about 2000; from Germany to Holland it is 350. This difference is comprehensible because Dutch inhabitants speak German. There are, however, many obstacles for commuters. These hindrances go back to national differences in social-security systems and fiscal systems.

In the design of policy instruments to overcome these obstacles the following actions are undertaken by the distinct government levels. On the level of the EC, recommendations are developed so as to promote the convergence of social-security systems. Recommendations are also in preparation to overcome differences in fiscal systems concerning the individual levying of taxes. National German and Dutch authorities deliberate about the same problems. Germany and Holland concluded a fiscal treaty, which eases tax paying considerably. Finally, the EUREGIO offers an open office in several municipalities to inform individuals on working across the border.

For *education and training* at an EC level, a licence exchange has been strongly promoted, especially for universities. For vocational training, however, the situation is bad. The EUREGIO therefore erected a foundation for cross-border vocational training. This foundation should lead to more licence exchanges, with the ultimate target of enlarging the labour mobility between the two countries.

An important issue in cross-border labour markets is the balancing of *labour supply and demand*. In the EUREGIO, with financial support from the EC, the information system JET (Job Euro Transfer) for vacancies has been installed on both sides of the border. Persons seeking employment may find vacancy information at a local bureau of employment.

3.1.2 *Economics*
Apart from the labour-market topics mentioned above, the EUREGIO designed other, economic, instruments to decrease unemployment. An interesting example has been the organisation of industrial fairs for Dutch and German local business, which are aimed at creating networks for industries.

3.1.3 *Transport and infrastructure*
A well-known problem of border regions is the design of infrastructure across borders. National governments design railway and motorway infrastructure in their own national interest, which results in networks that sometimes halt at the border, or that have to change to a different system. To function as a region, the EUREGIO had a natural interest in adjusting infrastructure. Therefore, the improvement of public transport links and the enlargement of cross-border roads and motorways were seen as necessary conditions for regional and cultural development.

An important location factor for the EUREGIO is its position on the West–East transport axis, along the motorway A1/A30 and the cross-border

4.2 Cooperation with high levels of spatial external effects

Border regions in most European countries are peripheral regions. In the network of urban regions in Europe, some border regions now play a special role. Channelling transport and designing new infrastructure not only is in the interest of the cultural and regional identity of these border regions, but also may be of major significance for the core regions. National governments thus have a clear interest in organising cross-border cooperation.

In the design of regional policy, equity and efficiency are the well-known elements. They are seen as antipoles. The interesting point with respect to border regions now is that by accompanying cross-border cooperation for peripheral regions, national governments can kill two birds with one stone. First, by institutionalising cross-border cooperation and by conducting this proces with national (infrastructure) instruments, former peripheral regions will improve their position; for infrastructure remains a major location factor. Second, for the core regions, cross-border cooperation is an efficient instrument to improve their position in the competition between urban regions in Europe. *Here, the surplus value of cross-border cooperation is the combination of equity and efficiency arguments.*

5 Surplus value of cooperation in the EUREGIO

Taking the example of the EUREGIO, local cooperation may have significant spatial external effects. Improving infrastructure in this region not only has consequences for regional development in the EUREGIO, but will spread to the core regions in the Netherlands and Germany. The conduction of this process by national government then is a necessary condition for an efficient supply of cross-border public goods.

At the moment the municipalities in the EUREGIO cooperate in a unique parliamentary assembly, the EUREGIO Council. It will be a challenge for national governments to yield rights to this Council and, perhaps, to design voting systems for the Council. If all levels of governments succeed in attaining this target, the EUREGIO preeminently is, and will be, the European example of cross-border cooperation.

References

Boadway R W, Wildasin D E, 1984 *Public Sector Economics* (Little, Brown, Boston, MA)
Cappellin R, 1990, "The role of interregional cooperation in international relations: the case of Mitteleuropa", paper presented at the 30th RSA European Conference, Istanbul, 1990; copy available from the author at Istituto di Economia Politica, Universita Bocconi, Milano, Italy
EUREGIO, 1991, "Cross-border cooperation in practice: institutional aspects of cross-border cooperation", EUREGIO, Enschede, the Netherlands
Oates W E, 1972 *Fiscal Federalism* (Harcourt Brace Jovanovich, New York)
Olson M, 1971 *The Logic of Collective Action: Public Goods and the Theory of Groups* (Harvard University Press, Cambridge, MA)
Vickerman R W, 1992 *The Single European Market: Prospects for Economic Integration* (Harvester Press, Hemel Hempstead, Herts)

Theory and Practice of Interregional Cooperation and Urban Networks in Economically Lagging Regions: The Experience of Galicia and the North of Portugal

A M Figueiredo
Oporto Faculty of Economics

In this chapter I analyse the cooperation and neighbourliness between the Portuguese region of Norte and the Spanish region of Galicia, as an example of transborder and interregional cooperation evolving in the context of a European lagging transnational area. In fact, not only is each region facing serious development gaps relative to the EC average income per head and other performance indicators, but also the whole territory is one of the least favoured parts of Europe as far as social and economic cohesion is concerned.

The aim in this chapter is to contribute to a more generalised approach to the theory and practice of interregional cooperation and urban networks in economically lagging regions, within the framework of comparative analysis with other models of interregional cooperation, such as the cooperation experiences between developed regions and between developed and lagging regions.

This chapter is divided into three main sections. In the next, the main structural adjustment problems in this transnational area are described, given the development models and trajectories evolving in the two regions. It is very important to analyse the development prospects of the northwest part of the Iberian Peninsula within the broad framework of patterns of development in European lagging regions. In this section, the results of GREMI's recent research on European lagging regions is seen to be an important point of reference for the analysis of structural adjustment problems emerging in this transnational area (Camagni, 1992; Quevit, 1992).

In the third section, I discuss the actual and the potential roles of transborder and interregional cooperation and of urban networks in helping the regional and Community development strategies underway in this territory. The role of interregional cooperation in providing new strategies of external regional policy for regional authorities and other regional actors, and in contributing to the creation of new territorial axes and areas in terms of social and economic cohesion of European territory, is emphasised in order to approach the specific dimension of interregional cooperation and urban networks in lagging regions. Urban networks are seen as a fundamental element of the cooperation strategy, given the change anticipated in the most important urban centres of Galicia and Norte and in the characteristics of their urban systems.

Eixo Atlântico (Atlantic Axis) is the name of the network formed by the seven most important cities of Galicia and the six most important cities of the North of Portugal. The creation of a new development space in the territory occupied by these thirteen cities calls for a cooperation process in which relations of complementarity and cultural neighbourliness tend to be the key dynamic factors. Nevertheless, I argue that it is important to combine this strategy with a variable geometry of interregional cooperation defined according a strategic view of the spatial organisation of European territory and the particular requirements for know-how, transfer of technologies, and new markets for lagging regions such as Galicia and Norte.

Finally, in the fourth section, I discuss what would be the role of interregional cooperation and urban networks as an instrument of regional policy for lagging regions following a development trajectory similar to that of Norte and Galicia.

I emphasise the need for a coherent integration of incentives for regional authorities, cities, and other institutional actors, and small and medium-sized enterprises in cooperation in the context of EC regional policy for lagging regions. It is important not to limit the model of EC technical and financial assistance for interregional cooperation to the experience of the most developed transnational European areas, where all the regional actors involved currently accept the principle of 'cooperation is business'.

The regional foreign policy for lagging territories and the improvement of internationalisation conditions of regional small and medium-sized enterprises should be approached from a similar strategic view and should reinforce each other, even though regional authorities and cities are not usually competent in terms of industrial policy. So, the role and aim of EC incentives and procedures should support the emergence of coherent strategies of the different actors and institutions involved in interregional cooperation schemes.

Community Framework Support in lagging regions for the period of 1994–99 provides an excellent opportunity for the introduction of the internationalisation vector in regional policy. Interregional cooperation and urban networks are one of the main instruments to succeed it.

2 The transnational lagging area of Galicia and Norte: structural adjustment problems in a context of diffuse urbanisation and different levels of political decentralisation

Even though Galicia and Norte are both members of the 'Objective 1' less-favoured group of European regions, this broad typology of European regional policy is not a useful one for identifying the key structural adjustment problems in that transnational lagging area. A dynamic perspective of development trajectories is needed to approach problems faced by this area in the scenario of European nominal and real convergence.

In any case, the main indicators published in the last CEC report on the socioeconomic development of European regions (CEC, 1991) allow for a deeper insight into development trajectories evolving in this area. As can be seen from table 1, some striking differences were evident between the two regions in the second half of the 1980s. The values of the unemployment rate, the percentage of agricultural employment, income per head, and productivity all suggest that the low level of development performance has been the result of different trajectories.

In the global context of high population density (principally in Norte) and of a very late process of modernisation in agriculture, a very impressive trade-off between the disequilibirium of labour markets and the levels of productivity and income per head is emerging in this area. So, in Norte, the weaker performance in terms of income per head and productivity is the price paid for having a low unemployment rate. As far as Galicia is concerned, the cost of better performances in terms of income per head and of productivity is higher unemployment (11.8% in 1990) and underemployment, namely in agriculture (the adjusted unemployment rate estimated by the CEC in 1990 is 15.9%).

Very different models of industrialisation, transition, and change explain these different development trajectories. In Norte, industrialisation is the result of export-led growth supported by small and medium-sized enterprises and endogenous private capital initiatives, with a very elastic supply of labour; in Galicia, on the contrary, public intervention, investments, and incentives are the main factors of the industrialisation process.

Moreover, the timing of industrial structural adjustment was very different. In Galicia, the crisis of the 1970s in sectors such as shipbuilding, aluminium, and car industries anticipated industrial adjustment. In Norte, traditional sectors such as the textiles, clothing, and footwear industries faced another kind of structural adjustment over a much longer period of time. Additionally, some hidden and artificial factors of competitiveness (low wages, flexible labour markets) explain the persistence of high employment levels in these sectors.

Put briefly, although public initiative preceded industrialisation in Galicia, in Norte one may speak of a reverse sequence of development (Hirschman,

Table 1. Galicia and Norte as a transnational lagging area in an EC context (source: CEC, 1990).

	Norte	Galicia	EC
Population, 1988	1.1	0.9	100.0
Unemployment rate, 1990 (%)	3.1	11.8	8.3
Average unemployment rate, 1988–90	35.7	137.3	100.0
Agricultural employment (%)	23.8	39.3	7.6
Average GDP per head, 1986–88 (PPC)	41.9	63.7	100.0
Average GDP per person employed, 1986–88	44.7	69.7	100.0

1984, page 96) in which endogenous capital and entrepreneurship often preceded public investments in social overhead capital. The industrialisation models of Galicia and Norte are thus apparently complementary, suggesting a high potential for cooperation. However, one should be aware of adjustment trajectories. In other words, it is necessary to analyse whether or not regional development trajectories, under way after adjustment problems, tend to converge. In Galicia, public investment can hardly be the engine of future industrial growth, given the debt burden of the central government and regional autonomies. In Norte, the low-profile model of low wages, flexible labour markets, and traditional export sectors is no longer creating new jobs and the unemployment rate will tend to rise.

The relevant question is not how to become a member of the Objective 1 group of regions; it is to identify regional-development trajectories after industrial adjustment and to appraise the potential for the cooperation emerging in this new context. Complementary growth and development sources may coexist with competition areas in the whole territory of Galicia and Norte, and the cooperation strategy should take account of this.

As regards infrastructure needs, this lagging area should combine the improvement of infrastructures that produce externalities to the competitiveness of local systems with the improvement of the quality of life in territories in which urbanisation dominates urban systems. Dispersed urbanisation runs counter to dispersed urban planning, particularly in a situation similar to that in Galicia and in Norte, where income per head is low. The high infrastructure costs of dispersed urbanisation present difficult budgetary problems for municipalities to solve. So, it is very difficult to extend the benefits of a process of sustained growth of income per head to this urbanisation model.

Striking examples of dispersed urbanisation characterise the territory of Galicia and Norte as a whole, particularly in those areas where the concentration and density of human settlements is high. This is one of the main reasons why, with the exception of the Oporto agglomeration, each one of the principal urban centres does not have enough potential to attract strategic services and to compete with other European agglomerations. Table 2 gives a broad perspective of this urban system, indicating the population and density of the principal cities and agglomerations presented in the Eixo Atlântico networks.

The chance of a new development space being created in the northwest of the Iberian Peninsula strongly depends on the structuring of a polycentric urban system focused on the principal cities of Galicia and Norte, probably led by the internationalisation potential of the Oporto agglomeration. The potential social and economic change introduced by this global urban system, which is served by an efficient internal transport network, compensate for the problems posed by dispersed urbanisation. Interregional cooperation and urban networks should provide an answer to these strategic needs.

Table 2. Cities and agglomerations of Galicia and Norte represented in the Eixo Atlântico network (sources: CCRN, 1993; Xunta de Galicia, 1990).

Area	Population 1991	Density (km^{-2})
Oporto city	302500	7203
Oporto agglomeration[a]	1013500	1814
Oporto metropolitan area[b]	1168000	1433
Viana do Castelo[c]	83100	263
Braga[c]	141300	789
Vila Real[c]	46300	125
Chaves[c]	40900	68
Bragança[c]	33100	29
La Coruña city[d]	241809	6535
La Coruña metropolitan area[d]	333585	676
Vigo city[d]	263998	2422
Vigo metropolitan area[d]	405118	520
Orense[d]	100143	1178
El Ferrol[d]	86154	1051
Santiago de Compostela[d]	86250	387
Lugo[d]	75623	228
Pontevedra[d]	67289	570

[a] 6 municipalities.

[b] 9 municipalities institutionalised as a metropolitan area.

[c] Including the whole municipality.

[d] Reported to 1986 and including the whole municipality.

---

3 The variable geometry of interregional cooperation as a strategy for a lagging region: the experience of Galicia and Norte

The interregional cooperation between Galicia and Norte is a good empirical example of the *role of the variable geometry of interregional cooperation as a strategy for a lagging region*. First, the experience is a highly successful example of the integration of transborder and interregional approaches (Figueiredo, 1990; Rich, 1988). Second, it illustrates that different stages of regional political autonomy are not a major obstacle to a cooperation strategy, given that autonomy in Galicia is very high compared with that in Norte, which lacks administrative and political autonomy. Third, it proves that the existence of common cultural values is, in fact, a precondition to implement any interregional cooperation scheme.

It is not difficult to identify the strategic factors of the interregional cooperation.

(1) Both regions are expecting the same impacts of the reform of the EC agriculture policy because of the disparities of their agriculture productivity compared with the EC average, the underemployment remaining, and the very high average age of farmers which is a common obstacle in the renovation of agriculture entrepreneurship supply.

(2) They both need a new period of intensive productivity growth and enhanced-value products, by means of improvement in sectoral and product diversification, upgrading, learning-by-doing, and technology transfer. In the case of Norte, this results from a need to upgrade the specialisation profile of its traditional sectors. In Galicia, it is because the declining sectors initially supported by public investments and companies are no longer credible for industrial development.

(3) The difficulties of communication (by road, train, or air) with the European concentration and developed areas, still present an obstacle to a better integration in European space for both regions.

(4) Both regions are lacking in critical mass in terms of human resources and research and development potential.

(5) The high-value-added business services in the main urban centres of the two regions are very weak, calling for the attraction of foreign investment into these areas in order to enhance the value of the existing services.

(6) The urban network of Norte and Galicia, when seen as a whole, is more competitive, depending on the reinforcement of economic and cultural links, between the Oporto agglomeration and Galician medium-sized urban centres.

(7) The Oporto–La Coruña axis, eventually extended to Lisbon, must be seen as an important aspect of the spatial organisation of Western European territories, following the conclusion of the recent exploratory study of the Atlantic regions (CEDRE, 1992).

The interregional cooperation has been recently institutionalised as a 'Comunità di Lavoro' (Cappellin, 1991b, pages 1–2). It corresponds to an increased activity of the two leading institutions (Xunta de Galicia and Commissão de Coordenação da Região do Norte) to diversify the cooperation strategy, extending it to other regional and local actors, and aiming to coordinate their actions.

Table 3 indicates the cooperation projects currently under way between the two regions, the regional and local actors involved, the kind of projects, and the expected results. Urban networks and agreements between entrepreneurial organisations are not integrated with those of the core areas of the EC.

As an urban network, the Eixo Atlântico is at a very early stage of cooperation agreement. A strategic study of cooperation potential emerging from the thirteen-city urban system will be the most important outcome of this phase. Some attempts to articulate this network with the Galicia–Norte network are underway. Nevertheless, the two networks will evolve in different institutional ways: the Eixo Atlântico network as an association seeking to be heard in Brussels; the Galicia–Norte community as a general agreement lacking juridical personality.

As far as entrepeneurial agreements are concerned, it has been difficult to integrate them into EC strategy. First, because of the lack of regional autonomy in Norte and the lack of regional incentives, the regional

Table 3. Cooperation projects within the Galicia – Norte region.

Sectorial commission	Cooperation projects	Main characteristics	Regional and local actors involved
1. Agriculture and fishing	Study on Galicia and Norte wines	Global characterisation and identification of all types of wine production supply	Agriculture Regional Board of Entre-Douro e Minho (DRAEDM), Estación Enologica de Galicia, Comissão de Vitivinicultura da Região dos Vinhos Verdes
2. Agricultural and fishing	Study on vineyard diseases	Common research and development projects of some vineyard diseases in order to improve the quality of wines and the profitability of investments	Tras-os-Montes University (UTAD), DRAEDM, Estación Enologica de Galicia, Estación Fitopatologica de Diputación, Provincial de Pontevedra
3. Agriculture and fishing	Development potential of indigenous cattle breeds	Exchanges of experiences, research projects, and reproduction techniques, aiming to conserve and to improve indigenous races	UTAD, Facultad de Veterinaria de Lugo, Xunta de Galicia
4. Agriculture and fishing	Development perspectives of agriculture and complementary activities in transborder areas	Global study of transborder agricultural areas in order to identify the most important production systems, their profitability, and the impacts of price changes	Institute for Norte Region Agriculture Development (IDARN), Xunta de Galicia
5. Culture and local development	Interregional cooperation as regards Development Agents Training programmes	Global meetings between local development agents working in both regions, development of common training actions for local development agents	Norte Region Association of Local Development Agencies (ADENOR), Conselleria de Trabajo e Servicios Sociales de Xunta de Galicia

,

Table 3 (continued)

Sectorial commission	Cooperation projects	Main characteristics	Regional and local actors involved
6. Culture and local development	GALLAECIA 92-93	A vast programme of cultural initiatives between the transborder areas of Ourense and Chaves in the fields of urban animation, art, painting, theatre, etc	Local associations, local authorities
7. Culture and local development	Santiago de Compostela roads	Inventory of historical roads to Santiago de Compostela as a factor of cultural animation of transborder areas and of promotion of cities integrated in those historical itineraries for pilgrimage	Cultural associations, Dirección Xeral de Cultura da Xunta de Galicia, Oporto University, Oporto traditional arts centre
8. Training	Exchanges of pupils, teachers, and experiences between professional schools (intermediate schools) for young people of 15-18 years old	The exchanges concern the fields of tourism, agriculture, and communication	GETAP—Technological, Artistic and Professional Education Department, intermediate schools, Conselleria de Educación e Ordenación Universitaria de Xunta de Galicia

administration is facing a lot of difficulties in involving entrepreneurial organisations in its cooperation strategy. Second, the already existing agreements between the regional confederations of Galician and Norte entrepreneurs are aimed at securing better transport infrastructures, improving the accessibility within Galicia–Norte, and reducing the physical distance to the European centres.

Despite this fact, the Galicia–Norte region is searching for an indirect involvement of enterprises and entrepreneurial organisations, developing other fields of cooperation with other regional actors and institutions in which regional economic operators could be interested; for example, professional training and research and development projects for the technological modernisation of traditional industrial sectors. The incentives to immaterial development actions included in the INTERREG programme between Portugal and Spain will help the diversification of cooperation projects, integrating the transborder and the interregional perspectives.

The experience of this community is anyway a good illustration of how INTERREG can be used as an instrument to help interregional cooperation. In this case, the experience is bilateral, but the extension to multilateral interregional cooperation is conceivable.

Viewed from this perspective, the community can also be an observatory of economic and social dynamics arising from the accomplishment of the Single Market in peripheral regions. But, as lagging regions, Galicia and Norte, in terms of interregional cooperation, need something more than the creation of synergies from the approach of common problems or from complementary endogenous resources.

Cappellin speaks of a "form of regional foreign policy" when "the various aspects of international relations within a single region were coordinated" (Cappellin, 1991a, page 7). The need for this foreign policy in lagging regions is obvious and interregional cooperation must be an operative way to achieve it.

Anyway, peripheral regions, such as Norte and Galicia, need to develop a cautious interregional cooperation policy, supported by a *variable geometry strategy*. First of all, regional authorities and actors must be able to distinguish the lobbying effect of some interregional organisations from their capability to develop credible cooperation networks and projects, and to be a source of enhanced know-how in promoting complementary endogenous resources (Cardoso and Figueiredo, 1990, page 154). The two aspects are both relevant for lagging regions. Nonetheless, they may be found in different interregional organisations. The geometry of cooperation axes may be variable, depending on the objectives that should be achieved as well as on the potential supply of cooperation emerging from the different networks created. Norte and Galicia are simultaneously members of the Atlantic Arc Commission and of the European South Atlantic (ESA) Regions Association.

A solid regional foreign policy should have a clear perspective on the strategic arguments justifying the need for a variable geometry strategy of interregional cooperation. As regards the Atlantic Arc movement, it is important to note that the political initiative of Atlantic regional leaders preceded cooperation dynamics: "Atlantic Arc is an idea, a mobilizing idea aiming to reinforce the solidarity of regions from the North of Scotland to the South of Portugal" (Guesnier, 1990, page 53).

In other words, as a concept in movement, the Atlantic Arc political initiative of regional actors, particularly of French ones, aimed to reduce the lack of economic solidarity between Atlantic regions, clearly represented in the weakness of trade flows between these regions, and to be heard in prospective discussions about the spatial organisation of European territory (Raffarin, 1991). If, in addition, one is aware that Atlantic French coastal areas are not included in the Objective 1 group of regions, the main reasons for a political initiative become more clear.

The construction of cooperation networks between Atlantic regions has evolved very slowly. The first package of projects submitted to the EC was in fact very poor in terms of strategic orientation, with the exception of a project on software modernisation at seaports. Actually, the main orientation is to press for an EC initiative in Atlantic regions following the prospective study promoted by the EC, in the framework of the Europe 2000 Programme.

Norte adopted a selective strategy of adhesion to the Atlantic Arc, in order to explore specific solidarities with other Atlantic regions, but refused a global approach of a loser's group. This approach of developing specific solidarities is featured strongly in the exploratory study by CEDRE, namely in the following cooperation fields:

(1) the networking of high-technology areas such as engineering science, marine science and biology, antipollution and environmental conservation technology, "creating wide areas of competence or otherwise of specialized poles with a sufficient and credible critical size";

(2) the building up of an Atlantic tourism product, exploring the existing complementarities, and probably in articulation with the American approach of the Atlantic Rim;

(3) the development of intermodal transport, applying not only to the transport of goods, but also to link-ups between regional airports and railway network.

These fields are good illustrations of specific solidarities justifying a nonexclusive adhesion to the Atlantic Arc. Nevertheless, the involvement of Norte regional actors, including the private sector, in interregional cooperation projects has proceeded further in the ESA Regions Association.

The main justification for this is a clearer perception of ESA strategy by all regional actors. The strategy began to be developed from an interregional agreement on infrastructure priorities, essentially promoted by Euskadi, Poitou-Charentes, and Aquitaine regions. Subsequently, it was extended to professional training, research and technological development, and forests.

The strategic interests of Galicia and of Norte in this network are obvious. Galicia, exploring the relationships of the Cantabric Axis with the node Euskadi–Aquitaine, will be able to participate in a new spatial development axis with the aim of being an interface between the northern and southern parts of Western Europe.

Norte, belonging to what Brunet (1990, pages 180–181) calls the North of the South of Europe, will be interested in exploring the natural access to continental Europe by Castilla y León and to approach the Ebro Valley and French regions such as Midi-Pyrénées. ESA regions realised very clearly that European territory and Atlantic regions in particular are crossed by several geo-logics (north–south, west–east, centre–periphery, and so on) and that interregional cooperation strategy could only be developed from a variable geometry of approaches (Figueiredo, 1992).

After considering the bilateral cooperation as a potential for an enlarged network, the ESA Association sought to develop the west-east territorial logic in order to promote a new development space in European territory, exploring the preeminence of the node Euskadi-Aquitaine. In the western part of this development space, Galicia and Norte play a role as the equilibrium factor within the network, benefitting from the magnitude and the internationalisation of the Oporto agglomeration. The structuring of the urban system of the two regions around the initiatives promoted by the network of thirteen cities is another relevant factor to be considered. Additionally, they are a natural bridge to Latin America, the United States, and Canada, considering the Galician and Norte immigrant colonies existing there.

The ESA network benefitted from RECITE programme support only in the case of the cooperation project on forests. Meanwhile, two other cooperation areas were underway. First, Poitou-Charentes leads a training programme of 'Développeurs Communautaires' supported by a budgetary line of one million ecus approved by the European Parliament. Second, the Exchange of Experiences Programme (EEP) managed by CEDRE supports the ESA network in research and development in the fields of biotechnology (animal and vegetal), automation, and new materials.

The frustrated expectations of stronger EC financial support produced some perverse effects concerning the adhesion of regional actors to the regional authorities' initiative. Nevertheless, in the forests project, private producers are fully represented. In this case, a virtuous effect has been produced in Norte and in Central Portugal. In order to be fully represented in the network, regional forest producers created a regional association of private interests, breaking the dependency on the existing national association.

The variable geometry strategy of interregional cooperation is then an operative approach to regional foreign policy. As regards know-how and technology transfer or markets diversification, Norte could be interested in searching for another network, in order to solve more specific needs. Oporto University and some regional research and development centres, for example, are well represented in other European networks, with a different territorial configuration.

The Oporto municipality is a leading member of EUROMETROPOLIS, which is an enlarged network of European cities, developing cooperation experiences in the fields of transport, universities, international trade, and industry and services. In addition, the Oporto municipality is the leader of the Atlantic Axis network with other cities of Galicia and of Norte, and very close relations with Barcelona are under way, exploring some political affinities between the two municipalities.

Meanwhile, the main challenge is to search for synergies between the initiatives under way in the framework of territorial networks (led by the regional authority and the Oporto municipality) and the strategies of internationalisation and cooperation led by the other representative regional actors and institutions.

The geometry of interregional cooperation and of urban networks in Norte begins to be complex. With Cappellin's definition of regional foreign policy—that is to say, a "co-ordinated approach of the various aspects of international relations within a region" (Cappellin, 1991a, page 7)—the variable-geometry strategy of cooperation reaches a critical point when the coordination ability of regional authorities becomes a scarce resource.

One may speak then of a critical level of coordination capacity of interregional cooperation networks and projects by regional authorities. Consequently, the variable-geometry strategy of interregional cooperation must be selective, particularly in relation to those projects affecting the internationalisation aspects of the community support frameworks. However, one may substantially reduce the need for coordination capacity if the relations between regional authorities and the various forms of the civil society tend to be flexible and transparent.

4 Interregional cooperation and EC regional policy: how to integrate the diversity of experiences

4.1 Virtues and limits of the principle of transfer of know-how

There is no tradition of using interregional cooperation as an instrument of regional policy. Article 10b of the ERDF regulation is based on a vague principle of helping the exchange of experiences and cooperation between regions. The EEP managed by CEDRE in Strasbourg and the RECITE programme developed by the CEC itself are very recent initiatives supported by Article 10b.

The central idea of considering interregional cooperation as a factor and as an opportunity for transfering know-how from the rich regions to the less-developed ones is the leading principle followed by the CEC in this matter. Curiously, if one considers the objectives of the RECITE programme diffused by DG-XVI, one may conclude that the CEC is thinking of a very wide concept of transfer of know-how and experiences. In fact, the objectives of promoting the rapid transfer of know-how and of experiences between the authorities of the developed and the peripheral regions include the improvement of the management of local and regional authorities in the less-developed European regions. The implementation of this principle runs the risk of ignoring the fact that community experiences of interregional cooperation are not automatically guided by the model of central versus peripheral regions.

There is evidence that regions are approaching each other according to their average development performances. The ability to cooperate in strategic terms depends on regional development performances. So, the diversity of interregional cooperation experiences tends to reproduce the clusters of European interregional disparities.

The experience of cooperation between Catalonia, Baden-Würtemberg, Lombardy, and Rhône-Alpes is widely quoted as an example of a high-level cooperation strategy. One of the fundamental reasons for the wider scope of cooperation objectives and actions is that the private sector is, in this case, more able to understand and to manage the competition/cooperation game. Development dynamics and innovation performances become significant factors in the selection of partners for the implementing of cooperation projects.

In any case, in a scenario of globalisation and of internal market achievement, the principle of the transfer of know-how is of course a good orientation for peripheral regions looking for a place in competitive markets. However, that is not the right point. The real problem is how to locate, and how to adapt, that principle within a more complex scenario of interregional cooperation experiences. Other geographies are possible. Thus, it is very important to create the right conditions for extending the principle of the transfer of knowledge and expertise to experiences of cooperation other than those commanded by private actors, namely enterprises.

A strategic view in terms of the interests of the lagging regions requires a deeper insight into other typologies of cooperation experience. The alternative is to ask for some paradigmatic illustrations of a more complex scenario of cooperation approaches, chosen in order to demonstrate the strategic implications for peripheral regions.

First, one should consider the experience of cooperation developed between peripheral regions aiming to achieve one or both of the following objectives: (a) to search for and to explore some potential or effective complementarities in order to ensure the intensification of economic and cultural flows within peripheral areas; (b) to achieve a kind of synergy in terms of international mobilisation and promotion of common resources or 'excellence poles'.

Second, it is necessary to take care of the emerging cooperation networks between regions aiming to stimulate and to manage new development spaces, following a strategic view of the process of spatial organisation of European territory, and searching for alternative concentration areas for human resources and activities (CEC, 1991). One should have in mind that such experiences become key factors for an important role in a broad approach to European economic and social cohesion, including the territorial dimension.

Third, it is necessary to work on the creation of networks at the same time as integrating regions and cities. The improvement of the efficiency and of the efficacy of economic and political cooperation efforts often requires a more cooperative way of selecting the right institution (region or local authority) to assume the leadership of the project. In fact, paradoxically, sometimes a cooperation project may create a conflictual relationship between regional and local authorities. In other words, sometimes cooperation experiences tend to produce noncooperative behaviour in regional actors.

None of these models of interregional cooperation fit easily into the general framework of developed regions approaching lagging ones. But more important than accepting the diversity of reality is realising that these experiences are not lacking credibility for having been promoted and managed by less-developed regions. Additionally, they are not condemned to become a 'loser's group' or an 'association of hunters looking for community incentives'. In other words, interregional cooperation following these three types of experiences is not necessarily one more factor contributing to the world of subsidised economies emerging in some peripheral areas.

As regards the first group of experiences, the emerging cooperation projects between some of the Atlantic regions may be seen as a good illustration of this tendency. For example, an interregional cooperation programme between Atlantic regions looking for a new product in the world market of tourism called 'Atlantic Tourism', including environmental, cultural, animation, and rural development factors, can contribute towards a denser structure of flows within the Atlantic regions to ensure the mobilisation of common and complementary resources.

One may discuss how it would be feasible to introduce the principle of the transfer of know-how and expertise within these models of interregional cooperation. It certainly depends on the concrete situations figured in the different experiences. As it is generally accepted, one may find a place for specific solidarities between peripheral regions, even though these regions may be very different in terms of regional disparities.

Thus, it will be possible to identify some sources of know-how and expertise within these experiences and to promote the right projects to implement the transfer. But the more important adaptation of the principle of the transfer of know-how is to profit from complementary factors in the context of the same 'product' in order to produce, by means of interregional cooperation, the upgrading of common knowledge. In the case of the creation of the product called Atlantic Tourism, interregional cooperation leads to a higher level of know-how and expertise in terms of entrepreneurial skills and promotion. In fact, not all regions have the same ability to explore the different elements of the product. However, there is a mutual interest in developing the new product, not only in terms of markets, but also in terms of entrepreneurial knowledge and skills.

The second group of experiences concerns cooperation networks between regions associated under a strategic objective of creating new development spaces in EC territory. There is an important role to be played by interregional cooperation, particularly when prospective studies and political decisions begin to shape the spatial organisation in Europe over the next few decades. In this case, as well as exploring complementarities between regions, the networks concern the potential of spatial contiguity and of neighbourliness in order to help create new spatial development axes.

The kind of agreements to be created in this network model may easily combine the interregional rationale with bilateral and/or multilateral transborder agreements and cooperation projects. Step by step, drawing on the experience accumulated by transborder agreements as a capital for extending mutual knowledge and trust in the interregional approach, this type of interregional cooperation network becomes an instrument to insure European internal cohesion in territorial terms. The strategy of the South Atlantic Europe Region appears to be a good illustration of this model.

Finally, as regards the third group of experiences, urban centres are, in peripheral regions, a key factor of regional economic recovery and of internationalisation. Regions (regional authorities) play an important role in promoting exchanges of experience and concerting and promoting agreements between regional and local actors. It is necessary to go further and to attempt to involve municipalities and cities in the process. In this matter, EC experience is unhelpful. The RECITE programme, in which the rules were not very clear, contributed indirectly to the reinforcement of competition between regional and urban networks.

The RECITE programme application rules were prepared and announced on the assumption that interregional and urban networks were independent forms of cooperation (EC, 1991). The cooperative procedures between regional authorities and municipalities were not specified as factors that would affect the credibility of the project. Competition is, of course, possible and sometimes useful between regional authorities and cities. Nevertheless, in order to ensure the credibility and feasibility of cooperation projects it is necessary for all the actors involved in the projects to be able to manage the operations. Thus, very often projects are presented by institutions which do not have either the legal capacity to interfere or the physical capacity to implement the projects. This is the main reason why there are cooperations in which the cooperative procedures between regional and local authorities are a precondition to success.

In brief, even though the three models presented are not an exhaustive description of European experience, they are a good illustration of the diversity of models. However, particularly from the point of view of lagging regions, one should recommend that EC regional policy on interregional cooperation should assume the right to diversity and not limit the community support to the model of the exchange of experience between developed regions and peripheral regions.

The RECITE programme gave priority to projects and networks having one or more Objective 1 regions as partners. This is just a formal criterion. In practical terms, the results achieved frustrated the expectations of a transfer of knowledge. In some projects and networks submitted to the DG-XVI General Board, the logic of the conception of projects was completely outside the peripheral regions or cities. The priority accorded to the presence of Objective 1 regions produced perverse effects contrary to the principle itself. The participation of these regions resulted from the bureaucratic procedures of application and not from a sustained approach of the transfer of knowledge.

As regards interregional organisations, such as the Conference of Maritime Peripheral Regions of the EC, this approach presents some difficult problems. First of all, it is not very easy to separate the role of the network as a lobby and its role as a forum stimulating the creation of cooperation networks and projects. In a typically defensive reaction, the EC refused many of the projects coming from these organisations, arguing that EC support cannot be an instrument to reinforce political lobbies in Europe.

Several misunderstandings and a number of frustrated expectations further complicated the situation. This is not the place to discuss the question of the effect of lobbying in regional policy. As regards the improvement of interregional cooperation networks and projects, interregional organisations need to be more rigorous in terms of technical assistance to the partners involved and in relation to the identification of strategic areas of cooperation.

4.2 Interregional cooperation, the 'hard' and the 'soft' dimension of regional development policy

The Objective 1 peripheral regions are strongly dependent on ERDF in terms of the financing of their infrastructure development needs. The cohesion fund will provide another opportunity to solve financing problems in this matter, because the agreements emerging from Maastricht would be respected.

Meanwhile, EC regional policy has started to emphasise the 'soft' or the 'immaterial' dimension of the structural adjustment of less-developed regions, and several EC instruments and initiatives are aimed at the most efficient combination of hard and soft dimensions of development programmes. Nevertheless, the very weak infrastructural base of some lagging regions, particularly in terms of infrastructures affecting the competitiveness of regional enterprises, justifies another approach. The search for the most efficient combination of hard and soft investments is a relevant question once the threshold of infrastructure resources endowment has been achieved. So the real convergence of peripheral areas to EC average development performances will continue to require a critical mass of infrastructures. Regional and local authorities tend normally to exaggerate those needs and this is the reason why immaterial community support finds some resistance to being accepted as the main priority of development interventions.

Apart from some transborder infrastructures (as for example roads and bridges, or others improving the quality of life in the transborder areas), admitted by the EC initiative INTERREG, EC incentives to interregional cooperation are mainly soft instruments.

In fact, EC incentives to interregional cooperation should not of course be just another source of finance for infrastructure projects for lagging regions. However, in a scenario of European spatial restructuring, interregional agreements on strategic infrastructures could be a vital instrument in order to promote new spatial development axes. European internal cohesion is not necessarily solely the concern of member states. If it were, the European spatial planning of Europe would run the risk of reinforcing the tendencies of concentration and being limited to the existing networks between the most important European metropolises.

Additionally, the EC Cohesion Fund will not cover all types of infrastructure projects. The urban renovation of historical centres, the infrastructural base of new touristic products, the modernisation of ports, are all examples of exchanges of experiences and interregional agreements that may combine the hard and the soft dimensions.

Regional and urban networks aiming to contribute to the promotion of new development spaces may find the right mix of the hard and soft dimensions of interregional agreements in order to stimulate more positive attitudes to cooperation strategies from regional and local political actors. Sometimes, as it is the case of the ESA, the agreements on strategic infrastructures become the leading factor contributing to further interregional cooperation projects.

4.3 Interregional cooperation and the creation of networks of regional and local actors within the regions

The experience of interregional cooperation studied in this chapter shows that the ability of regional authorities to promote the participation of regional and local actors and institutions (universities, research and development centres, entrepreneurial associations, and so on) in transnational networks is a key factor in the progress of interregional cooperation. The general situation in Europe is very heterogeneous. In some cases, regional actors are in a better position to have access to these networks, given their knowledge of the internationalisation of markets and of technology and expertise transfer, the more flexible management rules of private-sector budgetary facilities, or simply a faster perception of profitable investment opportunities in cooperation projects. Unfortunately, this is not usually the situation in peripheral areas.

So, regional authorities should play a role in mobilising regional actors (private sector and civil society) and providing them with important complete information about interregional cooperation opportunities, including EC incentives and programmes. However, regional authorities and entrepreneurial organisations are currently undergoing conflictual relationships. The entrepreneurs are often looking for financial support from regional authorities but they refuse to share the management and the follow-up of the cooperation projects. In other cases, regional authorities' strategies and enterprises do not fit each other and it is difficult to find the appropriate transnational networks in order to produce a common interest.

The empirical evidence shows that the ability of regional authorities to promote agreements within the region in order to ensure successful regional participation in transnational networks does not depend exclusively on the stage of regional autonomy that has been achieved. Regional authorities with more-decentralised powers are not necessarily in a better position to achieve that objective. The relevant task is then to analyse how the partnership is being implemented.

Interregional cooperation depends consequently on societal questions. What then are the consequences of this approach for EC regional policy support to interregional cooperation?

First of all, in what concerns management and follow-up models of interregional cooperation projects and programmes, the articulation between the CEC, regional authorities, and regional and local actors must be improved. The RECITE experience is a good support for this. In fact, in some projects it is not clear if they are submitted to the CEC after being discussed and assumed by regional authorities or if the reference to the regional authorities made by regional or local actors is only a question of bureaucratic procedure. Very often the leadership and the financial control and follow-up of the project are not clearly separated, producing a lot of misunderstandings within the region itself. The natural consequence is that the network will be in trouble or that the lagging region must quit.

The situation is globally different for cooperation projects developed in relevant areas for the implementation of the Community Support Framework in the region. It would be interesting if alongside the preparation of the next Community Programmes Support (1994–99) the lagging regions could integrate the interregional cooperation as an instrument of regional development policy, considering that internationalisation is a precondition for their structural adjustment programmes.

5 Conclusions

In sum, it is relevant to improve EC regional policy action in support of interregional cooperation in order to promote new attitudes in regional authorities and actors as regards the competition/cooperation game.

(1) Article 10b of ERDF is no longer an operative way to support interregional cooperation projects and networks, because it risks being a residual source of EC assistance.

(2) It would be very interesting to extend the EC initiative INTERREG to interregional cooperation, allowing a better combination of the hard and soft dimensions of structural adjustment in lagging regions and a close integration of transborder and interregional cooperation.

(3) One should emphasise the right to the diversity of interregional cooperation experiences and models, particularly concerning the implementation of the principle of transfer of knowledge.

(4) International regional organisations must be seen as frameworks stimulating the emergence of feasible and credible networks and not exclusively as lobbies searching for EC incentives.

(5) It is necessary to generalise the evaluation studies of interregional cooperation programmes, projects, and networks in order to see what kind of experiences should go on being supported.

(6) It will be necessary to implement a reform of management and of follow-up models in order to clarify the relationships between regional authorities and regional and local actors within regions that are members of European networks.

(7) EC support must look for a better integration of interregional and urban cooperation networks.

References
Brunet R, 1990 *Le Territoire dans les Turbulences* (The Territory in a Turbulent World) (Géographiques-Reclus, Montpellier)
Camagni R, 1992, "Development scenarios and policy guidelines for the lagging regions" *Regional Studies* **26** 361–374
Cappellin R, 1991a, "The international dimension of regional economies' interregional cooperation in Europe", paper presented in the V Workshop of the Joint Programme on Regional Science Studies in Southern Europe, Poitiers; copy available from Regional Economics Institute, Poitiers
Cappellin R, 1991b, "La cooperazione interregionale nelle Comunitá di Lavoro tra le regioni della Mittel Europa" (The interregional cooperation within the community between the regions of Mittel Europe), paper presented to the Conference 'I Parchi Tecnologici Nelle Sviluppo Economico Urbano'; copy available from Council of European Municipalities and Regions, Paris
Cardoso A, Figueiredo A M, 1990, "North of Portugal and the Atlantic Arc: some elements to a selective strategy of adhesion", paper submitted to the Seminar 'La Dynamique Atlantique,' Centre d'Économie Régionale, Poitiers; copy available from Regional Economics Institute, Poitiers
CCRN, 1993 *Recenseamento à População 1991—Dados Pré-definitivos* (Population Census 1991—Preliminary Data) (Comissão de Coordenação do Norte, Porto)
CEC, 1990 *The Regions in the 1990's: Fourth Periodic Report on the Socio-Economic Situation and Development of the Regions of the Community* (Commission of the European Communities, Bruxelles)
CEC, 1991 *Europe 2000: Outlook for the Development of the Community's Territory* (Commission of the European Communities, Bruxelles)
CEDRE, 1992 *Étude Prospective des Régions Atlantiques* (Prospective Study of Atlantic Regions), European Centre for Regional Development, Bruxelles
EC, 1991, "Appel de propositions de réseaux d'autorités régionales et locales désireuses de réaliser en commun des projets à caractère économique au titre de l'article 10 du règlement FEDER—Régions et Villes d'Europe (Recite)" [Call for propositions of regional and local authorities networks aiming in common to develop economic projects under article 10 of ERDF regulations—regions and cities of Europe (Recite)] *Journal Officiel des Communautés Européennes* June, number C 198/8

Figueiredo A M, 1990, "Do processo ao Programa Operaçional de Cooperação: novas perspectivas para o relacionamento Galiza – Norte de Portugal" (From the process to the Cooperation Operational Programme: new perspectives for the relations between Galicia and North of Portugal), in *Segundas Xornadas Tecnicas Galiza – Norte de Portugal* (Xunta de Galicia, Santiago de Compostela) pp 1 – 20

Figueiredo A M, 1992, "La stratégie de développement du SEA" (The ESA development strategy), rapport présenté aux Quatrièmes Rencontres Interrégionales du SEA (Association des Régions du Sud Europe Atlantique, Porto)

Guesnier B, 1990 *Potentialités et Stratégies de Développement des Régions de l'Arc Atlantique en Europe* (Development Potentialities and Strategies of European Atlantic Arc Regions), Colloque Scientifique International de Poitiers 'La Dynamique Atlantique' (Centre d'Économie Régionale, Poitiers)

Hirschman A O, 1984, "A dissenter's confession: the strategy of economic development revisited", in *Pioneers in Development* Eds G Meier, D Seers (Oxford University Press, New York) pp 87 – 111

Quevit M, 1992, "The regional impact of the internal market: a comparative analysis of traditional industrial regions and lagging regions" *Regional Studies* **26** 349 – 360

Raffarin J P, 1991, "La coopération interrégionale", report submitted to the European Parliament Conference on the European Regions; copy available from the European Parliament, Strasbourg

Ricq C, 1988, "Bilan et perspectives des Institutions Transfrontalières Hispano-Portugaises", paper presented to the Seminar 'Galice et Région Nord du Portugal avant 1992'; copy available from Xunta de Galicia, Santiago de Compostela, Spain

Xunta de Galicia, 1990 *Galicia en Cifras* Xunta de Galicia, Santiago de Compostela, Spain

The Channel Tunnel and Transfrontier Cooperation

R W Vickerman
The University of Kent at Canterbury

1 The regional context

The Channel Tunnel has become an interesting case study of the way in which a transport infrastructure project can be used as an instrument both of regional development and of transfrontier cooperation. Here I will examine the way in which the decision to construct the Channel Tunnel has led to different responses in the neighbouring regions of Kent (United Kingdom) and Nord – Pas de Calais (France). However, it has also led to an interesting range of cooperative ventures between these two regions as they sought to maximise the potential advantages they can obtain from the Tunnel. This is heightened by the very different political and administrative structures in existence in the two regions, reflecting the differing competences of the local or regional authorities in the United Kingdom and France. A further dimension to this is provided by the interest of Belgian regions in joining the transfrontier cooperation.

The cross-Channel transfrontier region is therefore somewhat different from many other transnational interregional arrangements. These typically involve:

(1) regions with similar industrial structures or economic characteristics, which seek scale economies in developing joint policies, such as the traditional industrial regions (RETI, 1990);

(2) regions with a common, largely artificial, land frontier, and hence typically a common cultural experience, which seek to complete a single functional geographical region, such as Franco-Belgian or Franco-Swiss regions (Quévit, 1988; Maillat, 1990);

(3) regions with similar geographical locations at the macro-European scale, which seek the development of a common set of policies, such as those in the Atlantic Arc (CEDRE, 1993).

In the case of the Channel Tunnel we have two very different regions in terms of economic experience, structure, and culture, separated by a significant physical barrier. They have similar geographical locations to some extent, within both a national and a wider European context, but the physical barrier of the English Channel has a very significant impact on this. The existing economic links are essentially not between the two regions; their common interests are largely concerned with the flow of traffic between the major metropolitan areas, between which they are located, which passes passes through them. Despite long-standing transport links by ferry, it is only the decision to construct the fixed link of the Channel Tunnel which has generated interest in, and acted as a catalyst for, cross-border cooperation. This is strange in that it can be argued that the construction of the Tunnel will have the effect of speeding up traffic flows through the regions and lessening rather than heightening the economic ties. Thus the increasing interest in cooperation is largely seen as a defensive one of attempting to identify and exploit the potential in the Tunnel. Moreover, there is a fear of these advantages being potentially more advantageous to the other region. The defensiveness is thus between the two regions as well as toward any third region. This explains the further interest of other neighbouring regions to join the cooperation.

2 The Channel Tunnel project—the decision

The decision to construct the Channel Tunnel was taken jointly by the British and French national governments in January 1986, following a competitive bidding process (see Holliday et al, 1991b, for a detailed discussion). The decision had already been taken that the Tunnel should be constructed and operated under a concession granted by the governments to a concessionaire who would have exclusive rights to the Tunnel's operation for a period of fifty-five years (until 2042) from ratification of a Treaty, and monopoly rights over the fixed-link operations until 2020. More significantly it had been determined that the Tunnel would be financed entirely by the private sector, through a mixture of loans and equity. The original (1985) estimate of the total cost was £4.5 billion, but this has escalated to a likely completion cost of (at constant prices) £9 billion or more.

The Channel Tunnel is more than just a simple fixed link between the British and French coasts, it involves two transport systems. One is a pure railway link between the British and French national railway systems, which will carry through passenger and freight trains. The other is a shuttle-train system which, by carrying road vehicles, would provide a link between the respective national road systems. This is important because the use of the tunnel requires the use of national road or rail networks in the two regions.

Thus, from the perspective of the most directly affected regions, the decision to construct the Tunnel and all day-to-day issues affecting its construction and exploitation were taken outside the region and with no formal mechanism for the representation of regional interests. It was agreed in the United Kingdom to establish the Channel Tunnel Joint Consultative Committee, chaired by a minister, but this was essentially viewed (by the UK central government at least) as a troubleshooting venture during construction rather than as a real involvement of regional interests in decisionmaking. The Committee has, however, been extended into the operational phase to deal with further issues.

As the governments had agreed there should be no public money in the project, there was no explicit role for the European Community, although the European Investment Bank has sought a continuing involvement in its financing. This now amounts to a total investment of £1.3 billion; £1 billion guaranteed by private-sector letters of credit and £0.3 billion loaned against the existing equity of the project.

3 Implications for the regions
3.1 The Kent and Nord–Pas de Calais regions
The two regions of Kent and Nord–Pas de Calais have certain similarities and dissimilarities. However, the most important point to note is that prior to the decision to construct the Tunnel they had virtually no formal contacts in place at either the political or the administrative level. Kent has traditionally been an agricultural and commuting region, with a range of lighter industries, but some concentrations of heavier industries in the north of the county (CTJCC, 1986). Nord–Pas de Calais, in contrast, is characterised by its range of older industries, although these have been in serious decline for a considerable time (Holliday et al, 1991a). The traditional coal-mining industry is now completely closed and the textile industry has lost over 40 000 jobs over the past five years. The region consists of a major urban conurbation around Lille, an area of smaller industrial centres in the mining basin, and the coastal area, centred on the three ports of Dunkerque, Calais, and Boulogne. In recent years the two regions have had very similar levels of GDP per capita, typically around 90% to 95% of the EC average (CEC, 1987; 1991; Eurostat, 1993). Nord–Pas de Calais has typically had rather higher rates of unemployment of up to 18% in places, but there are important pockets of very high unemployment in Kent as well, including two of the twenty worst areas of unemployment in the United Kingdom.

The completion of the Channel Tunnel poses major problems for the regions. First, it implies a need to restructure the traditional port industries. Cross-Channel ferries on the short sea routes between Ramsgate, Dover, and Folkestone in Kent, and Dunkerque, Calais, and Boulogne in Nord–Pas de Calais currently carry between fifteen and twenty million passengers a year out of a total market, including air, of sixty-five million passengers. The total cross-Channel freight market is around eighty million tonnes per year, of which some thirteen million tonnes passes through the Port of Dover, although this underestimates, by a substantial margin, the value of this traffic, which amounts to some 20% of the total value of all UK trade. It is estimated that the Channel Tunnel will take some 35% to 40% of the passenger market and up to 20% of the freight market (Le Maire and Pevsner, 1992; Vickerman and Flowerdew, 1990). This is likely to halve the ferry traffic and reduce employment by some two-thirds (up to 7500 jobs in Kent) given the need for the ferry companies to increase efficiency to enable them to compete effectively.

Second, the regions have had to accommodate the construction. This has brought benefits and costs. Benefits have accrued particularly to Nord–Pas de Calais where the traditional industries and the range of available skills of the labour force have been appropriate to such a major construction project. At the peak of the Tunnel construction some 88% of the employment on the French side was drawn from the region, meeting the requirements agreed with the contractor at the start. The employment in Kent, resulting from the construction, was never expected to be as large as that in France, but in the event rather more employment was created locally, some of this being because of the larger labour force necessary to catch up on early delays in tunnelling. However, the construction still had a substantial effect on local labour markets, both in terms of reducing unemployment in Kent, from 55 529 people in June 1987 to 24 230 in June 1990, and in pushing up local wage rates. The decline in construction since the period 1990 – 91 has coincided with the economic recession and unemployment had risen to 75 000 people by the end of 1992.

Third, there is the much broader question of how far the existence of the Tunnel will create secondary employment effects by enhancing the regions' attractiveness as a location for industry (Vickerman, 1994a). This will depend on several factors. The completion of the Tunnel will improve the accessibility of these regions to a wider potential market. However, the completion of the associated rail and road infrastructure provides the opportunity for speeding the flow of traffic through the regions. This could have the effect of removing the existing transshipment effect of port operations and replacing it with a through-transport corridor. More positively, however, the existence of the Tunnel could lead to a reevaluation of the regions' prospects by potential investors in much the same way as does accessibility to airports. I now take each of these issues in turn and relate them to the formation of policy in the regions.

3.2 Accessibility and economic potential

The effects on accessibility and economic potential are the obvious first response to a project such as the Channel Tunnel. Keeble et al (1982) demonstrated clearly how a tunnel which had the effect of removing the time and costs penalty associated with the ferry crossing would raise a simple measure of economic potential. The impacts would be strongest on the nearby regions, especially South East England, because there would be an immediate impact on the size of the hinterland. Such an analysis has a number of problems, however. It is aggregated and does not recognise the differing economic structures, specialisation, and trade potential of each region, as well as the intraregional accessibility factors (Vickerman, 1993; 1994a).

The localisation of industry tends to reflect an existing pattern of communications. Industries adjust to the relative location of a region such that they do not in practice suffer the implied transport cost penalty (Chisholm, 1992). Thus the process of centralisation that has been observed in Europe is more to do with the existence both of internal scale economies and of external economies of agglomeration and urbanisation than with accessibility per se (Krugman, 1991). Changes in accessibility may lead to long-term changes in localisation, but these are likely to be less abrupt than the analysis of potential suggests.

They are also driven by other factors. Changes in the overall level and pattern of demand, through both the business and the product cycles, affect the overall structure of industry and employment. The age and size structure of firms also affects the adaptability of firms and their ability to respond to change.

Studies of potential assume a coincidence of the geographic and economic centroid. It is assumed that the internal transport system of a region is reasonably uniform in quality and that regions do not differ substantially in the levels of service provided by the intraregional network or its connectivity to the interregional network. In practice a major difference in the performances of regions may be attributable to differences in the level and quality of service from the regional transport network.

Taken together these factors help to explain why some central regions of Europe, including regions such as Kent, Nord–Pas de Calais, and Wallonia, appear not to have benefitted substantially from their relatively central location in the European Community, whereas some of the faster growing or dynamic regions are more peripheral to this traditional core, such as Rhône-Alpes, Cataluña, Lombardia, or Oberbayern (Vickerman, 1992).

3.3 Corridor and network effects

A major concern for the affected regions is the need for investment in the regional transport infrastructure networks, both road and rail. This investment is necessary to ensure that increasing traffic flows through the Tunnel do not result in excessive congestion on the regional networks, to the detriment of the efficient operation of those networks for local traffic. However, these road and rail improvements may have the effect of reducing the relative attractiveness of locations close to the Tunnel. Currently, proximity to the ports can be an advantage. If more-distant locations have other advantages, they may be better able to exploit the improvements to the networks. This is particularly true of rail improvements, where access to the network is controlled, but may also be true of road improvements where, for example, motorway-standard routes are constructed with limited access to improve the flow of through traffic and, in the case of toll routes, to reduce the costs of toll collection (Vickerman, 1994b).

Road improvements have featured strongly both in Kent and in Nord–Pas de Calais. Both regions have recognised the need to balance the requirements of local and longer-distance traffic. Hence we have seen the completion in both regions of a major motorway route leading away from the tunnel. The A26 route in France leads inland from Calais to join the A1 at Arras, which provides access to Paris, and further to Reims and Dijon, thus giving access to the whole of eastern and southern France avoiding Paris. In Britain the completion of the M20 route provides access to the M25 London Orbital Motorway and hence to the remainder of the motorway network. In addition, both regions have been intent on improving access from otherwise bypassed areas to this spinal transport cord by upgrading existing regional roads. This affects such areas as Boulogne in Nord – Pas de Calais, and Thanet in Kent.

Where there are important differences between the two regions is in the development of other key corridors. In Nord – Pas de Calais the opportunity has been taken to use the Tunnel in order to develop the coastal corridor, not just to link the otherwise disadvantaged ports of Dunkerque and Boulogne to the new network, but to develop alternative routes into Belgium to the east and to Rouen and around Paris to the west (Bruyelle, 1994; Holliday et al, 1991a). This also provided the opportunity to develop a second, shorter route to Paris via Amiens. This is a reflection of the more strategic planning environment available in France through the Schéma Directeur Autoroutier. This provides both a national planning framework and the scope for regional and local plans which fit inside it. In Kent the geography does not provide quite the same opportunities for the creation of a transport node based on the Tunnel terminal. However, it is notable that there has been no planning of a coastal route to the west to provide a link to the major urban areas of Brighton, Portsmouth, and Southampton, and also provide a route other than the congested M25 route for access to the South West and South Wales. All that has been achieved is a proposed planning study of a Kent – Hampshire route.

3.4 The development of rail networks
More substantial, however, is the difference in attitudes to rail planning. First, it is clear that the two countries, France and the United Kingdom, had already embarked on rather different strategic courses towards the long-term development of rail. In France the first new high-speed rail line, the TGV (Train à Grande Vitesse) Sud-Est between Paris and Lyon, had been opened progressively between 1981 and 1983. This system, operating at speeds of up to 280 km per hour, had been an immediate and greater than expected success in terms of the number of passengers carried and profitability. In Britain, despite early experiments with a high-speed train (the Advanced Passenger Train, designed to run at speeds of up to 240 km per hour on existing tracks) there were no such general plans for high-speed operation. Increasingly during the 1980s British Rail (BR) was being required to operate as a commercial undertaking. Not only were any new investments required to meet increasingly stringent financial criteria on rates of return, but also whole sectors of operation were expected to operate at an overall profit. These included the InterCity operations.

Thus it is not surprising to find that the UK government regarded any rail development as an accompaniment to the Tunnel, needing to be justified on the basis of the existing commercial criteria for rail investment of an 8% return on capital. This would apply to any track improvements, rolling-stock investment, new station construction, as well as any decision on a new, high-speed line.

In fact, at the time of the decision to construct the Tunnel in 1986, the high-speed line was effectively ruled out on political grounds. The aborted scheme to build a similar Channel Tunnel in the 1970s had been abandoned largely as a result of escalating costs, particularly of the new line through Kent, then considered essential (Holliday et al, 1991b). To some extent the long-term decline in commuter rail traffic into London during the 1970s and early 1980s helped this argument as BR could now claim that there was sufficient capacity to cater for an increase in international traffic. However, from the government's point of view it was essentially a political decision, to avoid the environmental problems associated with such a major project becoming confused with the decision on the Tunnel itself, which dominated. It was felt that the delicate financing operation of the Tunnel would be upset by any reference to a new railway line. Furthermore, the Channel Tunnel Act, 1987, included an explicit reference (Section 42) prohibiting any UK government from subsidising international rail services. This prohibition was introduced overtly to assure port and ferry interests that the Tunnel, to which rail traffic would be captive, would not receive an unfair competitive advantage. However, it also protected the government from subsequent pressure to subsidise a new line.

The situation was rapidly overtaken by events. The long-term reduction in commuter traffic was reversed from 1984 and by 1988 it was clear that BR would have severe difficulty in coping with international traffic on the crowded Kent rail network by the mid-1990s. Even at the Tunnel's opening it is likely that some peak-hour international trains will have to be diverted via alternative routes because of capacity constraints at critical points. From 1988 onwards, BR sought possible solutions. This would need new construction and the most efficient solution would be construction of a new line from the Tunnel to London. It was also clear that the capacity at the initial London terminal at Waterloo would be reached after some five years of operation, so it was also decided to try and combine this with the development of a second London terminal at Kings Cross. This would have the advantage of providing much better through and interchange facilities for access to other UK regions beyond London.

Two major problems have emerged. First, environmental considerations have proved extremely difficult. A new high-speed line would involve around 120 km of new route built through one of the most densely populated regions in the United Kingdom (indeed in Europe), where the nonurban areas are almost entirely covered by some form of environmental protection. This suggested that large sections of the railway would need to be in expensive tunnels. Costs escalated from an initial £1.5 billion to a high of £4.5 billion. Following a long period of delay and a rethinking of the routes and the engineering requirements, the government finally announced in March 1993 a preferred route with a cost of around £2.5 billion. This will allow the process of environmental consultation to begin with a view to passing the necessary legislation in order for the line to be in service by around the turn of the century.

Second, the government's insistence on at least partial private finance, even allowing for some subsidy to the construction of a new line for use by regional trains from East Kent to London, has so far proved impossible to realise. Private investors have shown an understandable reluctance to invest in a project which does not have the monopoly rent of the Channel Tunnel and on which government policy has in any case been unclear, especially with regard to the conditions under which privatisation or franchising of BR's operations will occur. The announcement of March 1993 provides for a joint venture between public and private sectors, with the private sector taking the lead in the design and building, but the public sector guaranteeing the project in some form. The public-sector involvement is being justified on the provision of half of the line's capacity for domestic rail traffic between Kent and London. This is the current UK government's preferred mode of financing new infrastructure projects, but it remains to be seen whether this can be realised within the committed timescale. After a delay of five years from the first routes being proposed, further prevarication would be a major embarrassment.

In France, in contrast, the decision to construct the TGV Nord from Paris to Lille and the Tunnel was taken by the government in October 1987, just prior to the public flotation of Eurotunnel. In other words, the French government could be seen to some extent to be underwriting the Channel Tunnel's financing by agreeing to a key piece of supporting infrastructure. The issuing of the Déclaration d'Utilité Publique at this stage ensured rapid completion of the planning process. Construction started in 1988 and will be complete by the opening of the Channel Tunnel—in fact services commenced on part of the new line in May 1993, with full operation in September 1993. This 330 km of new line is also part of the proposed northern European high-speed rail network, the so-called PBKAL (Paris – Brussels – Köln – Amsterdam – London), which will have further links to Frankfurt am Main, via a new Köln – Frankfurt line, and to the rest of the French TGV network, via the Paris Interconnexion. This also provides access to the Charles de Gaulle airport in Paris, as well as the airports at Brussels – Zaventem and Amsterdam – Schiphol.

For the two regions, it is clear that decisions on high-speed rail links are even more remote than those for roads, given the levels of finance required and their essentially interregional impacts. However, the rail developments are crucial for the regions in two respects, where again there are important contrasts. One relates to the provision of stations; the second to parallel investment in the regional rail network. Both of these are concerned with connectivity to the network.

3.5 Rail-related developments

In Nord–Pas de Calais the key development has been in Lille. The original plans of SNCF (Société Nationale des Chemins de fer Français) considered a series of alternative routes between Paris and the Tunnel. The route finally selected had the aim of economising as much as possible on the amount of new track, by combining the Paris–Tunnel and Paris–Brussels routes with a junction at Lille, instead of more direct routes via Amiens or direct across the Plain of Flanders from Arras to Calais. This would have included a station on a green-field site outside Lille. Local interests considered that a central Lille site for a new station was vital to local business developments; such a site was available adjacent to the existing railway station. The extra cost of between FFr 800 million and FFr 900 million was accepted by local and regional authorities (the Communauté Urbaine and Conseil Régional), although the final costs were shared with the national government. This is a good example of local interests being able to respond to a new development and achieve significant local advantages. The region and Lille were not able to influence the basic decision on the route, but were able to secure detailed modifications. The new station complex in Lille is being used as the basis for a major commercial development, the Euralille Métropole (a joint public–private venture), which will serve to regenerate a major part of the urban core of Lille. This is capitalising on the unique geographical position Lille will have within the core European-capitals region, especially its future position as a major interchange point on high-speed rail routes in the PBKAL network (Bruyelle, 1994).

Although the developments in Lille are the key ones in Nord–Pas de Calais, there are other significant rail-related developments at Arras (based on the TGV station) and at Calais (based on the Tunnel terminal and adjacent TGV station). In addition to the direct station access to the TGV network and associated commercial developments, a key feature of the French TGV philosophy has been the use of trains which can use existing electrified rail routes at normal speeds and new lines at high speeds. A further dimension to the development of TGV Nord has therefore been the construction of key turnouts from the new line to link it to the regional network, coupled with the electrification of some routes, to ensure that all major urban centres in the region can be served by direct TGV services. This is important for towns off the main line of the new transport corridors, such as Dunkerque, Boulogne, Valenciennes, and Roubaix–Tourcoing. Again these additional works have been financially underwritten by the region (and in some cases the local authorities or Chambres de Commerce et d'Industrie), although part of the cost is in most cases shared with the central government.

A similar strategy has been apparent in Kent. The need to develop a key access gateway to the new rail network in the county as a basis for attracting new industrial and commercial activity, whilst also developing the regional network in a complementary way, was recognised in the plans for Ashford. Here it was planned to develop an international passenger station, independently of future long-term plans for a high-speed rail link. However, there is a complete contrast in terms of the ability to make progress on this strategy, principally because the mechanisms do not exist in Britain to enable local authorities to secure rail developments in anything other than a limited way. The local authorities in Kent have had to rely on their lobbying of BR and central government (PACEC, 1991).

BR and the government have had problems in coming to an agreement on the financing of a station. BR needs to have guaranteed access to the necessary funds and to be able to present the investment as a financially viable venture to the government before it can go ahead. It is not able to include potential future business gains to the area, nor is it able to use local-authority (or EC) finance as an additional source of funding. Hence, after an agreement, during the passage of the Channel Tunnel Act 1987, committing the government to ensure provision of a station at Ashford, a firm commitment to the station was not made until March 1993. The government is still seeking private-sector involvement of up to £50 million in the total cost of £80 million, and it is now impossible for a station to be in service by the inauguration of through passenger services expected for Spring 1994. This means that rail passengers to and from destinations in Kent will probably need to travel into London and out again (return distances of up to 250 km) to use international passenger services. In the absence of the high-speed rail line this implies additional journey times of some $2\frac{1}{2}$ hours.

A similar situation applies to ancillary rail investment in Kent. The government has sanctioned a substantial investment in track and signalling improvements, new international trains, and a new terminal at London Waterloo, amounting to over £1.5 billion. Much-needed track and signalling improvements on routes other than those that will carry international trains has been left undone and the provision of new trains for regional and commuter services in Kent has been deferred indefinitely. From the point of view of the region it is this supporting investment in its own services which is a critical factor in ensuring the attraction of new investment and the development of local businesses.

3.6 Business developments

The approaches to business development in the two regions also show some similarities and some differences. As a region which has been coping with long-term decline in its traditional industries, Nord – Pas de Calais has been used to restructuring policies. Many of the traditional heavy industrial sectors have undergone a characteristically French process of the establishment of joint public – private Sociétés de Reconversion. These have not stemmed the rate of decline in industries such as textiles or steel, and have failed to prevent the complete closure of shipbuilding and coal mining.

At the time of the announcement of the Tunnel project the region was in desperate need of further help. The response to the Tunnel has been principally to use it as a lever to change the profile of the regions' industries by attracting firms in new and high-technology sectors (Holliday et al, 1991a).

The creation of major business development areas in Lille (the Euralille project) and around Calais (both at the terminal and in a number of other locations) is an attempt to build on their strategic locational advantages. These are backed up by land prices which are only a fraction of those in Kent, around one-tenth or less is typical. As well as the emphasis on new activities, transport developments also feature strongly in the form of multimodal interchanges. However, the region also faces a long-term problem of low skill levels, which generally militate against the attraction of new, high-technology industries. Complementing the policy of investment in transport infrastructure is also a major policy of investment in education and training, the human capital infrastructure.

Nord–Pas de Calais faces the additional problem that it has benefitted substantially from the construction phase of the Channel Tunnel. The reduction in the construction work force poses problems of redeployment and retraining. In a sense the construction phase of the Tunnel served to delay difficult decisions about the long-term restructuring of regional employment opportunities.

In Kent the lack of traditional heavy industries, with the exception of a small coalfield which finally ceased production in 1990, meant that the Tunnel construction was less significant for employment. Unemployment levels, with the exception of the 1987–90 period, have remained high. For the county as a whole unemployment was 11% in December 1992. The worst unemployment area, Thanet in the extreme northeast of the county, had a rate of over 16%. As in Nord–Pas de Calais, one of the main difficulties has been the planning of appropriate training of the work force to ensure its compatibility with future demands from new industries (*Kent Economic Report* 1993).

Business-park developments have been to the fore here also. Several sites have been selected, at or near to good access points to the infrastructure, especially at Ashford. However, these are on a generally smaller scale than in Nord–Pas de Calais, with the total area available in the whole of Kent (around 800 hectares) being equivalent to that available just at the Tunnel Terminal in Calais. Initial development concepts based on the growth of distribution have been shown to be less appropriate in Kent. The location is less favourable for European distribution than are sites in Nord–Pas de Calais, for reasons both of accessibility and of land costs. For UK distribution, the problems of the access to major markets, given the congestion imposed by the intervening presence of London, make Kent less attractive than sites closer to or beyond the capital (PACEC, 1991). Kent had been less successful than other parts of South East England in attracting high-technology industry—the location quotient for high-technology manufacturing in 1981 was 0.70, compared with an average of 1.77 for other counties of the South East outside London, and a high of 2.89 in Hertfordshire to the north of London. For high-technology services the figures were 1.06 for Kent, 2.67 for the region outside London, and a high of 6.13 in Oxfordshire (SERPLAN, 1985). Nevertheless the general overheating experienced in the late 1980s in these other counties suggested that substantial spillover investment could be attracted by the improved accessibility of which the Tunnel (and its international rail services) was one element. Both service and manufacturing activity in this sector, and financial services, largely because of the push-out effect from other areas, could be attracted to appropriately developed sites in Kent. Such activity could be reinforced by a development of tourism.

In 1987, the first estimates of the *Kent Impact Study* suggested a total secondary employment effect of around 12 500 jobs (CTJCC, 1987). However, later reanalysis of this suggested that such a figure was rather optimistic as an estimate of the directly induced effects of the Tunnel. In 1991, following the onset of recession, this figure was revised downwards to just 2500, with much of the reduction being accounted for by more realistic assessments of the employment-generation potential of development in the distribution and tourist sectors (PACEC, 1991). An initial proposal to establish an East Kent Development Agency (CTJCC, 1987) was not successful given the disagreements between the District Councils. Following the review in 1991, an East Kent Initiative was established as a public–private partnership, strongly promoted by Eurotunnel, with a specific short-term remit to identify and promote the interests of the East Kent area.

Although a sensible development strategy of providing modern sites with good access to roads (and, where possible, rail) has been followed, Kent does continue to have major disadvantages. It is close to London, which has suffered relatively badly in the recent recession. Its position to the southeast of London makes Kent highly dependent on London both for markets and for job opportunities. In common with other peripheral areas, the coastal belt faces particular problems. A relatively old population and a relatively unskilled work force, traditionally employed in the old-style holiday industry which has suffered badly from competition from newer holiday destinations in the Mediterranean, have led to the high levels of unemployment already referred to. These areas are also the ones likely to directly benefit least from the Tunnel because they are off the main corridor of communication from the Tunnel to London. This has led to the application for Assisted Area status which would enable these coastal areas to benefit from regional policy assistance, including direct access to funding from European Regional Development Fund (ERDF) as well as to the small amount of INTERREG funding, which will be discussed below. A decision on this was due to be taken in April 1993 but has been deferred. Further consideration is being given to an application under the current review of Objective 2 regions in the ERDF. Although it may seem a retrograde step for a region attempting to position itself as part of the core region of the European Community, the availability of investment assistance may prove to be the crucial factor in breaking the present log-jam on development. It also reflects clearly the way in which regions such as Kent may suffer from the cumulative problems of being the border region and of the development of new transport corridors encouraging development opportunities to pass them by.

4 Transfrontier cooperation and collaboration

It is against this background that increasing cooperation and collaboration has taken place between Kent and Nord–Pas de Calais, extending to include the Belgian regions as well. Collaboration in this context involves both a learning process and the potential to exploit new opportunities. This has a defensive, negative, purpose of identifying and responding to interregional competition, and a constructive, positive, purpose of building complementary activities and exploiting spillovers between the regions.

4.1 The development background—contrasts in experience

The history of interregional collaboration is very short. Despite Kent and Nord–Pas de Calais being bordering regions, the Channel has acted as an effective barrier between them in the past. Even the common economic interest in the ferry industry and the mutual concern about traffic passing through the regions did not lead to any real contact. The initial official contacts over the present Channel Tunnel scheme in the Anglo-French Study of 1982 were at central-government level. Some consultation of the Nord–Pas de Calais regional interests appears to have been made, but Kent County Council was kept firmly out of any negotiations by the British government. Nord–Pas de Calais presented its own regional development plan for the Tunnel—the Plan Transmanche (CR, 1986)—in January 1986, but this was drawn up without any reference to Kent (or other neighbouring regions). The *Kent Impact Study* of 1987 (the nearest equivalent British study) did include reference to Nord–Pas de Calais, but essentially in terms of identifying the competitive threat from the neighbouring region, although some reference to collaboration was made (CTJCC, 1987).

Two factors appear to have promoted increasing interest in interregional collaboration. The generally hostile attitude of national government, especially that shown by the UK government to genuine development concerns in Kent, led to a desire to learn more about the French approach for use as a bargaining weapon. Second, the availability of INTERREG funds under Article 10 of ERDF Regulation 4254/88 for use in border regions not otherwise eligible for ERDF funding under the new Structural Fund regulations of the EC, highlighted the advantages which could be obtained at the EC level from formal collaboration.

Since regular contact between the two authorities in France and Britain began, largely as a result of their needs to respond to the *fait accompli* of the Tunnel, there is substantial evidence of mutual learning. Kent had been a traditionally conservative county in terms of party politics until the elections of May 1993, with a reputation based on relatively low spending. Nord – Pas de Calais was a traditionally socialist region, until the regional elections of 1992, serving as the local power base of several national politicians and with strong pockets under the control of the Communist Party, notably in Calais. This may not seem to have been a fruitful basis for cooperation. Nevertheless, Kent has learned much about the role of infrastructure in the process of economic development, the need for public-sector commitment to new development projects and the benefits of being able to harness several levels of financial assistance (for example, see Holliday, 1991; 1992).

Nord – Pas de Calais, on the other hand has emerged from the recent past with a more diversified approach to local development. The traditional reliance on the Sociétés de Conversion has been replaced by a more aggressive policy towards attracting new industries and a public – private mix through the Société d'Économie Mixte, such as in the Euralille Métropole project (Langrand, 1992). Furthermore, the management of the Zone d'Aménagement Concertée (ZAC) created around the Tunnel Terminal was entrusted initially to Eurotunnel itself, the first time in France that the management of a ZAC had been left to the private sector. Note the parallel with the direct involvement of Eurotunnel in the East Kent Initiative which followed later. The ZAC was later split into two parts and the management of one zone was transferred to the public authorities in Calais.

A further example of common approaches in the two regions is through the use of Enterprise Zones (EZs). In Kent an EZ was established in 1983 mainly as a response to the closure of the Chatham Naval Dockyard. This was not directly related to the Channel Tunnel, but it has been the only EZ in South East England outside London. In 1986 the NORMED shipyards in Dunkerque, a traditional Société de Conversion, collapsed, and partly building on the British experience, an EZ was proposed and, despite some reservations, accepted by the EC. Again the Dunkerque EZ was not directly Tunnel related, but its proximity to Calais, the development of the Rocade Littoral which improves access to the various EZ sites, and the profile of the region itself in the context of the Plan Transmanche, have served to make the EZ successful.

Development has been extremely slow in both regions. Initial enthusiasm for the redevelopment opportunities occasioned by the Tunnel shown by the local authorities were not always matched by the private sector. In the first place there was an initial boom in the property market in Kent. The shortage of developable land placed it immediately at a premium so developers wishing not to lose out took up options. Land values in Ashford rose to over £1 million per acre compared with around

£200000 per acre in Thanet, although even these prices were up to ten times those in Nord–Pas de Calais. However, the reluctance of option holders to turn their options into firm developments was the result initially of uncertainty about the Tunnel project itself and then later was caught in the economic recession. Despite the successful flotation of Eurotunnel in 1987, the project's success was in doubt in the eyes of many until after the refinancing and rights issue of late 1990. Only when the initial break-through of the service tunnel was achieved in December 1990 did the Tunnel's completion become generally accepted as certain. By this stage the UK economy was moving into serious recession. This downturn was led by the construction and development sector and those sectors which had formed the basis of the 1980s boom in South East England and on which Kent's future economic success was thought to depend.

There was a generally less pessimistic view taken of the Tunnel in France, including a much more enthusiastic response to its financing with a higher proportion of both debt and equity being held by French banks, institutions, and individuals. However, this did not prevent a similar slow response to Tunnel opportunities in Nord–Pas de Calais. Two factors could be important here. One is the generally low level of development experience in the regions, especially by outside investors. Second, the most enthusiastic investors, especially in the coastal region, were British-based companies. This follows a long history of British involvement, especially in Calais itself where the three largest employers were British companies. British investors saw the Tunnel as providing a major bridge-head on the continent for exploiting the Single European Market, but risk minimising suggested this should be done from a relatively near location. This was perceived as a threat from the Kent perspective, but also from a French perspective because it made development in the region dependent on nonlocal decisions. Such a view was justified by the subsequent experience as the recession took its toll on several of the developers who were accordingly reluctant to capitalise on their sites in France. At the time of writing, in early 1993, firms were showing a rather cautious response to economic recovery in the United Kingdom, and at the same time the French economy was moving into deeper recession.

4.2 The development of collaboration

The development of formal links between Kent and Nord–Pas de Calais started in earnest in 1986 following the announcement of the Tunnel project (Luchaire, 1992). This has occurred at various levels and between various organisations. At the political level meetings between the Leader of Kent County Council and the President of the Conseil Régional, Nord–Pas de Calais, evolved into a forum involving the chairmen of the French and British companies constituting Eurotunnel (André Benard and Sir Alastair Morton). These have an important symbolic significance, but the real work was being carried out at the official level. This involved not just regular meetings, but also an increasing use of secondments and work experience in the partner authority. Such links involved not just the County Council and Conseil Régional, but also other local authorities and government agencies such as the Employment Service in the United Kingdom (later joined by the newly formed Training and Enterprise Council, TEC) and the corresponding body in France, the Agence Nationale pour l'Emploi (ANPE).

Within Kent County Council a European Team was established in 1987 in the Chief Executive's Department to advise and coordinate policy, both to Nord–Pas de Calais and towards the European Dimension generally. By 1993, when this responsibility was transferred to the Economic Development Department, seven departments had their own European Officers.

Building on the experience of the existing links of Nord–Pas de Calais with its neighbouring provinces in Belgium, a Euroregion covering Kent, Nord–Pas de Calais, and the three regions of Wallonia, Flanders, and Brussels was formed. Within this a Transfrontier Programme Region comprising East Kent and the coastal region of Nord–Pas de Calais was defined. This opened up the prospect of direct EC funding for Kent other than through Infrastructure Funds and the European Social Fund (ESF). Kent's lack of designation as an Assisted Area prevented it from access to the ERDF funding enjoyed by large parts of Nord–Pas de Calais, which had benefitted from such funding for a long period and which received Objective 2 status in the redefinition of structural funds from 1989. INTERREG enabled otherwise ineligible border regions to obtain limited ERDF and ESF funding for collaborative transfrontier projects. The new transfontier region secured a total of £6 million for Kent and £11 million for Nord–Pas de Calais for the period 1990–94, although delays in approval meant that projects only came on stream in the period 1992–93. These projects fall under five main headings: infrastructure and telecommunications; land, planning, and the environment; economic development; tourism development; and education and training. Some 80% of the funds had been allocated by March 1993, although there have been some problems in the securing of final approval by the national authorities in the United Kingdom because of problems in identifying the public-expenditure cover required under the additionality principle.

In line with the priorities of the regions themselves, much of the emphasis in agreed transfrontier projects has been on two major areas: training and labour-market development; and infrastructure. Joint work on labour markets and training dates back to 1986 when the emphasis was on recruitment for the Channel Tunnel construction, but this has evolved into programmes for training, apprenticeships, and the exchange of young workers. There is now liaison between the job centres in Dover and Folkestone and that in Calais, and the possibility of exchanging vacancy details is being explored. Documentation on job seeking and on working in the other country has been prepared for both the English and the French markets.

This cross-border work is now coming within the ambit of EURES Crossborder. EURES is the European linking of employment services at a national level to encourage mobility. Much of the early work has concentrated on cross-border links between France and Belgium with four main missions: exchange of job vacancies; collection of information on training; information on local labour-market conditions; and information on living and working conditions for movers. This is the type of basic support which is essential to the creation of any real single transfrontier market for labour.

At the infrastructure level, joint work within the wider Euroregion has been concentrated on the coordination of strategic planning information towards the early publication of a framework for the entire region, supported by an 'Observatoire' for the collection and monitoring of planning information. More detailed work is also proceeding on a joint project on the impact on the port economies and their access needs. This also fits into the more general question of the review of regional assistance, both at the national and at the EC levels.

5 Conclusion

The main theme of the transfrontier cooperation between Kent and Nord – Pas de Calais is that it has been forged between two dissimilar, in terms of economy and culture, regions as a result of the creation of a new transport infrastructure link. Although this is the first fixed link between the regions, links through a growing ferry industry have existed for a long period with rapidly increasing flows. These flows have, however, tended to be regarded as through traffic with no real impacts on the regions.

The decision to construct that link was taken outside the regions, and as a private-sector venture; the regions have had no formal part in its development. Moreover, key decisions affecting the regions, principally concerning connecting infrastructure, have been taken outside the regions, or frequently, in the UK case, have not been taken. Although Nord – Pas de Calais has been in a position to formulate a more strategic planning response, there is nevertheless the feeling that both regions have essentially been responding to, and attempting to cope with, inevitable changes, rather than being able to control these. It is not clear that the existence of a fixed link will change the corridor status of the regions; it has, however, galvanised them into believing that it creates the opportunity to change this situation.

The move to transfrontier cooperation has been partly a defensive move to understand and hopefully contain competitive pressures. This is found in both directions: a British fear that activity will drain away to France, attracted by cheap land and regional development incentives; a French fear of an inability to compete with the environmental attractiveness of Kent and the benefits of an English-language business environment.

Increasingly, however, greater understanding has led to greater emphasis on the more positive aspects of cooperation: the ability to create a Euroregion which can compete more effectively *as a whole* with other regions. At various levels there are moves to develop the crossborder cultures which did not exist.

References

Bruyelle P, 1994, "The impact of the Channel Tunnel on the Nord – Pas de Calais" *Applied Geography* **14** forthcoming

CEC, 1987 *The Regions of the Enlarged Community: Third Periodic Report on the Social and Economic Situation and Development of the Regions of the Community* Commission of the European Communities (Office for Official Publications, Luxembourg)

CEC, 1991 *The Regions in the 1990s: Fourth Periodic Report on the Social and Economic Situation and Development of the Regions of the Community* Commission of the European Communities (Office for Official Publications, Luxembourg)

CEDRE, 1993 *Étude Prospective des Régions Atlantiques* (Study of Future Trends for the Atlantic Regions) final report to Commission of the European Communities, Centre Européen de Développement Régional, 20 Place des Halles, 6700 Strasbourg

Chisholm M, 1992, "Britain, the European Community and the centralisation of production: theory and evidence, freight movements" *Environment and Planning A* **24** 551 – 570

CR, 1986 *Lien Fixe Transmanche: Éléments pour un Plan de Développement de la Région Nord – Pas de Calais* (Channel Fixed Link. Elements of a Development Plan for the Nord – Pas de Calais Region), Conseil Régional Nord – Pas de Calais, 7 Square Morisson, BP 2035, 59014 Lille

CTJCC, 1986 *Kent Impact Study: A Preliminary Assessment* Channel Tunnel Joint Consultative Committee, Department of Transport, 2 Marsham Street, London

CTJCC, 1987 *Kent Impact Study: Overall Assessment* Channel Tunnel Joint Consultative Committee (HMSO, London)

Eurostat, 1993 *Rapid Reports: Regions 1993/ 1* (Eurostat, Luxembourg)

Holliday I M, 1991, "The new suburban right in British local government—conservative views of the local" *Local Government Studies* **17**(6) 45 – 62

Holliday I M, 1992, "The politics of the Channel Tunnel" *Parliamentary Affairs* **45** 188 – 204

Holliday I M, Langrand M, Vickerman R W, 1991a *Nord – Pas de Calais in the 1990s* Special Report M601 (Economist Intelligence Unit, London)

Holliday I M, Marcou G, Vickerman R W, 1991b *The Channel Tunnel: Public Policy, Regional Development and European Integration* (Belhaven Press, London)

Keeble D, Owens P L, Thompson C, 1982, "Economic potential and the Channel Tunnel" *Area* **14** 97 – 103

Kent Economic Report 1993 report by Kent County Council, Kent TEC Ltd, University of Kent at Canterbury, The Employment Service, Kent County Council, Springfield, Maidstone

Krugman P, 1991 *Geography and Trade* (MIT Press, Cambridge, MA)

Langrand M, 1992, "L'insertion locale du tunnel" (Local impact of the tunnel), in *Le Tunnel sous la Manche: Entre États et Marchés* Eds G Marcou, R Vickerman, Y Luchaire (Presses Universitaires de Lille, Lille) pp 291 – 327

Le Maire D, Pevsner M, 1992, "Eurotunnel: the development of traffic forecasts for a private sector project", in *Financing European Transport* Eds P H L Bovy, H G Smith, European Transport Planning Colloquium Foundation, INRO-TNO, PO Box 6041, NL-2600JA Delft, pp 61 – 77

Luchaire Y, 1992, "L'euro-région, fille naturelle du tunnel sous la Manche?" (The Euro-region: a natural development of the Channel Tunnel?), in *Le Tunnel sous la Manche: Entre États et Marchés* Eds G Marcou, R Vickerman, Y Luchaire (Presses Universitaires de Lille, Lille) pp 379–429

Maillat D, 1990, "Transborder regions between members of the EC and non-member countries" *Built Environment* **16**(1) 38–51

PACEC, 1991 *Kent Impact Study 1991 Review: The Channel Study—A Strategy for Kent* report by PA Cambridge Economic Consultants, Halcrow Fox and Associates, and MDS Transmodal; copy available from Kent County Council, Springfield, Maidstone

Quévit M, 1988 *Le Potentiel de Développement de la Zone du Hainaut Occidental, de Mons-Borinage et du Centre et la Coopération Transfrontalière avec le Nord–Pas de Calais* (Development Potential of Western Hainaut, Mons-Borinage and Centre and Transfrontier Cooperation with Nord–Pas de Calais), RIDER, Université Catholique de Louvain, Louvain-la-Neuve, Belgium

RETI, 1990 *The Traditional Industrial Regions of Europe: Problems and Perspectives* (RETI Conference, Brussels)

SERPLAN, 1985 *Regional Trends in the South East* RPC369 London and South East Regional Planning Conference, 50–56 Broadway, London SW1H 0DB, London

Vickerman R W, 1992 *The Single European Market: Prospects for Economic Integration* (Harvester Press, Hemel Hempstead, Herts)

Vickerman R W, 1993, "Analysing the regional impacts of new transport infrastructure", in *Regional Development, Economic Restructuring and Emerging Networks* Eds J Cuadrado Rouro, P Nikjamp, P Salva (forthcoming)

Vickerman R W, 1994a, "The Channel Tunnel and regional development in Europe" *Applied Geography* **14** forthcoming

Vickerman R W, 1994b, "Transport infrastructure and region building in the European Community" *Journal of Common Market Studies* **32**(1) forthcoming

Vickerman R W, Flowerdew A D J, 1990 *The Channel Tunnel: The Economic and Regional Impact* Special Report 2024 (Economist Intelligence Unit, London)

The Baltic Region and the New Europe

J Storm Pedersen
Roskilde University

1 Introduction

After the removal of the Iron Curtain in Europe, it is relevant to analyse the possibilities of the creation of a flourishing Baltic region in the new Europe. The Baltic region will be defined and the development of the region is analysed on the basis of the concepts of Randkerne regions and meso-regions.

No sustainable cooperation and hence regional development can be created without regional trade and economic integration based on mutual economic interest. Therefore, the development of markets and private business enterprises in the eastern part of the Baltic region is analysed. And programmes made for, and initiatives taken in, the Nordic countries and Germany supporting the reform process and promoting regional cooperation are discussed.

2 The Baltic region[1]

The collapse of the USSR, the end of the Cold War, and the removal of the Berlin Wall and the Iron Curtain in Europe have created a new situation in Europe and the Baltic region. In the Baltic region an atmosphere of curiosity and readiness to cooperate has developed.

Many governmental and many local, small-scale initiatives to cooperate have been taken in the Baltic region, involving all types of actors. But neither the many small initiatives nor the larger national programmes are coordinated. Seen from a general perspective the 'model' of regional cooperation must, for the time being, be described as a 'model of chaos'. There are no strong visions of how the Baltic region should be developed and what role the region should play in a European context. One reason for this is that until 1990 there was almost no contact between the eastern and the western part of the Baltic Sea because the Iron Curtain divided the Baltic region into an eastern and a western part. The Nordic countries of Denmark, Finland, and Sweden,[2] and Germany belonged to the West, and Russia, the Baltic States, Poland, and East Germany, belonged to the Eastern Bloc. The NATO embargo of high-quality and low-quality technology and products in the 1980s to the former USSR and Eastern Europe reinforced this lack of regional cooperation. Finland was

---

[1] Definitions and statistical information given in this section are based on various reports from the Denkfabrik in Kiel and public statistical data in Denmark.

[2] All the Nordic countries are Iceland, Norway, Denmark, Sweden, and Finland. At present only Denmark is a member of the EC.

squeezed politically and economically between the East and West during the postwar period.

Today most political barriers to economic, political, and social cooperation across the Baltic Sea have been removed. The basic question is then: will the new situation create large-scale regional cooperation? Will the Baltic region become a European region of some importance? Before an attempt to answer these questions, two definitions of the Baltic region will be given—a broad and a narrow one.

The broad definition of the Baltic region is that this region consists of the Nordic countries (minus Iceland), Russia, the Baltic States, Poland, and Germany. Given this definition the Baltic region is very big. The population in the Nordic countries ranges from 4 million inhabitants in Norway to 8 million in Sweden. The Baltic States have, all in all, a population of about 18 million people. In comparison with this there are about 150 million inhabitants in Russia, 80 million in the reunified Germany, and 40 million in Poland. One may find this broad definition of the Baltic region rather artificial because not all the countries in the Baltic region have a general interest in the creation of regional cooperation. For example, Russia, Poland, and Germany have no particular interest in creating regional cooperation in the Baltic region. Besides, in the Nordic countries regional cooperation in the Baltic region has low priority compared with the question of European integration within the framework of the EC at present. These facts form, however, the basic conditions for the creation of regional cooperation in the Baltic region. Therefore, the broad definition of the Baltic region is used in section 3.1 in the description of the basic conditions for regional cooperation in the Baltic region and the integration of the region into the new Europe.

The narrow definition of the Baltic region is used in the description and analysis of the regional cooperation in practice in section 3.2. According to this definition, the Baltic region includes Denmark, Sweden, Finland, the Baltic States, the areas of St Petersburg (Leningrad) and Königsberg (Kaliningrad), those of Mecklenburg-Vorpommern (the northern part of the former East Germany) and Schleswig-Holstein (the northern part of the former West Germany), and the vojvoidships of Szczecin, Kozalin, Slupsk, Gdansk, Elbag, Ostyn, and Suwalki in Poland. This area has a total population of 35 million inhabitants.

On the basis of national and regional statistical data it is possible to give a short and general description of the situation in the Baltic region. In Denmark and Sweden the GNP per person is about US$20 000 and about US$16 000 in Schleswig-Holstein. In East Germany the income was about US$9000 per capita, in Poland it is about US$5500, and in the Baltic States about US$6000 (this is above the Russian average which is about US$5000). If these figures are compared with those in the EC, the Nordic countries and Germany are above average and the Eastern Europe are below average.

Using some conventional and simple indicators of welfare to describe the situation, one finds that in the Nordic countries the numbers of telephones per 1000 people are from 614 in Finland to 890 in Sweden. In Schleswig-Holstein one finds 420 phones per 1000 people compared with 195 in Mecklenburg-Vorpommern and 122 in the northern part of Poland. In Estonia one finds 225 phones per 1000 people compared with 182 in Latvia and 208 in Lithuania. The same pattern is repeated in terms of cars with the exception that one finds most cars per 1000 people in Schleswig-Holstein.

The Nordic countries have many more students per 1000 inhabitants than do any of the other countries in the Baltic region. However, Eastern Europe has a considerably higher rate of students per 1000 inhabitants than do countries in the Third World. This is advantageous when seen from the perspective of the current reform process in Eastern Europe. The potential of human resources is big in Eastern Europe.

Furthermore, the labour force is used quite differently in the countries in the Baltic region. In the Eastern countries about 50% of the labour force is employed in the agriculture and industrial sectors, compared with about 30% in Germany and the Nordic countries. More importantly, in the Eastern countries only about 40% of the labour force is concerned with service production (public as well as business service), compared with 60%–70% in Germany and in the Nordic countries. Service production is now the most important activity in the modern Western societies (Bévort et al, 1992, pages 6–21). Therefore, the reform process in Eastern Europe has to go beyond a 'simple' reorganisation and renewal of the industrial sector. To realise the aim of the reform process, namely to catch up with societies in the West, public services and business services must be extensively developed. This is the only way to make the industrial system flexible and efficient and to create a public sector which can support the development of a modern economy.

The internal trade of the Baltic region has not formed a solid basis for economic and hence social and political cooperation in the region. Although, internal trade is equivalent to about 4%–6% of world exports and the total exports from the Baltic region amount to about 20% of world exports (if the broad definition of the Baltic region is used), regional cooperation is very limited. Among the Scandinavian countries, Russia, and the Eastern European countries there is no trade of importance for the social and economic development of these countries. For example, only 2.5% of the Danish exports are sold to Eastern Europe, including to the CIS.

However, for Finland and Germany the situation is quite different. In the 1980s about one third of all Finnish exports went to the USSR. Since the collapse of the USSR, Finland has been confronted with a severe economic crisis and has to find new export markets. Before the collapse, West Germany was the most important country in the Baltic region regarding imports and exports. This position has been reinforced by the reunification of Germany. Exports from Germany amount to more than one third of the total exports in the Baltic region.

The overall conclusion is that until now external trade in the Baltic region has been much more important than has internal trade as such. Will this situation now change? Will the removal of the Iron Curtain create more trade and, hence, economic cooperation in the Baltic region?

One of several methods to indicate the size of the economic potential of trade and cooperation after the removal of the Iron Curtain is to calculate the income potentials and analyse the changes in their spatial pattern as a result of the removal of the Iron Curtain. This has been done by Ziesmer (1992) on the basis of Bröcher's (1989) revision of Clark, Wilson, and Bradley's (1969) formula for income potentials (see Peschel, 1992a, page 12). The result is that no major changes will happen in the Baltic region concerning trade and hence economic cooperation. With this relatively pessimistic scenario in mind, the development of the Baltic region will be analysed in more detail. The analysis will be based on the concepts of Randkerne regions and meso-regions.

3 Randkerne regions and meso-regions
The concept of Randkerne regions can be used to indicate how the *countries* located near to the Baltic Sea will be integrated into the new Europe. The concept of meso-regions can be used to identify social, political, and economic forces *within* the countries in the Baltic region which will try to create regional cooperation.

3.1 Two Randkerne regions in the Baltic region?
The starting point for the concept of the Randkerne region is the work of Predöhl (1949) as described in *Räumliche Strukturen im internationalen Handel* by Hass and Peschel (1992). The basic idea is that there exists industrial centres of gravity in the world economy. Before World War 2, the world economy was dominated by two large industrial centres of gravity, namely Europe and North America. Russia as an industrial centre was linked to Europe until the Bolshevik Revolution. After that time the USSR formed its own centre of gravity (see Peschel, 1992b).

Related to centres of economic gravity one can find Randkerne regions (peripheral centres), which are strongly related to the centre of gravity in terms of exports and imports and hence through economic integration.

"Small centres (peripheral centres) are created outside the centre of economic gravity, but are under strong influence from this ... We define these small centres (peripheral centres) as Randkerne" (Hass and Peschel, 1982, page 9, my translation).

On the basis of international trade statistics from the UN for 104 countries it can be shown that the concepts of Predöhl were still valid in the 1980s.

Scandinavia (Denmark, Sweden, and Norway) is seen as a good example of a Randkerne region (Peschel, 1992a, pages 9 – 10). Eastern Europe also formed a Randkerne region related to the European centre of gravity up until World War 2. After the war, Eastern Europe was uncoupled from the European centre and formed a Randkerne to the newly established centre of economic gravity, the USSR. In Predöhl's view the Eastern European countries would form a Randkerne to the European centre of gravity if the market-driven forces of development were not distorted by political factors (Peschel, 1992b). In this perspective the Eastern European countries can 'go back' to a kind of 'historical normality' after the collapse of the USSR. This is, however, not so easy. In accordance with Predöhl's theory, one can identify four groups of barriers to economic integration (Peschel, 1992a, page 8)
(1) distance-bridging costs such as transport and communication costs;
(2) linguistic and cultural dissimilarities;
(3) differences in the scope of social and political life; and
(4) political influences, deliberately or unintentionally resulting in the separation of countries.

Because of the postwar development of Eastern Europe these barriers are in force now as Eastern Europe tries to become integrated into the West and the EC. However, in the long run the barriers can be broken via the reform process in Eastern Europe. The reform process, if successful, will break barriers (3) and (4). In relation to barrier (2), some positive options exist. French or German has been the second language in most of Eastern Europe and, for example, people in Estonia can communicate with the Finnish people. Seen from a cultural point of view, the countries are as strongly connected with Western Europe as with Russia. The Baltic States are, perhaps, a little atypical. They are more attached to the Nordic countries than to Central Europe.

The situation for barrier (1) is that the distance from Poland, Czechoslovakia (now the Czech and the Slovak republics), and Hungary to Berlin, Vienna, and even Frankfurt am Main is shorter than that to Moscow. In the Baltic States the distance to Moscow is about 1000 km compared with about 200 km between Tallinn and Helsinki, 500 km between Riga and Stockholm, and 800 km between Vilnius and Copenhagen.

If the Eastern European countries can break through the four barriers, and if the new enterprises in Eastern Europe meet the preconditions of rational behaviour as described by conventional microeconomic theory, then Eastern Europe will have an opportunity to form a Randkerne region to the European centre of gravity.

Before this possibility can be realised the trade barriers created by the EC to prevent Eastern Europe from becoming integrated into the EC have to be abolished. In the short run Eastern Europe has four groups of products for export to the EC: steel and iron products, textile products, chemical products, and agricultural products. Exports to the EC of products within these four categories are essential for the Eastern European countries if they are to be able to finance the reform process themselves. Unfortunately, exports from Eastern Europe are sold on markets in the EC with 'sunset' industries lobbying for political protection. The result is that in the market for agricultural products an index of 106 exists. [An index of 100 indicates full political control of a market, compared with 0 indicating a market without political regulation (*Dansk Økonomi* 1992, page 131).]

Another precondition for realising the opportunity for Eastern European countries to form a Randkerne region is that they cooperate with the aim of creating a regional centre on the basis of economic integration, as given by the definition of a Randkerne region. In practice the countries in Eastern Europe compete to achieve the best positions in the process of economic and political integration into Western Europe and the EC. The result is that very little cooperation between the Eastern European countries exists. This might again lead to a situation where Eastern Europe forms only a Rand region (a periphery region).[3] In this case local and regional resources in Eastern Europe will not be utilised fully and the capacity to shape the development of Eastern Europe itself will be reduced considerably compared with a situation in which it forms a Randkerne region. One way to illustrate this theme is to describe the Scandinavian Randkerne region.

The Scandinavian countries can be characterised as small countries with open economies. The result is that they are strongly integrated in the European centre of gravity. In a simple trade perspective they also form a Rand region to central Europe. However, three important factors in the Scandinavian countries have created a situation which has made it possible for them to achieve a status of a Randkerne region.

First, in the three Scandinavian countries, a vision of regional development was already formed by the 1920s and 1930s by the Social Democrats. That is, the vision of the creation of 'democratic socialism' based on democracy, equality among the citizens, a welfare state, optimal utilisation of the human resources based on democratic and humanistic principles, and a mixed-economy system (Storm Pedersen, 1988). This vision has served as a guideline for development in these countries for many decades and has led to the creation of the so-called Scandinavian model.

Second, the realisation of the vision was reinforced by a strong cooperation between the different Scandinavian countries. The intratrade in Scandinavia is over 20% and a common labour market exists. Besides this there is mutual recognition of the educational structures of the different countries, the same privileges are given to citizens no matter which

---

[3] These observations come from my own experiences during my work in Eastern Europe as a UNISTAR 1992/1993.

country they are living in, passports are not needed when crossing borders, there is similar environmental regulation, and so forth (Storm Pedersen, 1989).

Third, the integration of the Scandinavian countries is based on 'bottom-up' principles. It has not been necessary to apply strong supranational bodies to create strong regional cooperation. On this basis the Scandinavian countries have formed one of the strongest Randkerne regions in the world (Peschel, 1992a, page 9). The result is that it has been possible to shape the regional development by a combination of regional visions and resources and free international trade. The Scandinavian countries have fully utilised both the economic integration in the European centre of gravity and regional resources to shape regional development in accordance with regional needs as reflected in the so-called Scandinavian model. This situation does not exist in Eastern Europe. Here, only a few, half-hearted initiatives have been taken to push the development of Eastern Europe into a situation which makes the creation of a Randkerne region possible.

The conclusion is that the Eastern Europe might be (re)integrated into the European centre of gravity as a Rand region. It remains to be seen whether or not it will be able to form a Randkerne region.

The overall conclusion is that, if the development of the Baltic region is analysed on the basis of the concept of Randkerne regions and the present situation is taken into account, the Scandinavian and the Eastern European countries are being integrated into the European centre of economic gravity in different ways, Finland has to be (re)integrated into both the Baltic region and the new Europe, and Germany will play a key role in the creation of a Baltic region. The basic trend, that the Scandinavian and the Eastern European countries are being integrated into the European centre of gravity in different ways, is reinforced in these years.

The Scandinavian model has run into a severe crisis. It seems to be impossible to control the economic performance and hence the rate of unemployment within the framework of the Scandinavian model. The result is that the welfare state and the model of a mixed economy are being eroded in the 1990s. Instead of revitalising the Scandinavian model, social and political forces at the national level pressurise countries into applying for membership of the EC and for further integration within the EC. Membership of the EC and further integration are seen as the way out of the economic crisis in the Nordic countries, although the internal market will not create more economic growth according to the Danish EC Commissioner, Mr Christopfersen.

In Eastern Europe the strategy at the national political level is also to apply for membership of the EC as soon as possible. That the question of European integration is in focus in the Nordic countries, as it is in the Eastern European countries, is a negative indication for the creation of regional cooperation in the Baltic region. Political priority is given to handling the cooperation related to the question of European integration in appropriate ways.

On the other hand, social, political, and economic forces do exist in the Baltic region, which do not strongly support a Randkerne-region scenario. Many people in the Nordic countries show a great scepticism towards the EC and further integration within its framework. The Danes voted 'Nej' to the Maastricht treaty in the first place, as is well known. In Norway, polls show that the Norwegians are against membership of the EC (*Information* 1993). In Sweden and Finland the situation is not clear. However, the people in the Nordic countries are not, as such, against European economic integration. As mentioned, the strong Scandinavian Randkerne region is based on European economic integration. What the Scandinavians do not want is political, military, and monetary cooperation based on strong supranational bodies without democratic control combined with big bureaucratic organisations based on 'top-down' principles. This is against all the political and social traditions in Scandinavia. Recent polls in Denmark and Norway can be interpreted in this way: many people want more cooperation among the Nordic countries and more European integration based on pragmatism (*Information* 1993); that is, European integration with the aim of creating more free trade in Europe and of handling common problems such as environmental problems, unemployment, the large number of refugees, and similar common European problems. In the Nordic countries, one finds initiatives to create cooperation in the Baltic region. The Nordic countries have created programmes to support the reform process in Eastern Europe, with a focus on the Baltic region. Also, in Eastern Europe some economic and political forces support the creation of regional cooperation. The Baltic States have a strong orientation towards the Nordic countries, and vice versa. Social and political contacts exist for historical reasons, especially among the Baltic States, Finland, and Sweden.

The area of St Petersburg and Königsberg is trying to establish cooperation with the Nordic countries and Germany. For example, the city of St Petersburg is twinned with several Nordic cities. Königsberg is also trying to become a 'free-trade zone'. The idea is to become an attractive gateway for Western companies to the Eastern markets, and vice versa. The northwest part of Poland has been part of Germany and has, therefore, a strong tradition of cooperation with Germany, both for good and for bad. Furthermore, Finland has a strong commitment to supporting the development of the Baltic States, the area of St Petersburg, plus other areas of Russia near to the Finnish border. Finland fears that if Russia collapses many refugees will arrive in Finland.

The former Prime Minister of Schleswig-Holstein and former leader of the SPD in Germany, Mr Engholm, has suggested the creation of a strong regional cooperation because he fears that the Baltic region will be marginalised in the new Europe (Engholm, 1990). The political and economic forces promoting regional cooperation will be discussed in more detail in the next section, on the basis of the concept of a meso-region.

3.2 A meso-region

In the Baltic region, cooperation must be based on transborder cooperation and it is likely that the main actors will be local politicians, enterprises, interest groups, and institutions. A basic motive for initiating regional cooperation could be to avoid marginalisation in a national or in a European context. Regional cooperation on a big scale, based on such criteria, forms a meso-region.

The meso-region is "a type of region which is peripheral in Western, Northern, and Southern Europe and contains transborder cooperation. The main goal of cooperation is to achieve an independent economic development in the region" (Gerner, 1991, page 14, my translation). According to Gerner, one finds several visions with the goal to create a meso-region in Europe. For example, the powerful efforts to create the so-called Mitteleuropa can be seen as an attempt to create a meso-region. The driving forces in the creation of this meso-region are "German capital and investments which involve Poland, Czechoslovakia and Hungary directly in German activities and interest sphere, and where the Ukraine and White Russia will be involved as well" (Gerner, 1991, page 14, my translation).

The vision of Engholm to create regional cooperation in the Baltic region is also seen as a strategy to create a new meso-region in Europe; that is, "To gain power through a strategy that changes a relatively poor periphery in the wealthy Germany to a dynamic centre in the peripheral Northern Europe" (Gerner, 1991, page 14, my translation).

However, cooperation in the Baltic region does not, for the time being, meet the criteria for regional cooperation within a meso-region if, for example, Cappellin's criteria are used. In accordance with Cappellin (1992, pages 14–15) the following preconditions for regional cooperation have to be met in a meso-region:
(a) common values and history;
(b) common local 'industrial atmosphere';
(c) transportation linkages;
(d) producer services distribution;
(e) common urban-system pattern;
(f) single-issue contractual agreements;
(g) coordination procedures;
(h) common administrative regulations;
(i) common public institutions; and
(j) common sociopolitical identity.
The previous discussion on the Baltic region shows clearly that these preconditions are not met in the Baltic region at present. It will take years or even decades before they are met because of the four barriers to economic integration previously mentioned. These barriers will also be

active in the case of regional cooperation in the Baltic region, although the configuration of problems relating to them will be different from those in the situation in which the Eastern European countries try to become integrated into the EC and the West. For example, barrier (1) will probably be relatively easy to break down whereas barrier (2) will take some time. However, on the basis of the existing conditions some serious initiatives have been taken, and programmes made, which can strengthen the cooperation in the Baltic region within the concept of a meso-region. These initiatives are presented in the following five points.

3.2.1 *The Denkfabrik*

It is peculiar that the most forthright and thoroughly prepared initiative for creating regional cooperation in the Baltic region, and hence to form a meso-region, has been made by the former Prime Minister of Schleswig-Holstein and the former Leader of the German SPD, instead of key people in Scandinavia or in Eastern Europe. Engholm's point of departure is that he fears a situation "where the Southern Regions in Europe will have a positive development and the Northern part of Europe could be placed in a situation without any progress. This could be the case for the Northern parts of Germany and Poland, the Baltic States plus Sweden, Denmark, Finland and Norway" (Engholm, 1990, my translation).

According to Engholm the challenge of such a scenario can only be met by one strategy "We must renew our efforts, create transborder cooperation and utilize our potentials" (Engholm, 1990, my translation). Seen from a strategic point of view, the basic vision of Engholm is to create regional development as a political instrument for preventing marginalisation of the Baltic region in the new Europe in the 1990s. That is to create one big Randkerne region out of the Baltic region by the creation of a meso-region.

3.2.2 *The Baltic region as an agro-industrial centre in the new Europe*

A vision which to some extent is parallel to Engholm's vision has been put forward by the former Danish Foreign Minister, Mr Ellemann-Jensen. His idea is that the Baltic region should become one of four prosperous European regions related to the so-called 'Blue Banana' (the European centre of gravity). According to Ellemann-Jensen (1991) the Baltic region has the potential to become a European growth centre primarily based on a new agro-industrial complex, with Copenhagen in Denmark as the centre. With the current problems of the agricultural sector in Europe and within the EC taken into account, this vision seems to be rather optimistic. However, the vision reflects a typical Danish – Scandinavian – Randkerne region thinking. The starting point is that Denmark participates in European economic integration, then tries to strengthen its position as far as possible by utilising regional resources.

3.2.3 The council of the Baltic region

A council for the Baltic region was established in March 1992. The goal of the council is to promote and support further cooperation across the Baltic Sea. Special working fields are economics, traffic, the environment, and issues related to the development of democracy in the former Eastern Europe (Storm Pedersen and Fuglsang, 1992, page 44). Until now the council has not played a major role in the creation of visions which could serve as guidelines for the development of the Baltic region, or in promoting more networks and networking in the region. In fact not one major initiative has been taken by the council.

3.2.4 Meso-regions and Randkerne regions

In the northern part of Germany, in the Nordic countries, and in Eastern Europe, many strategies have been drafted to link parts of the Baltic region with the Blue Banana (the European centre of gravity). The basic idea is that strong links to the Blue Banana will generate regional development. For example, it has been decided that a bridge should be built between Copenhagen and Malmö in an attempt to generate a huge city that in the future could become a centre both in Northern Europe and in the Baltic region. This vision has now been developed in more detail by politicians in greater Copenhagen. Here, initiatives have been taken to identify markets in the Baltic region which could attract big European companies into using Copenhagen as a gateway to the Baltic region (Ernest and Young, 1992). In addition, leaders of the Danish Chamber of Commerce now suggest that instead of promoting Denmark in Europe one should promote the Baltic region as an appropriate way to promote Denmark in the new Europe. That is, cooperation within the concept of a meso-region is a strategy for achieving a stronger position in a Randkerne-region scenario. This shows that there is no definitive contradiction between the creation of a meso-region in the Baltic region and the Randkerne-region scenario.

3.2.5 Support from Nordic governments[4]

Since the collapse of the USSR, the Nordic countries have formed programmes with the aim of supporting the reform process in Eastern Europe. I shall briefly describe these.

Denmark The first programmes were established in September 1989. In principle, aid and support to the reform process is given to all countries in Central and Eastern Europe and the CIS countries recognised by Denmark. In practice priority is given to the countries in the Baltic region. Currently, the major programmes are given below.

(1) The Investment Fund for Central and Eastern Europe, with a capital of about ecu 40 million (1990–92), is a fund which buys shares in joint-venture

[4] Information given in this section is based on information and publications provided by the Foreign Ministries in the Nordic countries.

companies if a Danish partner is involved. In 1992 the Investment Fund made investments in twenty-seven joint-venture companies (among others, nine in Poland, eight in the Baltic States and the CIS, and five in Czechoslovakia). The Investment Fund expects to become self-financing after 5–6 years.

(2) The Investment Insurance Scheme and the Scheme for Special Export Credit Facility guarantee investments in Eastern Europe and in the CIS.

(3) The Project Fund grants economic support to projects promoting economic and educational aspects of the reform process. Since 1990, about ecu 30 million has been spent on 330 projects.

(4) The Democracy Fund has, since 1990, used about ecu 10 million on projects promoting democracy.

(5) The Environmental Support Scheme has a budget of about ecu 65 million for the period 1991–95. Support is given to projects concerned with environmental improvements.

(6) A number of small programmes exist such as humanitarian aid for St Petersburg and the Baltic countries, and the Danish Cultural Institute in the Baltic States.

In 1992 about ecu 125 million was used on the programmes mentioned and the expectation is that the same amount of money will be used in 1993.

A similar amount of money is given to international organisations supporting the reform process in the Eastern Europe, such as the EC, G-24, The Bush Plan, and the European Bank for Reconstruction and Development (EBRD).

Sweden In Sweden almost the same amount of money is used on bilateral programmes as in Denmark to support the reform process in the former Eastern Bloc (SKr 1 billion in 1992/93, 1993/94, and 1994/95). Less money is spent on multilateral programmes. In Sweden, as in Denmark, priority is given to the Baltic region. In December 1992, Poland received about 30% of the money given by Sweden to the former Eastern Bloc. The Baltic States received about 50%, and Russia only about 15%.

The major programmes in Sweden are as follows.

(1) BITS is a programme for technical assistance involving about SKr 200 million (1992/93). 50% of the money is used on environmental projects. Another 30% of the money is used to promote industrial renewal.

(2) SIDA, which normally takes care of the Swedish aid to the Third World, administers SKr 45 million (1992/93) with the purpose of promoting social aspects of the reform process.

(3) SwedeCorp channels the governmental subsidy to Swedish companies operating in Eastern Europe. The capital involved is about SKr 60 million (1992/93).

(4) As in Denmark a number of smaller programmes exist for education, humanitarian aid, and so on.

Finland In 1991 and 1992 Finland gave, in bilateral as well as multilateral support to Central and Eastern European grants, about Fmk 470 million and offered credits and guarantees for about Fmk 930 million; that is, a much smaller amount of financial support compared with that of Denmark and Sweden. The aim of Finland's bilateral support to Eastern Europe is to promote democracy and economic development. The focus is on the Baltic States and areas of the former USSR close to the Finnish border.

In 1991 and 1992 the Baltic States received Fmk 122 million. Fmk 50 million was used for environmental projects, Fmk 26 million for supporting agricultural and food production, and Fmk 20 million was used for the Nordic Baltic Investment Programme. Also, Fmk 330 million was used for credits and guarantees.

In 1991 and 1992, the parts of the former USSR close to the Finnish border received Fmk 160 million. The money (Fmk 60 million) was used for environmental projects, promotion of food and agricultural production, and Fmk 30 million was given to humanitarian aid. Furthermore, Fmk 70 million was involved in reducing the energy consumption in Poland. Finally, some arrangements have been made in the former Czechoslovakia and Hungary, promoting Finnish export.

Nordic initiatives

(1) A Baltic investment programme has been made to support the creation of small and medium-sized enterprises (SMEs) in the Baltic States. The capital involved is ecu 75 million paid by the Nordic countries, and the EBRD will cofinance up to ecu 30 million. The basic idea is that the SMEs will play a key role in the creation of markets in the Baltic States and hence regional cooperation. Therefore, the capital is used to facilitate credits and loans to the SMEs in the Baltic States directly or indirectly through the three national investment banks in the Baltic States (controlled by Nordic and international institutions).

(2) The Nordic Environment Finance Corporation (NEFCO) is a Nordic institution promoting environmental investment of Nordic interest in Eastern Europe on a long-term basis.

(3) The Nordic Investment Bank (NIB) is also a Nordic institution which grants long-term loans to, for example, infrastructure projects.

The programmes in the Nordic countries, combined with other initiatives taken in the region, might be thought to be so comprehensive that they would be able to contribute significantly to the reform process in the eastern part of the Baltic region, and hence promote regional cooperation; that is, promotion of markets, enterprises, and economic and political cooperation in the region. However, to be more precise in the evaluation of the effects of the programmes and other initiatives taken, one must compare the support given to the reform process with some rough estimates of the preconditions for a successful reform process.

The ultimate goal of the reform process is that the population in Eastern Europe will achieve, after some years, the same living standard as in the EC. If the growth rate in the EC is estimated to be 2.5% per year for the next twenty years, the growth rate in Eastern Europe must be 7% per year. Massive investments are needed to achieve such a situation (US$165 billion in the first year, US$315 billion in year 10, and US$640 billion in year 20). Investments at this scale will influence the balance of trade in a negative way (with US$15 billion in the first year, US$55 billion in year 10, and US$180 billion in year 20).

If the negative effects on the balance of trade were compensated for by a Marshall plan involving all OECD member countries, these would have to pay less than 1% of their GNP to Eastern Europe. That is less than the UN norm for aid to the Third World from the OECD countries. At present Denmark pays US$8 billion per year to the Third World.

From the EC 'only' US$10 billion have been transferred to Eastern Europe (calculated Spring 1992). That is, that the EC offers Portugal, Spain, Greece, and Italy ten times more money per head through the structural funds than that offered to Eastern European countries. If Eastern Europe is offered by the EC about US$200 billion to US$300 billion per year over 5-10 years to promote and finance the reform process, this will be equal to 0.7% to 0.8% of the GNP in the EC and equal to about 4% of the GNP in Eastern Europe. In comparison the money given by the USA under the Marshall plan to sixteen European countries after the Second World War in the period from 1948-51 was equal to about 2% of the GNP in these countries on average, and 1% of the GNP in the USA.[5]

If one assumes that the OECD member countries should contribute substantially to financing the reform process in Eastern Europe, the Nordic countries should pay US$2 billion to US$6 billion per year depending on how the support is organised and shared between the OECD member countries. If this amount of money is compared with what the Nordic countries actually give to the Eastern Europe, only Denmark pays enough money. Sweden, and especially, Finland should contribute more. However, this might be difficult as Finland is confronted with a severe economic crisis. Although the Nordic countries should pay more to the Eastern part of the Baltic region, enough money is paid to influence the development of the region, if the estimates for a successful reform process above are correct. The main problem is to utilise fully the support provided (given the lack of appropriate institutions and organisations in Eastern Europe) and persuade the OECD and the EC to pay more money.

However, in the long run the development of markets and business enterprises in Eastern Europe will be essential for the development of a

[5] The information and estimations given in this and the two previous paragraphs are based on data from *Dansk Økonomi* (1992).

sustainable cooperation in the Baltic region. No sustainable cooperation can be created without regional trade and economic integration based on mutual economic interest. Therefore, the development of markets and private enterprises in the eastern part of the Baltic region is analysed in the following section and the promotion of markets and private enterprises seen from the perspective of regional cooperation discussed; that is, how to utilise the support given to the reform programme.

4 Regional cooperation, markets, and private enterprises
Until now the results of many market analyses in the eastern part of the Baltic region, as done by Nordic companies, have been negative. The price and quality of the Nordic products are in general too high for the Eastern European market. Besides, the quality of the Eastern European products is too low and the price too high for the Nordic markets compared with products from the Far East. The result is that not many Nordic firms operate in the eastern part of the Baltic region without financial support from one of the programmes presented. This situation will only change if markets and enterprises are created in Eastern Europe on a massive scale. What is the situation in the Eastern part of the Baltic region like regarding the creation of private enterprises and markets? Although many strategies are used in Eastern Europe to create new private companies the following four general strategies can be identified: privatization of old state-owned companies; the creation of new private SMEs; the creation of new companies based on foreign investment; and the creation of joint-venture and joint-stock companies.

It is often believed that the creation of private companies and the abolition of the planned economy in itself will create a market economy. This is not the case. In the eastern part of the Baltic region a bazaar economy is developing: a type of economy on the basis of which it will be impossible to create regional trade and economic cooperation on a large scale with markets and private enerprises. Besides, this type of economy cannot, in the long run, utilise and improve the economic potential in the region and hence give the population a better standard of living. The bazaar economy tends to undermine the reform process and might create a situation where the money given to support the reform process is wasted. With this in mind, a short description of the creation of markets and private enterprises is given after some background information.

In the Baltic States, Poland, and the area of St Petersburg and Königsberg (which are parts of Russia) there has been a drop in production and high inflation. In the Baltic States there was a drop in production of about 11% in 1991 and 25% in 1992 in Estonia, in Latvia there was a drop in production of 4% in 1991 and of 30% in 1992, compared with a drop in production of 13% in 1991 and 25% in 1992 in Lithuania. In Russia (St Petersburg and Königsberg) the drop in production was 11% in 1991 and 20% in 1992, compared with a drop in production in Poland of only 7%

in 1991 and 2% in 1992. Inflation in the Baltic States was 212% in 1991 and 1050% in 1992 in Estonia. In Latvia, inflation was 125% in 1991 and 700% in 1992, compared with 216% in 1991 and 1200% in 1992 in Lithuania. In Russia, inflation was 90% in 1991 and 1450% in 1992, compared with a rate of inflation in Poland of only 70% in 1991 and 45% in 1992 all data from EBRD, 1992, page 35).

In the countries mentioned, the rate of unemployment is increasing very quickly and the standard of living for the average person is falling dramatically because of inflation and the reform process.

Many prognoses for 1993 concerning changes in production, inflation, and the rate of unemployment are primarily based on an evaluation of how far the countries have progressed in the reform process; that is, how close the countries are to a market economy. If the prognoses are made in this way the expectations are that Poland will stabilise production at the present level, combined with a further decrease in the rate of inflation. In the Baltic States, where the reform process has just begun, the situation is critical compared with Poland. One can only hope for economic stabilisation. The same applies to Russia.

It is impossible in Poland, the Baltic States, and Russia to obtain credits and loans to establish production. The banks prefer to lend money and to give short-term credits (up to six months) to consumption and business activities with a fast turnover; that is, trade, catering in various forms, and small-scale activities in business services. Besides, the banks have little experience in analysing business projects and in analysing the capacity of a firm to earn money. Furthermore, the new tax systems in Eastern Europe are not created in ways appropriate to stimulating the creation of new enterprises. For example, taxation is made before investments, and in many cases there is much red tape related to the import of modern equipment. In spite of this negative situation, new private companies are created daily.

The Baltic States were strongly integrated into the USSR economy with oligopolies and a high degree of specialisation, as is well known. Latvia had, for example, complete monopoly on electric railway cars in the Soviet market. Latvia also produced 58% of all telephones, 43% of automatic milking machinery, and 29% of all cooling equipment (Storm Pedersen and Fuglsang, 1992, page 14). One consequence is that most of the enterprises in Latvia are large enterprises: the average company has 850 employees, against 167 in the EC (van Arkadie et al, 1991). Furthermore, after the collapse of the former USSR, both the comprehensive network the companies participate in and the markets in which they operated are eroding. This complicates the reform process in the Baltic States.

In the period before 1991, 82% of imports and 91% of exports went to the USSR. Where can new export markets be found? In the Baltic region? The Baltic States are committed to the reform process and want to become independent of Russia. For example, in 1992 Estonia and Latvia introduced a national currency as a way to get out of the Rouble Zone, which is a precondition for forming national strategies of development.

The implementation of the programmes for privatisation is very slow and has in many cases stalled. Some joint ventures and joint stock companies have been registered in the Baltic States within the last years. The external partners come mostly from the Nordic countries (Storm Pedersen and Fuglsang, 1992). Besides, many small private companies have been established. Rough estimates suggest that 10% to 20% of economic activities are now undertaken by private companies. However, only 10% of these economic activities involve material production. The main activity in the private economic sector is trade and business services related to economic speculation.[6]

New small private companies expect to achieve up to 500% profit. In the Czech republic, for example, a medium-sized company producing material products expects a profit of about 20% of its turnover (Storm Pedersen, 1993). Furthermore, many black and grey markets exist in the economic system in the Baltic States, as do 'mafia' activities. The consequence is that the private enterprises in the Baltic States do not produce for local needs and hence do not contribute to the improvement of the standard of living.

What does exist in the Baltic States is a bazaar economy which, at present, is necessary to avoid total disintegration of the economic system. Unfortunately, the bazaar economy directs the economic system towards a kind of casino economy instead of an economy promoting production on the basis of 'best practice' for local needs. This problem will be discussed in more detail in section 5.

Poland has problems with the implementation of the privatisation programmes. For example, as late as March 1993 the government's model for the privatisation of 600 large state-owned companies was rejected by parliament. In contrast many new private companies are created in Poland. Here, 1.5 million SMEs were registered at the beginning of the year 1992. About 50 000 of these companies had more than 5 employees. And the SMEs had created about 2.6 million jobs by the beginning of 1992. The SMEs accounted for 20% of the industrial output and for 45% of the activities in the construction sector. Besides, the SMEs counted for 15% of the exports from Poland and for 45% of the imports. In 1993 it is expected that the private sector in Poland will contribute about 50% to the GNP. The percentage of SMEs in Poland is now equal to that in Western Europe. The activities undertaken by the SMEs are primarily service activities (trade, catering, transport, and consulting). Over two thirds of all SMEs are involved in service activities in broad terms, and the growth rate

[6] Estimations are based on interviews made during the preparation of the report by Storm Pedersen and Fuglsang (1992) and by students from Roskilde University in the Spring of 1992.

in this category is 50% in terms of the number of companies (EBRD, 1992; Piasecki, 1992, pages 143–169).

Although the situation is much better in Poland than in the Baltic States, the economic system in Poland is in many respects similar to the bazaar economy mentioned, which will be discussed in more detail in section 5. The main problem in Poland is the creation of financial institutions which can provide the SMEs with credits and loans. Also, the rate of company mortality has to be reduced. In Poland only a few SMEs survive the first two years, whereas, for example, about 35% of the SME survive more than six years in Denmark (Vejrup-Hansen, 1993).

St Petersburg and Königsberg present a situation that is in all respects worse than in the Baltic States.

East Germany represents a special case in the reform process in Eastern Europe because of its reunification with West Germany. Therefore, the case of East Germany will not be discussed here.

The *conclusion* regarding the development of private enterprises and markets in the Eastern part of the Baltic region, and in Eastern Europe in general, is that the situation is critical. In the Baltic States and the area of St Petersburg and Königsberg, relatively few private companies have been created until now. In Poland it is primarily SMEs which have been created. However, this has been done to a remarkable extent, although most of the SMEs operate in the service market. One basic problem in the Eastern part of the Baltic region is that too much of the economic activity is based on trade, services, and economic speculation; that is, on, and organised in, a bazaar economy.

5 Bazaar economy and local needs [7]

The bazaar economy reflects the attempts of companies and households to do business in every possible way in a situation where neither plans nor markets exist. Basically, 'bazaar' means that little information about the prices, quality, and quantity of the products are available because of the lack of plans and markets. This situation is unproductive because it stimulates actors to make money on the basis of speculations and to trade on a short-term basis; that is, the actors earn money on having special knowledge about the prices, quality, and quantity of products in the bazaar.

The result is that the work incentives in firms producing material products for local needs are undermined. The salaries in such companies are too small compared with what can be earned in the bazaar economy or activities related to the bazaar economy. The bazaar economy is no longer only an economic institution where SMEs and households operate in their attempts to survive under extremely hard business and living conditions.

[7] See Storm Pedersen and Fuglsang, 1992, for a more detailed discussion of the bazaar economy.

Also, big companies have to use the bazaar economy as a way to survive because of the collapse of the old networks in the planned economy. The scale of operations have become substantial in the bazaar economy. When equipment producers in Tallinn, for example, purchase sheet steel on the black market at a price ten times the official plan price, the minimum volume os 60 tons, the weight of a railwagon shipment (Grahm and Königson, 1991, page 9).

It is, however, difficult to provide statistical material about the role and significance of the bazaar economy in St Petersburg and Königsberg, the Baltic States, and Poland. If one considers the economic situation and the living conditions in the countries, it is understandable that people and companies survive only by taking into account the bazaar economy. Hence, almost everybody may be potentially connected to the Baltic bazaar and there are neither social basis or values nor institutional constraints to hold people back from earning quick money in the bazaar economy. The slowdown of the reform process in Eastern Europe at present reinforces the development and importance of the bazaar economy, and within a short time the bazaar economy might become the basic economic institution.

Seen from the perspective of economic development the bazaar economy creates a basic problem. Within the bazaar economy it is rational economic behaviour to engage in short-term speculative business instead of productive business based on profound skills and 'best practice'. One important consequence of this is that the eastern part of the Baltic region cannot utilise and develop its economic potential and hence contribute to the development of regional markets in appropriate ways.

The bazaar economy will become a barrier for regional cooperation. Therefore, one important aim of the Nordic programmes supporting the reform process in the eastern part of the Baltic region must be to facilitate conditions for productive activities. That is to support the creation of SMEs in the productive economic sectors and the privatisation of state-owned companies producing material products for local and regional needs. If one takes the situation of the slow process of privatisation in the eastern part of the Baltic region into account, the SMEs will play a key role in the creation of private business enterprises and hence in the new economic system. As a consequence of this one has to give massive support to the SMEs in the Baltic region as a way to support the reform process and promote regional cooperation.

Although the big companies in the eastern part of the Baltic region prefer to 'go West' to the big Western markets, some of the smaller Nordic markets might be attractive for the big companies in Eastern Europe. These big companies might see some possibilities in the still-increasing discount markets in the Nordic countries. The short distance to Nordic markets combined with the tradition of open economies there might make the Nordic discount markets attractive. Therefore, support to the reorganising of big companies in the eastern part of the Baltic region, so these can operate at the Nordic discount markets, might also contribute to the creation of regional cooperation.

6 Policy recommendations

The policy recommendations are made with the aim of supporting SMEs in the eastern part of the Baltic region and to promote regional cooperation on the basis of SMEs and to some extent on the basis of reorganised state-owned companies.

6.1 Support to SMEs

(1) Salaries have to be calculated in accordance with classic Western principles. That is on bonus-and-accord systems. A number of cases show that the introduction of salaries calculated in this way increase the work productivity by up to several hundred percent (Storm Pedersen, 1993).

(2) The flow of raw material and semifinish products inside the SMEs has to be improved considerably. There is a 'hidden' fortune inside the SMEs as a result of a slow and badly organised flow of raw material and semifinished products (Storm Pedersen, 1993).

(3) SMEs are generally too inflexible, partly because of old production equipment and partly because of old-fashioned human resource management and old work culture. It will, however, take some years for the SMEs to generate a cash flow which will make it possible for them to finance a renewal of the production equipment by themselves. Also, the workers in Eastern Europe are not trained and prepared to take initiatives by themselves and to be responsible for decisions and initiatives made by themselves (Storm Pedersen, 1993).

Existing Nordic programmes should be directed or newly designed to promote a renewal of the production system, and modern human resource management should be introduced. A renewal of the production system and the introduction of modern human resource management is the only way to improve the work environment in the SMEs physically as well as mentally.

(4) The SMEs have to be trained in marketing which will also promote regional cooperation.

(5) Incubators for SMEs should be created in the eastern part of the Baltic region with support from the Nordic countries. It is important to create institutions where experiences with SMEs are accumulated and used quickly to promote the further creation of SMEs and to bring down their mortality rate. More emphasis in the Nordic support to the reform process should be given to create incubators and technology and science parks.

(6) Financial institutions for SMEs have to be developed in the Baltic region with the aim of giving credits and loans to SMEs operating in the region. The Baltic Investment Programme mentioned previously should be developed to cover the whole of the eastern part of the Baltic region.

6.2 The creation of institutions promoting regional cooperation

(1) 'Baltic' institutions in the Nordic countries and in the northern part of Germany should be established with the strategic aim of making it possible for business people and persons from various institutions and organisations in the eastern part of the Baltic region to visit the Nordic countries and Germany for a longer period. During the visits these people could be educated, market analyses could be made, products presented, and companies and organisations promoted with the strategic aim to establish permanent networks and networking which is urgently needed.

(2) The transfer of the know-how of management, technology, marketing, human resource management, and similar issues should be related to the incubators for SMEs.

(3) A regional body should be created with the aim of improving the infrastructure in the region.

(4) 'Islands of communications' should be created and improved; that is, the improvement and the creation of institutions, such as the Information Office of the Nordic Council and the Office of Danish Cultural Institute in the Baltic States, which on a nonprofit basis generate dialogue and cooperation between the various Nordic and Eastern countries in the Baltic region. This again promotes all types of regional cooperation with a long-term perspective (see Storm Pedersen and Fuglsang, 1992, for a more detailed discussion of this type of institution in the Baltic region).

(5) Proper market analysis should be made to evaluate which markets have the biggest potential for trade in the region. On this basis strategies should be designed to develop the markets found.

If these recommendations are followed, a meso-region scenario might become of some importance in the Baltic region. Besides, if the Baltic region becomes an EC region in the 1990s the meso-region scenario might be strengthened. However, the risk of an unsuccessful reform process in Eastern Europe still exists. Therefore, regional cooperation in the Baltic region might also be based on a fear of political and social unrest in the region.

References

Bévort F, Storm Pedersen J, Sundbo J, 1992, "Human resource management in Denmark—recent trends", in *Human Resource Management in the European Community, Part 1* Eds J Berridge, I Brunstein (MCB University Press, Manchester) pp 6–12

Bröcher J, 1989, "How to eliminate certain defects of the potential formula" *Environment and Planning A* **21** 817–830

Cappellin R, 1992, "Theories of local endogenous development and international cooperation", in *Development Issues and Strategies in the New Europe* Ed. M Tykkyläinen (Avebury, Aldershot, Hants) pp 1–20

Clark C, Wilson F, Bradley J, 1969, "Industrial location and economic potential in Western Europe" *Regional Studies* **3** 197–212

Dansk Økonomi 1992, "Østeuropas integration i verdensøkonomien. Handel og støtteforanstaltninger" (The integration of Eastern Europe into world trade. Trade and support) May, pp 87–148 (Det Økonomiske Råds sekretariat, Copenhagen)

EBRD, 1992 *Annual Economic Reviews* European Bank for Reconstruction and Development, 1 Exchange Square, London EC2A 2EH

Ellemann-Jensen U, 1991, "Arkitekturen i den kommende baltiske region" (The structure of the emerging Baltic region) *Nord Revy* 5/6, 67–70

Engholm B, 1990, "Nordeuropas Middelhav" (The Baltic Sea as the Mediterranean of Northern Europe) *Politikens* 23 July

Ernst and Young, 1992, "Copenhagen—securing future advantage I and II" consulting reports, Tagensveg 86, 2200 Copenhagen, Denmark

Gerner, 1991, "Två hundra års europæisk felutveckling" (Two hundred years of development in the wrong direction) *Nord Revy* 3/4 14

Grahm L, Königson L, 1991, "Baltic industry—a survey of potentials and constraints" Development Cooperation Studies in Policy and Practice, number 1, Stockholm

Hass J M, Peschel K, 1982 *Räumliche Strukturen im internationalen Handel* (The Spatial Structure of International Trade) (Verlag V Florentz, München)

Information 1993, 1 March (a newspaper, Denmark)

Peschel K, 1992a, "Perspectives of regional economic development around the Baltic" Institut für Regionalforschung, Kiel Universität, Kiel (unpublished)

Peschel K, 1992b, "European integration and regional development in Northern Europe" Institut für Regionalforschung, Kiel Universität, Kiel

Piasecki P (Ed.), 1992, "Policy on SME in Central and Eastern European countries" Department of Entrepreneurship and Industrial Policy, University of Lodz, Poland

Predöhl A, 1949 *Aussenwirtschaft* (Foreign Trade) (second edition) (Vandenhoeck and Ruprecht, Göttingen)

Storm Pedersen J, 1988 *The Contemporary Society with Mixed Economy* PhD thesis, Department of Economics and Planning, Roskilde University, Denmark (only summary in English)

Storm Pedersen J, 1989, "The internal market and European political and economic integration. Prospects and challenges", in *The Internal Market in EEC: A Debate on Eurotrends* Eds J Storm Pedersen, B Greve (Forlaget for Samfundsøkonomi og Planlægning, Roskilde) pp 122–138

Storm Pedersen J, 1993, "15 cases of SME in Eastern Europe", research paper, Department of Economics and Planning, Roskilde University, Denmark

Storm Pedersen J, Fuglsang L, 1992 *The Baltic Region—Why Regional Cooperation Matters* (Commission of the European Communities, Luxembourg)

van Arkadie B (Ed.), 1991 *Economic Survey of the Baltic Republics* volumes I and II, Swedish Ministry of Foreign Affairs, Stockholm

Vejrup-Hansen J, 1993, "Virksomhedsdemografi: overlevelse og vækst i nye virksomheder" (The structure of firms: survival and growth in the new firms) *Samfundsøkonomen* 2 21–28

Ziesmer K, 1992, "Räumliche Wirkung der ökonomischen Öffnung Osteuropas— eine Analyse auf Basis des Potentialansatzes" (Spatial effects of the opening-up of East European economies—an analysis based on their potential contributions), unpublished thesis, Fakultät of the Christian-Albrechts University, Kiel

Restructuring and Interregional Cooperation in Central Europe: The Case of Hungary

G Horváth
Hungarian Academy of Sciences, Pecs

1 Introduction

The collapse of the socialist planned economy and the transformation of the ownership structure in Hungary have increased regional tensions in the country. The economic recession has revitalised the traditional spatial differences between the capital and its agglomeration, between the eastern and the western part of the country. In the core region of the country the unemployment rate is relatively low (4%); the withdrawal of state industries is balanced by the fast development of private business. In the eastern rural areas and in the large industrial centres of the country, a deep depression has appeared (the unemployment rate is between 15% and 25%, there is little launching of new business, and economic restructuring is hindered by, quite apart from the lack of capital, the termination of the former foreign trade relations of the region). The territories west of the Danube are in a transitional state; it remains to be seen which of the above types of regions they will join. When one considers their development endowments and initial success, the western and southwestern counties along the border are in a favourable position [the unemployment rate is around the national average (12%), and although industrial production is diminishing here too, the rapidly increasing new enterprises have strengthened the tertiary sector—although they were needed to compensate for the loss of jobs].

The transition to a market economy built on diversified administrative and decision centres will increase the task of choosing among regional development models in Hungary, too, in the near future. As the country is at an important crossroads of development, there are several possible options. These development directions differ from each other according to the economic ideas and the desired economic policy of their representatives. They also differ in the ways that are proposed for granting rights—also with respect to political issues—to the local and regional organisations of public administration (and central institutions) in the organising and coordinating of regional processes. Regarding these points of view, there are a wide range of possible solutions. A strategy controlled from one centre—following the traditional regional development models of market economies—is just as likely to succeed as an innovation-oriented regional policy with many actors, being built from the bottom upwards.

For the western and the southwestern Hungarian counties, because of their development characteristics and their institutional relations with regions of the Alpe–Adria working community, the second development option puts itself forward unequivocally. Here I seek to establish the common characteristics of economic development and the strategies of regions of the Alpe-Adria community, and to study the available conditions for the application of this model and the possible changes in the Hungarian counties necessary for them to enter the Central European regional division of labour.

2 The Alpe-Adria working community
2.1 The goals of the community
In 1978, when Europe was still quite divided and the germs of the idea for a unified common market had just emerged, the representatives of two Northeastern Italian regions (Friuli-Venezia Giulia and Veneto) and four Central Austrian provinces (Carinthia, Styria, Upper Austria, and Salzburg),

Figure 1. The Alpe-Adria working community, 1993.

and Bavaria, Slovenia, and Croatia decided, in Venice, to form an action association for harmonising the most different fields of regional development. In 1981 the Italian region of Trentino-Alto Adige joined this association, as did Lombardy in 1985 and the Austrian Burgenland in 1987. And between 1986 and 1989 five Hungarian territorial administration units—Gyôr-Moson-Sopron, Vas, Zala Somogy, and Baranya counties—participated in the work of the interregional organisation. With the admission of the Swiss Ticino canton in 1990, the organisational foundation of the working community was completed (figure 1). Except for the founding regions, all member provinces participated as observers in the working community's work for a couple of years.

The task of the working community was formulated in the founding Joint Declaration (Venice, 20 November 1978) as a common informative, professional discussion, and harmonisation concerning problems falling within the interests of the members. The following areas were emphasised: transportation crossing points in the Alps; traffic at ports; energy production and transportation; agriculture and forestry; economy of water supplies; tourism; environment protection and nature conservation; landscape planning; settlement development; cultural relations; and relations between academic and higher educational institutions.

The participants declared, first in the founding declaration and later, in 1988, in the declaration of the foreign ministers in Millstatt (Austria), that their activity and programme corresponded with the provisions of the final declaration of the European Security and Cooperation Conference; thus it represented European interests. The national governments expressed their willingness to help in promoting and encouraging the interregional cooperation of the Alpe–Adria area. In 1990 the Standpoint of Pentagonale Initiative given in Venice underlined the importance of offering encouragement to cooperative development among those provinces already interacting (Horváth, 1990; 1991a; 1991b).

Thus the political preconditions exist which guarantee that this association could become the integrator of the EC, the European Free Trade Association (EFTA), and the regions of Eastern Europe. It is worth pointing out that the Hexagonale—nowadays the Central European Initiative—cooperation between nations covers a larger area than the eighteen regions, but it could increase the efficiency of its activities if the working groups of the Initiative would consider *cooperation between regions as the driving force of cooperation, so that it would become possible to represent regional interests in the state decisionmaking process.*

2.2 Core and periphery in the working community
The Italian and the German regions have decisive weight in the Alpe–Adria working community, occupying an area of $28\,000$ km^2, with 38 million inhabitants. Some 40% of the population and 42% of the GDP are in Italy; the equivalent percentages for Germany are 29% and 39%. The Hungarian

counties account for 4.6% of the population and 2.2% of the GDP [figures 2(a) and 2(b)].

There are great differences in the economic productivity and the sectoral structures of the member provinces. Though the eastern peripheral provinces are the developed regions of Hungary and the former Yugoslavia, their gross regional production indicators per capita reach only one half to one third of the average in the working community. (This statement is the result of an expert estimation, earlier the regional indicators could be determined only roughly.) Remarkable differences are demonstrated by the competitiveness and comparativeness of regional economic structures. The sectoral structure of the core regions is characterised by the economic structure of a postindustrial society (the tertiary sectors account for close to, or more than, 50% of the gross regional product, whereas in the provinces not yet modernised—even in Burgenland—this figure is under 40%). The ratio of agricultural production is high in the peripheries (figure 3).

The development path of this traditionally rural area is determined by the characteristics of the postindustrial economy: the service sector, which is spatially more mobile and has new locational requirements, has become the engine of economic growth. In 1988 in the Alpe–Adria community, 49.6% of the employees worked in the tertiary and quaternary sectors, 41% in industry, and 9.4% in agriculture. The eastern peripheral regions, however, still have a traditional economic structure: there is a high proportion of agricultural employees, in a number of regions the weight of industry is decisive, and service sectors are underdeveloped (figure 4, over). The proportion of agricultural employees is highest in the Hungarian member counties (24.9% in Somogy, 21.2% in Gyôr-Sopron-Moson,

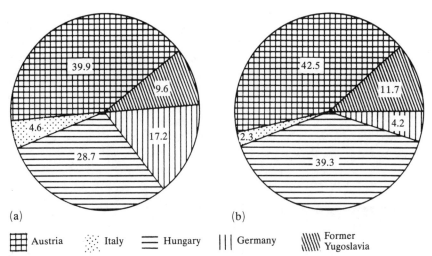

Figure 2. (a) The population of the Alpe–Adria working community by country, 1990. (b) The share of the GDP of the Alpe–Adria community by country, 1990.

21.0% in Vas) and in Croatia. Because the weight of backward regions is relatively significant (17.5%), the indicators of economic structure of the working community are less favourable than the EC average.

The economically developed regions have a modern, complete, physical infrastructure. The density of the backbone of the road system, the motorway network, is 15.9 km per 1000 km^2 (the EC average is 13.2 km); only the Hungarian countries and Burgenland do not have a motorway. The majority of the provinces (with the exception of the Hungarian counties, Trentino-South Tirol, and Burgenland) have been connected to the European air traffic network. In the region 19 airports produce 200 000 metric tonnes of freight and 25 million passenger transactions annually (figure 5, over).

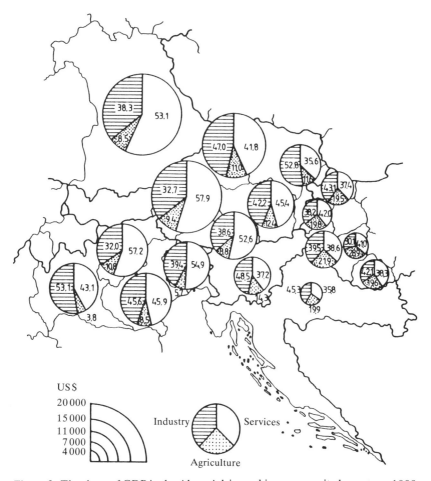

Figure 3. The share of GDP in the Alpe–Adria working community by sectors, 1988.

Significant development can be observed in other service sector industries, too. Not only is the number of employees growing in the sector
but—more dynamically—so is the production value. Typical of this are the
Italian Veneto regions where between 1971 and 1983 the number of
employees in the tertiary sectors increased by 30%, and the output by
56%. In the core regions the internal structure of the tertiary sector shows
the peculiarities of a modern economy. Although in the peripheries the

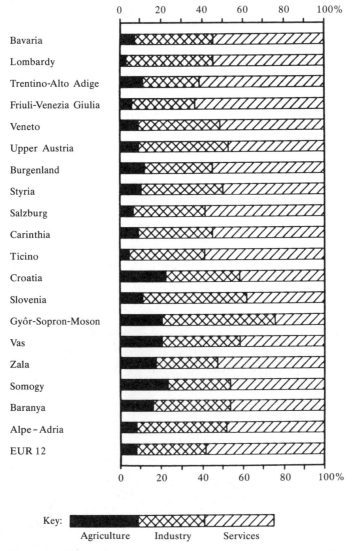

Figure 4. The share of employment in the Alpe–Adria working community by
sectors, 1988.

growth industry of services is almost exclusively commerce (and tourism in Croatia and Somogy county), in the core regions financial, research and development, and productive services play an important role. In the five Hungarian counties between 1.7% and 3.3% of the employees work in personal and economic services, whereas, for example, in the Austrian Lands between 6.2% and 13.2% of the labour force is employed just in the financial services sector.

In the 1980s there was a significant reorganisation of the interior industrial structure of the core regions: traditional industries fell behind, and production of microelectronics, biotechnology, and information technology replaced them. The traditional clothing industry and the food

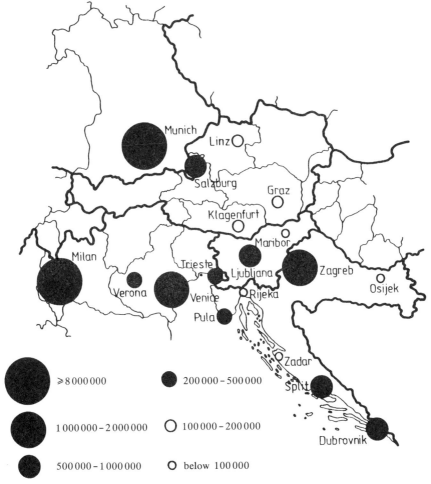

Figure 5. The number of passengers at the airports of the Alpe–Adria working community (designed by the author on the basis of national yearbooks of statistics).

industry changed from mass production to diversified quality products complying with market demands. The most characteristic example of this is the Benetton company operating in the Veneto region: the small family business grew to become a world company by changing the content of its product and by using an entirely new business organisational concept for its manufacturing (Conti and Julien, 1991).

Parallel with the economic restructuring in the western part of the Alpe–Adria community, the size composition of the enterprises has also changed. Although in this area small and medium companies have been predominant, the change of paradigm of market economies—replacing the Fordism of economic organisations with a decentralised structure and a view that emphasises differentiated market needs—resulted in a rapid growth of the number of enterprises in the German, Austrian, and Italian regions. Small firms have dominant positions in the Italian regions: the number of business organisations per 1000 people here is double that of the other regions (table 1). Only Salzburg Land is close to the density of Italian enterprises, where 83.9% of the enterprises operate in the tertiary sector. Despite the large wave of business start-ups that emerged in Hungary and the former Yugoslavian territories in the end of the 1980s, the indices of these regions are one tenth to one quarter of those for the core regions.

Table 1. Enterprises in the Alpe–Adria working community, 1988 (source: ISTAT, 1988; 1990).

Member region	Number of firms	Employees per firm	Firms per 1000 inhabitants
Bavaria	390 353	13.7	35.3
Lombardy	672 336	5.6	75.6
Trentino-South Tirol	65 352	5.7	73.9
Friuli-Venezia Giulia	81 554	5.6	67.6
Veneto	321 343	5.6	73.4
Upper Austria	51 938	11.6	39.9
Burgenland	10 527	10.9	39.5
Styria	55 073	9.5	46.6
Salzburg	33 870	6.4	72.9
Carinthia	26 435	8.5	48.8
Croatia[a]	92 932	22.3	19.9
Slovenia[a]	49 798	19.7	24.9
Gyôr-Moson-Sopron[a]	3 518	47.1	8.3
Vas[a]	1 802	60.0	6.5
Zala[a]	2 576	44.5	8.4
Somogy[a]	2 739	40.2	8.0
Baranya[a]	3 050	50.2	7.3
Total	1 865 196	9.3	47.9

[a] 1990.

The operation of what amount to nearly two million enterprises is supported by an expanded market-service institution system: thousands of economic consulting, marketing, engineering development, and information service organisations are at the disposal of small businesses, and they are helped by institutions that assist them to enter the international market and to organise fairs and expos, and regional professional fairs and exhibitions. (The largest European fairs are held in Milan and Munich; the expos of Verona, Trieste, Pordenone, Graz, Klagenfurt, and Ljubljana also have international importance.)

As well as the differences in economic potential and structural characteristics we can see differences in the other interior components of the economies of the core and the periphery. An example of the qualitative differences in the integration capability and degree of modernisation can be shown by giving one peculiarity of both: export indicators and R&D data for the two spatial divisions of the Alpe–Adria community (tables 2 and 3).

The Northern Italian regions have great export capacity, they provide nearly half of the Italian exports, whereas the Hungarian counties account for only 10% of their national exports. In the Italian member-provinces, the export quantity per employee is double the Hungarian indicator, though with respect to the participation ratio of export production, only slight differences can be registered. A similar ratio can be found in the R&D capacity of the two areas.

In comparisons of the export indicators there were methodological difficulties because of the contents of the data available. The Italian data show the total export computed for the active income earners of the

Table 2. Export potential of Italian regions and Hungarian counties, 1988 (sources: calculated by the author on the basis of: Cappellin, 1990; ISTAT, 1988; Hungarian yearbooks of county statistics, 1989).

Region	Volumes		Percentages	
	(US$ million)	per employee (US$ 1000)	of country's exports	of country's production
Lombardy	39 875.8	10.84	31.1	38.0
Trentino-South Tirol	12 128.1	5.94	1.7	24.4
Friuli-Venezia Giulia	3 637.3	8.10	2.8	21.6
Veneto	15 280.0	8.63	11.9	34.6
Italian regions (total)	60 921.14	9.74	7.5	34.8
Gyôr-Moson-Sopron	568.3	8.29	5.9	31.0
Vas	79.0	2.93	0.8	21.0
Zala	88.9	2.78	0.9	12.4
Somogy	55.8	3.75	0.6	20.7
Baranya	139.0	2.31	1.5	16.7
Hungarian counties (total)	931.0	4.53	0.7	23.1

regions. In the case of the Hungarian counties, only the export activity of industrial companies located in the capitals of the counties and the exports falling to one industrial employee were considered. Thus the conclusions drawn from data comparison could be only relative. I have to point out that European integration requires drastic changes in the regional statistical information system.

During the first decade of the Alpe-Adria working community it primarily arranged the exchange of information, the coordination of linear infrastructure (first of all within the triangle of the Italian-Austrian-Slovenian borders), and the organisation of cultural relations. In the past few years, however, partly because of the changes taking place in Eastern Europe, and the capital expansion of the Italian regions, the professional exchange meetings of the economic organisations of the member provinces have become regular. Economic cooperation began in 1989-90, in which period the Lombardy region played the role of the coordinating centre of the working community. Innovative features can be strengthened as a consequence of programmes started in 1990, and not only can their advantages be enjoyed by the economically developed member regions, but also the Eastern peripheral regions can gather ideas for transforming their economic structure. For the actual integration, however, adequate *institutions and measures* are needed. One of the cooperation programmes is intended to establish two important institutions, the common regional development fund and a common financial institution, that are the prerequisites of developing economic integration. These institutions, on the

Table 3. Research and development expenditure in the Italian regions (1985) and Hungarian counties (1990) (sources: Costa and De Marchi, 1989; *Tudományos kutatás és fejlesztés* 1991).

Region	Total expenditure		Percentages [a]	
	(US$1000)	per inhabitant (US$)	total	per inhabitant
Lombardy	900861.2	101.4	28.9	185.2
Trentino-South Tirol	14353.6	16.3	0.5	29.9
Friuli-Venezia Giulia	42432.1	35.1	1.4	63.2
Veneto	81282.9	18.6	2.6	34.0
Italian regions (total)	1038929.8	67.7	33.4	123.8
Gyôr-Moson-Sopron	12628.7	29.6	2.2	54.8
Vas	423.3	1.9	0.1	3.5
Zala	1409.5	4.5	0.3	8.3
Somogy	955.7	2.7	0.2	5.0
Baranya	4865.6	11.3	0.9	20.9
Hungarian counties (total)	20282.8	11.6	3.7	21.5

[a] These are percentages of the country average.

basis of the Common Market norms, could promote the eastern regions in joining the European integration, partly by using the financial resources of the EC.

2.3 Development models of core regions

The new economic policy has also made a significant impact on regional policy. The former consensus between central and regional governments broke up. The traditional means of regional policy (a significant central role in regional development, an incentive system built from the top down, and so on) lost their economic and political motives, and new regional strategies have been formed.

As opposed to the centrally managed regional development policy, the fundamental feature of the new models is that, instead of exogenous factors, endogenous endowments gain major significance in the development of regions. Centrally controlled policy was realised primarily in sectoral development programs. The regional branch offices of central authorities could, at most, technically coordinate these, but they were inadequate for the mobilisation of local resources. The new development policies, however, emphasised local actors, democratic decision procedures, and complex utilisation of resources and innovation. The development models of the core regions of the Alpe–Adria community show a number of individual peculiarities as well as a lot of common characteristics. The major part of the regionally specific characteristics is rooted in the variety of regional policies, and in the social and economic position of the regions within the country (Fuà, 1991). Although the Italian regions are among the most developed territories of the country, Carinthia, Burgenland, and the eastern border zone of Bavaria are relatively less-developed areas compared with the average of their own countries, and receive significant government subsidies. The heavy-industry areas of Styria and Upper Austria are hit by depression, and in the Rovigo district of the Veneto region the recession in the sugar industry has caused a crisis. Naturally, the development of these areas requires individual solutions. Without doubt, however, even these development concepts will not follow the traditional models, but I will emphasise innovative elements (Marinucci, 1988).

The new regional policy generally applied in this region, which may be called the innovation-oriented or local–regional initiative development model, is focused on the establishing of and systematic renewal of marketable products, industrial processes, and services. Therefore, this model enhances the development of the adaptability of regions. The local and regional decisions are not influenced by central standards any more, but local–regional economic decisions, based on signals from the market and economic cycle, mobilise in order to produce the performance necessary for the changes. The common goals of these strategies can usefully be outlined in the following way (Stöhr, 1990):

(1) a search for new development resources and the systemisation of them, and the creation of the institutions necessary for the operation of this system;

(2) the building of regional, local, and entrepreneurial cooperation networks (the industrial parts of the Italian regions have reached this objective most completely where traditional entrepreneurial cooperation has been combined with breaking down the production process into spatially separated phases);

(3) the institutionalisation of information, innovative, and entrepreneurial incentive transfers (industrial parks, business-innovation centres, R&D consortiums);

(4) the organising of local and regional development coalitions of various interest groups, harmonising rigid local hierarchies, and building flexible decision systems; and

(5) transforming the quality of living in neighbourhoods, their cultural and scientific atmosphere, and favourable environmental status into economic growth factors, and the complex settlement supply into capital attraction factors.

In these regional communities the system of norms of cooperation has become the motivation force of economic rationality, so it may not be accidental that a prefigurement of the new economic cooperation, the Alpe–Adria working community, was formed in this area of Europe. The other reason for the transboundary regional cooperation is rooted in the political realism induced by this development model, which means the relatively high degree of spatial decentralisation of power, and the possibility of joining independently to the international regional division of labour. (Naturally, the Central European historical precedents cannot be neglected either.)

3 The possible role of international factors in regional development in Hungary

Historic events, especially the Trianon Peace Treaty, had serious consequences for the spatial structure of counties. The new borders fragmented natural economic units; the built-up area of cities in frontier regions became smaller; their economic connections with inland areas is still weak. These factors have a strong influence on the development possibilities of border regions. Up to now the borderland situation was a factor hindering economic and settlement development. Provided that there are favourable political changes in future, the borderland situation may turn out to be a factor of regional development. The integration of socialist states made possible only a low level of integration between frontier regions. It cannot be defined as a territorial integration for there were almost no incentives for the economic realisation of political declarations. That is why there were only local examples of the exchange of manpower, the coordination of regional development organisations was exclusively directed by the government, and the exchange of goods between borderland regions—which is now the most common form of cooperation—was regulated by intergovernmental agreements and strict monetary regulations. In practice, there were no cases of direct company or local territorial administrational initiatives at that time.

Because of the collapse of Yugoslavia and the Soviet Union, and the uncertainty of these countries' development, a dynamic interregional cooperation with them has not yet proved possible. However, a more detailed analysis of these two border regions is necessary in the long run, for they include some backward settlement groups as well. The consequences of the possible trading and cooperation in production should also be taken into account in the plans of economic development programmes. Another important factor is the way that economic cooperation of mutual benefit—the most important target of cooperation between organisations situated at a reasonable distance from the point of economy—can be achieved.

A cross-border economic cooperation is defined as a system of economic cooperation, based on trading and more complex cooperation systems, that functions between economic organisations participating in cooperation. Development should be an important factor in this special form of cooperation. Cooperation in production—which is dominant in any form of cooperation—is based on a certain level of mutual investment. If it is so, then cooperation has a primary dependency on regional potentials, a secondary dependency on the economic potentials of economic organisations participating in cooperation, and a tertiary dependency on the regional development policy of central–local–regional administration systems.

The future implies that the incentives and advantages of regional policy can be applied to frontier regions as well if central and local authorities consider the increase in the economic production of frontier regions as an important task. Until now, the problem was that regional development concepts did not include such priorities which could be applied directly for the elimination of cross-border cooperation problems.

We should learn a lesson from the recent practice of resource allocation for the development of lagging regions. In spite of the fact that the development of frontier regions gave clear possibilities for a greater intensification of cross-border cooperations, there were only a few cases for its realisation in practice.

Hungary's present economic structure, with the exporting capacities of its industry, is unfavourable for the country's present and future cross-border and general foreign relations. During the last forty years the specialisation, the structure, the institutional system, the government, and the main features of the political and social environment of Hungary's economic development were largely determined by its cooperation with COMECON states. I do not want to mention here the slow transformation of foreign trade orientation as well as the well-known problems of foreign trade regulation and its institutional structure. We should concentrate on the regional differences of foreign trade which have not as yet been investigated in any detail. In Hungary, there are large regional differences in the participation intensity of foreign trade, just as there are in other fields of the country's socioeconomic structure. Research results indicate larger differences than any other previous studies. Although, as a result of the past forty years, the spatial diffusion at the majority of quantitative production units shows a smooth, or at least a slackening, pattern of differences, the differences are still sharp at the qualitative components of economy. To illustrate this I could cite the unilateral R&D environment needed for the territorial concentration of innovative economic development, but the regional spread of modern enterprise forms is following a similar pattern to the example of the spatial division of foreign trade. In the 1980s, 41.2% of Hungary's foreign trade of industrial products was performed by companies located in Budapest. Only 20% of industrial workers are employed in Budapest (table 4). Five counties (Borsod-Abaúj-Zemplén,

Table 4. Regional structure of the foreign trade of industrial products in Hungary, 1981–90 (source: calculated by the author on the basis of *Megyei Statisztikai Evkónyvek* 1981–1990).

County	Proportion of foreign trade in total trade	Distribution of foreign trade (%)	Increase[a] 1981–90 (%)	Foreign trade per employee
Baranya	18.8	2.1	136.7	2.27
Bács-Kiskun	31.7	2.9	121.0	3.25
Békés	28.0	2.2	173.2	3.26
Borsod-Abaúj-Zemplén	19.3	7.8	148.9	3.91
Csongrád	23.2	2.7	152.1	3.47
Fejér	30.4	5.7	288.5	8.11
Gyôr-Moson-Sopron	31.8	7.4	165.3	8.45
Hajdú-Bihar	22.6	3.3	205.0	4.59
Heves	14.5	1.1	127.8	1.43
Jász-Nagykun-Szolnok	12.0	2.7	178.9	3.94
Komárom-Esztergom	15.6	2.0	160.9	2.51
Nógrád	12.8	0.5	342.5	1.51
Pest	16.8	7.2	244.8	6.28
Somogy	27.1	1.0	95.9	1.74
Szabolcs-Szatmár-Bereg	25.6	1.7	159.9	2.18
Tolna	20.9	1.2	192.5	2.36
Vas	22.5	1.2	141.6	2.17
Veszprém	30.0	4.9	160.8	5.83
Zala	12.2	1.2	144.9	1.93
Budapest	28.1	41.2	170.4	11.44
Total	23.7	100.0	179.2	5.38

[a] 1981 = US$1 001 000.

Fejér, Gyôr-Moson-Sopron, Pest, and Veszprém) had another 33% share of the foreign trade of industrial products, whereas the equivalent figures were 15.5% in the six counties of Central and Eastern Hungary and 4.5% in the four southern trans-Danubian counties (Baranya, Somogy, Tolna, Zala).

The predominance of Budapest is significant both in the quantitative and qualitative indexes of foreign trade. It has a foreign trade index three times larger than the national average; this index is one-third of the national average in the four southern trans-Danubian counties. The dynamics of foreign trade shows a similar difference.

During the period of investigation, the qualitative parameters of foreign trade depended much more on macroeconomic decisions and changes in foreign trade regulation than on the use of the given regional geopolitical situation. The priority of macroeconomic regulation in foreign trade regulation indicates a strong correlation with general regional economic development; first, with the pattern of industrial development that Hungary's underdeveloped regions—southern trans-Danubian counties and the counties of Central and East Hungary—underwent in the past.

Those elements that are determinant in the outlook of these two parts of Hungary as a consquence of a deindustrialisation policy in the 1960s, are weak points in the competitiveness of the Western European economy as well. The lack of economic autonomy and the high rate of movement of industrial complexes from low-tech levels in other regions are the components of the present foreign economic situation. Radical structural and institutional changes are necessary for converting geographical position into an internal source of regional development, and these regions could thus have a role in international regional competition.

4 Can the Alpe–Adria model be applied to Hungary?

Those European regions that were able to formulate a development strategy suitable for their own needs and to have it accepted and enforced achieved stability in a relatively short period of time, and their new structures began to grow. The regions, however, that were unable to formulate an independent programme (in many cases because of their endogenous endowments) could expect their regeneration to occur only through central support. However, the restructuring of the system led by the centre, following the solutions of the traditional regional development model, brought about only a temporary stabilisation. The economic structure of these regions was conserved, their growth potentials and competitiveness remained poor, and their integration with the international regional division of labour still meets with difficulties.

The regional development of market economies is not based on a uniform model, but strategies diversified and different in their elements are developed for the regions in different geographical locations and with different structural endowments. It is inconceivable that the regional development in Hungary would evolve according to a general pattern.

The regional strategy of the government should include the general goals of regional policy, financial incentives, and forms of support. But formulating the direction of regional development, choosing an adequate model of the path of development, and finding financing are the tasks of the actors of local economic activity and of the local government.

It is clear that the regionally initiated development policy based on associations of regional actors cannot be the only solution in Hungary. Favourable changes can be brought about only in those regions (for example, in the Hungarian Alpe–Adria zone) where the need to transform the traditional, formerly relatively strong, economic structure, and the demand to activate the backward areas connected to the core territories, formulated in accordance with public opinion, are, together with the new types of driving forces of international regional development, and their human resources, intellectual capacity, and also the forming market and interest asserting organisational net, give adequate frames to formulate the direction of development.

The central government in Hungary is not yet capable of intervening in the regional crises consequent upon the transition to a market economy. The business sphere instinctively drifted towards adaptation strategies unfavourable for the region: decreasing the production capacity and relocating the productive units. The transformation of the administration system, particularly, the disparagement of the counties' role, and the underdevelopment of the regional institutional system of the market did not give the regions any chance to initiate other adaptation strategies such as developing a model based on the combination of new products and markets. Now the important obstacle to the economic restructuring of the region (and of the country) is the lack of a complex development strategy for spatial units and larger areas (and cities).

The formulation of a new course of development calls for the revaluation of the economic resources and endowments of the southern and southwestern counties in Hungary. The new economy could rely primarily on the development of regional infrastructure, human resources, the mobilisation of capital goods, and an organisational–institutional system capable of attracting foreign working capital. The appreciation of mental ability, technical development, and management activity could be determinants in the transformation of the economic structure. Thus, it seems advisable for the development strategy of the border zone to be based on new combinations of the endogenous resources. The exogenous (Hungarian and foreign) means of economic development should be used only for the utilisation of the spatial endowments and to increase the ability of the market to react, based on the preferences of endogenous demands. This is the only way to prevent a repetition of the consequences of the former regional policy, and to avoid the situation where the solution of the acute employment problems would lead to the formation of a fragile economy in which the components do not link up with each other, but are based on a strong regional external dependence. Thus in the future there is a need for an innovative strategy of regional policy to develop economic modernisation rather than one-sidedly to acquire factors from outside the region.

The new economic structure in many respects could be advantageous enough for Hungary to join the international regional integration, and it is conceivable that perspectively innovative development, similar to courses of development in Western Europe, could evolve in lots of places. For development of the foundations which rely on small and medium-sized firms, the following favourable endowments are available.

(a) The traditions of enterprise are very strong in agriculture, small town industry, and tourist services in the region. This is particularly true for the agricultural zones surrounding the cities where production for market, the reaction to changes in the market, and the establishment of the necessary independent organisations related to them, infiltrated the traditions of the farming economy. It is also true for the regions involved in tourism where there are precedents in services organised on the basis of private ownership.

(b) The institutions of higher education in the region could provide a framework for regional human development programmes, and could serve as a basis for the development of quality tourism (conferences, therapeutic tourism) and for the diffusion of technical innovations and professional culture.

(c) The educational level of one fifth of the population (living in small towns) is good, and the conditions are in favour of their trainability.

(d) There are relatively favourable conditions in the residential districts of the medium-sized towns and large cities in the region (the aesthetic appearance of downtowns, the existence of norms of residential districts similar to the Western European ones, the cultural–educational–academic milieu). These signs of quality can be attractive to foreign capital investors.

The key to the structural transformation of the Alpe–Adria region in Hungary is to link up the Central European growth centre. The following development objectives should be accomplished:

(a) the development of transportation and communication (modernisation of the main traffic roads, highways, airports) and the evolution of a modern information system (from the European development experience, it is inconceivable to integrate Hungary with the international division of labour by linking up a single centre—the capital; only a network of regional subcentres can link Hungary with the European markets);

(b) the development of an institutional system of regional markets (business, banking and financial services, exhibitions, fairs, regional market information systems, enterprise and export incentive centers);

(c) industrial parks promoting technological change and changes in product mix, and the organisation of technological centers;

(d) the building up of a close network of vocational training and retraining in towns, the expansion of higher education both in quantity and curriculum, and particular attention to technical research and training;

(e) the establishment of associations (agencies) for regional economic development in order to harmonise the development ideas and to organise the composition of conceptions.

The complex regional development planning and the formation of strategy are still impeded by numerous factors from an organisational point of view.

(1) The local governments (despite their jurisdiction or, in case of existing policy, the lack of methodologies in organising the economy or operation routine) are cautious in formulating a complex concept of settlement development. So far, the cooperation of local governments has not been characteristic at the level of small districts, town surroundings, or, particularly, regions.

(2) The county governments (lacking jurisdiction and a system of policy means) can only be voluntary actors of regional development.

(3) The separation of the cities with county rank (there are twenty of these) from the administration of the county governments (because of the underdevelopment of the coordination of regional development) protects the dichotomy of the regional economy and prevents the separation of the modernising, innovative centres from their area-wide planning districts. Tearing the cities with county rank (which account for 38% of the country's population, 57% of the employees in industry, and 46% of the investment in financial sectors) away from the complexity of regional economic and social processes could raise questions about the successfulness of the restructuring of the economy in Hungary.

(4) The existing net of decentralised organisations (county offices of central state organisations) articulates sectoral interests. The intersectoral coordination does not prevail, the regional interdependency of particular decisions is not considered, and the activity of these organisations primarily follows the logic of the administration.

(5) The office of the representative of the republic (prefect) does not coordinate the economy, though it demonstrates a tendency to develop its harmonising activity despite the fact that its organisational principle, information base, relation system, and professional structure are not suitable for bringing about an agreement on economic and social objectives or political decisions.

(6) The institutional system of the regional market has not yet developed. Its elements (because of their function to observe, to register, and to foresee economic processes) could provide information about the endogenous and exogenous market factors of economic development for the selection of the directions of a regional development strategy.

A general task of regional administration is to represent and defend the interests of this cooperation in front of the central government. The organisation of the Alpe–Adria working community was not free from conflicts between central and regional interests either. Because of the specific constitutional system the Free State of Bavaria has the greatest amount of freedom; on the other hand, the Italian regions and the Austrian Lands are able to expand their international cooperation rights only through long-lasting constitutional debates which have not yet been concluded. In the former Yugoslavia, even the member republics had only limited foreign trade autonomy, and in Hungary this question was hardly even raised.

Constitutional debates flared up, especially after 1980, when the Council of Europe in Madrid reached an enabling agreement that pointed out the necessity of decentralised organisation of transboundary cooperations. This agreement prescribes the freedom of regions to choose the forms of borderline cooperation, on the one hand, and contains guarantees for the central state to have the means to inspect and control the maintenance of state sovereignty, on the other. Although the agreement has not obliged the ratifying states to reform their internal legal system, it was an important measure to develop the institutional and legal means of regional cooperation, and ensure that these autonomous endeavours of the regions should not be considered anticonstitutional. After the ratification of this agreement, further national laws were enacted: the 1987 decree of the Italian Constitutional Court has extended the rules of the basic agreement to regions further than borderlines (from the Italian side this has legitimated the Alpe–Adria working community). In the preparation of the Austrian constitutional reform it has been unanimously accepted that the Lands should be able to sign international agreements on issues in their authority.

Independently of all these legal results, and of the definitely more-extended rights, power positions, and financial means of the regional medium level compared with those of Hungary, the centre–region conflicts of interests are continuously present. In the case of the Alpe–Adria working community the Italian, Austrian, Yugoslavian, and Hungarian states have endeavoured to diminish, rather than to incite, the rate of development of this Central European integration, especially after the organisation of the Pentagonale (Central European) Initiative.

For the Hungarian economy to be able to integrate, on a regional basis, into Europe (which is on the way to unification) a radical renewal of regional policy and administration is necessary. Power must be divided among the state, the local governments, and their regional communities in a way such that the adaptation to modern centres should be influenced by central norms. It should also be possible to respond to market signals with autonomous local and regional decisions (Pálné Kovács, 1993).

The reform of the regional and administrative structure of the country is a condition of the realisation of an innovative regional development strategy, and of establishing the international regional competitiveness, that cannot be neglected. The current Hungarian counties, because of their economic potential, market size, and the extreme weakness of their market organising power, are not appropriate to fulfill the role of independent fields of action in the international division of labour and to be equivalent partners of Western European regions. The solution can partly be in the organisation of a medium level on a representative basis (which can be the county, but, in international relations, is the association of counties).

References

Cappellin R, 1990 *L'Internazionalizzazione delle Economie di Alpe–Adria e la Cooperazione Interregionali* (Internationalisation of the Alpe–Adria Economy and Interregional Cooperation) (ISPI, Milano)

Conti S, Julien P-A, 1991 *Miti e Realtà del 'Modello' Italiano. Letture sull'Economia Periferica* (Myth and Reality of the Italian Model. Lecture on the Peripheral Economy) (Pàtron, Bologna)

Costa G, De Marchi G, 1989 *Indagine sulla Ricerca e le Tecnologie nel Friuli-Venezia Giulia* (Survey of Research and Technology in the Friuli-Venezia Giulia Region) (L'Immaginarie Scientifice, Trieste)

Fuà G (Ed.), 1991 *Orientamenti per la Politica del Territorio* (Information on Regional Policy) (Il Mulino, Bologna)

Horváth G, 1990, "Integrazione europea, competizione internazionale, cooperazione regionale" (European integration, international competition, regional cooperation), in *La Cooperazione Economica in Alpe–Adria e l'Integrazione delle Economie Europee* (Regione Lombardia, Milano) pp 151–167

Horváth G, 1991a, "International division of labour and regional policy", in *Regional Policy and Local Governments* Ed. G Horváth, Centre for Regional Studies, Pécs, pp 11–24

Horváth G, 1991b, "European integration and internationalization of regional economies as new point of view in the Hungarian regional policy", in *The Local and the International in the XXI Century. The Importance of Collaboration Networks* Ed. J Castillo (Diputación Foral Bizkaja, Bilbao) pp 246–263

Horváth G, Hrubi L, 1992, "Restructuring and regional policy in Hungary", DP-12, Centre for Regional Studies, Pécs

ISTAT, 1988; 1990 *Annuario Statistico Italiano* (Statistical Yearbook of Italy) (ISTAT, Roma)

Marinucci M, 1988, "Il Veneto: elementi continuità e di innovazione" (Veneto region: elements of continuity and innovation), in *Nuova Città, Nuova Campagna, Spazio Fizico e Territorio* Eds A Celant, P P Federici (Pàtron, Bologna) pp 483–491

Megyei Statisztikai Evkönyvek 1981–1990 (Yearbooks of County Statistics) (Központi Statisztikai Hivatal, Budapest)

Pálné Kovács I, 1993, "The basic political and structural problems in the workings of local governments in Hungary", DP-14, Centre for Regional Studies, Pécs

Stöhr W B (Ed.), 1990 *Global Challenge and Local Response* (Mansell, London)

Tudományos Kutatás és Fejlesztés 1991 (Scientific Research and Development) (Központi Statisztikai Hivatal, Budapest)

Interregional Cooperation and Transborder Activities in a Middle European Context

M Steiner
University of Graz
D Sturn
Joanneum Research, Graz

1 Introduction

What is Middle Europe? Eduard Goldstücker, Professor of Literature in Prague, who had to leave this town twice (in 1939 and again in 1968), defines it as the European core between Germany and Russia, extending from the Baltic to the Adria regions and the Black Sea, sharing long periods of occupation (with the notable exception of Austria—tu felix), and establishing a certain form of living and thinking (Goldstücker, 1991). To many others, nevertheless, the term Middle Europe is merely fiction and a part of a nostalgic Habsburg myth. Certainly there are, and were, some terms and notions hinting to maybe never very realistic cultural, political, and economic union even after World War 1: the Mitropa Cup in the 1930s was a forerunner of the European Cup of nowadays, in which football teams of Hungary, Czechoslovakia, Austria, and Italy participated. For a long while there existed a train coach 'Mitteleuropa' although it was not quite as luxurious as the Orient Express. But Peter Handke dismissed it altogether as a term merely to be used for meteorological purposes.

From myth to reality? Claudio Magris, Professor of German literature in the north Italian town Trieste, used the term again in the 1960s and assigned a special role to it: a laboratory for the design of the essence of a 'new' Europe—a small world in which a bigger Europe could work out its problems (Magris, 1967). In the 1980s, for opposition circles in the former East European communist countries, this notion did not refer to a past, but to a hopefully coming future. In the recent past, Alpe–Adria, a working community of regions in Hungary, former Yugoslavia (now the independent states of Slovenia and Croatia), Northern Italy, Austria, and Germany (Bavaria), revived this idea. Founded in 1978, it tried to find means of cooperation and consultation beyond borders (even beyond borders separating economic and political systems), and an important characteristic of this working community was that these contacts were established not between states but between regions.

Looking at this European Core in economic terms, one can even find close ties in terms of trade relations over considerable stretches of time and in spite of the political break up of former unions (Karner et al, 1987). Even after the demise of the Austro-Hungarian Empire and despite special prohibitions in regular trade between the follow-up states in the treaty of Saint Germain and Trianon, Austria again had strong ties with Hungary,

Czechoslovakia, and Yugoslavia by 1928, and all bilateral links between these four countries were remarkably strong. Even after World War 1, therefore, and even in 'real' economic terms, Middle Europe was an integrated spatial unity. This unity has continued to recent times: in the 1980s Austria, Hungary, and Yugoslavia formed—in terms of normalised trade flows—a strong trilateral centre within European trade (Kubin et al, 1986).

Thus, with these very real phenomena taken into consideration, Middle Europe stands not only for a certain cultural and historical background, but also for complementarities and things in common, and for closeness. It also stands, in the sense of Magris, for a kind of laboratory: countries and regions in close vicinity, at borders which suddenly change in character. It is this specific situation which makes it possible to pose two sensible questions: how far is there a movement towards regional cooperation across borders and how far can this cooperation alleviate the process of transformation?

2 Border regions in Eastern Austria
Until 1989 the term 'border region' had a quite unidimensional meaning in Austria. The so-called border regions consisted of the eastern parts of the country close to the (then) CSSR, Hungary, and (then) Yugoslavia. They comprised parts of upper and lower Austria, almost all of Burgenland, and the southern parts of Styria and Carinthia.

They were deliberately called 'border regions' because they were handicapped owing to their geographical situation bordering the former planned economies of COMECON. The western part of Austria—Vorarlberg, Tirol, Salzburg—of course has borders, too. Yet they are of a very different kind: they are and always were open frontiers with intensive close border activities—an intensive exchange of material goods and immaterial services. But these regions not only profited from their contact with cross-border partners and from their nearness to the economic centres of Europe (Munich, Baden-Württemberg, Lombardia) but also were stronger trading partners to the former COMECON countries than were their East Austrian counterparts. And in everyday language (and even in the regional economic literature) they were never termed as border regions: they were considered as the prosperous West in contrast to the less developed East with its handicapped 'dead' border.

The handicap character of these eastern borders was quite clear: they showed all the features of peripheral regions reinforced by the fact that they were situated at a 'dead' border with hardly any economic flows going beyond that border. There was of course trade between Austria as a whole and those countries (it was even the most intense of all OECD countries; Kubin et al, 1986), but there were hardly any close border activities, especially with the CSSR and Hungary. Moreover the advantages of the special situation of Austria (being the most easterly part of the

Western economic world and sharing a common cultural and political heritage) mainly accrued to the centres; the border regions themselves hardly profited from the material and immaterial transactions between these countries.

This specific frontier situation meant an almost complete disruption of economic transborder activities. This enforced the underprivileged character of these regions: they were typical peripheral, backward, mainly rural regions, where qualification levels were very low and infrastructure scarcely existed. In the 1970s there was a shift from the agrarian to the industrial sector—mainly low-wage industries with few dispositive functions (mature or standardised phase of the product cycle). With reform of the education system the qualification levels increased, but most of the better qualified young people were not able to find appropriate jobs in the regions, so they constituted a large group of commuters who often spent hours travelling from home to their workplace. A considerable number of them were weekly commuters, leaving their home early Monday morning and returning Friday afternoon. It was mainly the less mobile and less qualified women who were highly represented in the typical low-wage industries (textiles, clothing, food). The regions show low productivity, low value added per capita, and consequently low per capita income, low tax yield, and consequently low infrastructural supply, especially immaterial infrastructure.

3 From separation to cooperation?

In the traditional sense of the term 'border', the eastern regions of Austria represented a specific kind of periphery: it was the end of the world. It was—almost to an extreme—a typical border area as described by traditional location theory: the political separation led to an artificial interruption of a former common and central market area (Christaller, 1933) and/or to a separation of complementary economic areas (Lösch, 1940). This was, for example, the case between Styria and Northern Slovenia after 1918, where this (former) part of Yugoslavia had served as an economic hinterland delivering basic resources which, after World War 1, were cut off because of severe limitations by the treaty of St Germain, an interruption which was ended after 1945.

This strong 'traditional' aspect of a border region—interruption and separation of economic ties and flows between close areas and representing a strong impermeability—was of course based on the different economic systems on each side of the border. Permeability presupposes some basic elements common to both sides: an economic regime allowing at least some mobility of labour, guaranteeing the institutions for entrepreneurial behaviour, being able to perform some forms of cooperation. The different regimes led to an almost complete immobility of labour, there was little possibility of private property and of profit transfer, and hence no incentives for the foundation of firms or the deployment of plant.

The strong impermeability therefore was not so much the result of the different forms of transaction costs as explored in foreign and regional trade theory (see Amelung, 1991; Haass and Peschel, 1982; Herrmann et al, 1982) and which influence the direction and composition of trade; it was of a radical kind allowing no close border trade at all.

There were slight differences in this traditional border character. The separation effect was almost complete regarding the border with the (then) CSSR—the 'barrier effect' of the border was dominant. The border with Hungary was less severe. Hungary began economic reforms relatively early, so economic ties already existed at an interregional level, although trade was rather of a complementary kind (Kubin and Steiner, 1985). Yugoslavia always had a substantial amount of mobility: not only was the labour force mobile, but so were the consumers. Hence this border had, to a certain extent, a control function for labour-market segmentation. There was also room for 'tariff factories'—especially in the southern part of Styria, retail trade flourished in the last decade—hence the 'filtering effect' was dominant. (Specific goods were, of course, very sensitive to temporary import restrictions made by Yugoslavia. A famous coffee shop in Graz had to close down because of quotas on imports of consumption goods.)

The opening of the borders and the removal of obvious barriers, such as the Iron Curtain, does not mean that these are open borders, especially in the economic sense. A high degree of uncertainty still impedes strong economic linkages and concerns such fundamental questions as property rights, capital transfer, tax systems, as well as less fundamental ones as bureaucratic handling, language barriers, reliability, and so on. However, it does open the opportunity for changes in the character of these border regions and for them to take up the roles and functions that accrue to open borders. They may become dynamic frontier regions offering themselves as possible locations for specific segments of economic activity (Ratti, 1988; 1991).

(a) They might take advantage of a *closeness effect*: they might turn out to be the regions with the best knowledge of the mentality of the other side, of its political and social institutions, and of its specific weaknesses. Historical and cultural ties might enable a better understanding and reduce mental barriers.

(b) They might be the first ones to exploit the complementarity of (labour) markets on the two sides of the border and hence profit from the *control and singling-out effect* exercised by an (open) border.

(c) They might gain from the new impulses and incentives coming from beyond the border. There will be new opportunities (economic, political, cultural ones) to be seized; there will be the need for higher flexibility and a greater necessity for adaptation. The pressure already exercised by the probable enlargement of the Common Market is enforced by the opening to the East. Hence they may take profit from a *polarising effect*.

4 Some tentative empirical approaches

The situation is still very new, the changing character of the borders is very recent. So it is not yet possible to decide if these areas will succeed in the transformation from traditional to dynamic border regions. This uncertainty in future developments is not only because of a lack of the 'hard facts' of an economic data base, but also because the expectations concerning the future situation falter between hopes and fears (Steiner and Sturn, 1993). These regions are especially afraid of competition from Eastern European low-wage industries, of an uncontrolled influx of foreign labour, and of the Hungarian agrarian exports. There are also widespread fears that the economic impulses in a first phase will be low and might accrue to others and not to border regions. These fears are not without justification. The regions on the other side of the border currently have their comparative advantage in exactly those economic activities which dominate in the Austrian border regions and which form the economic base of these regions: timber, leather, textile, and clothing are strongly represented in West Hungarian regions; the Czech republic and Slovakia have large capacities in the shoe industry. In the agrarian sector the most important products of the Austrian border regions—fruits, vegetables, and special cultures—are under severe competition from Eastern European, especially Hungarian, producers.

Because of the short timespan since the change, and because of wavering expectations, it is not (yet) possible to give a precise description of the effects of this change, to present a coherent interpretation of the results and of the direction of development; we will probably not know the results before the next millenium. Nevertheless, there are some tentative attempts to find out if there is change at all and if this change supports hopes rather than fears.

One approach is to construct *scenarios* for possible developments in the reform countries and to ask for possible consequences of interregional cooperation. Four possibilities can be differentiated (ÖIR, 1992):

Scenario 1 has as a basic assumption that the positive measures in the reforming countries of the East are supported by the West and lead, after a short phase of transition, to a positive path of development and stability. In this case these countries will politically and economically move closer to Western Europe and will become a 'second Europe'.

Scenario 2 assumes a positive development policy on the part of the Eastern countries which is met by a passive, rather defensive, strategy of the West. The phase of transition, therefore, is prolonged and entails political troubles—the Eastern countries remain the 'European periphery'.

Scenario 3 starts with severe difficulties in the reform process, endangering economic and political stability. Western countries do assist, but rather in the form of crisis management. The economic upswing happens after long troubles and leads to only a modest dynamism—the phase of 'Euro Crisis Management' cannot be overcome.

Scenario 4 is the worst case assumption in which reforms are met by heavy resistance. Despite radical measures—privatisation, liberalisation of prices, tight fiscal policy—economic performance declines. The West refrains from active cooperation, and the economic status deteriorates to a 'Chaos/Third World' position.

All these scenarios—from the best to the worst case—have one essential consequence in common: the differences between East and West in income, wages, and demand will remain pronounced at least for the next eight to fifteen years. Instead of the Iron Curtain there will be a social border with remarkable differences in the levels of welfare. This gap might become smaller if we take a regionally differentiated view. The countries bordering Austria especially are the ones with the best chances of revival and of an early economic take off: Czech Republic, Slovakia, Hungary, and Slovenia. Nevertheless it means that even in the optimistic case there are hardly any 'backwash' effects to be expected in the short term: the gap between the West and the East will persist for quite a while.

A second approach consists of an analysis of *trade patterns*. Even if we study the very short period since 1989 we see one striking fact: enormous growth rates in Austria's exports and imports to and from its immediate Eastern neighbours. The annual growth rate of recent years was above 30% which is more than twice the growth rates among OECD countries. On the export side this increase brought about a higher diversification and a decreasing concentration on a limited range of Austria's export products; the change in the import structure may be interpreted as an increase in product quality in the exporting Eastern countries. Generally speaking, the trade between Austria and its Eastern neighbours becomes increasingly similar to the trade patterns of developed countries.

Preliminary attempts to regionalise this trade from a national level to border areas give an even more accentuated picture (Steiner and Sturn, 1992a). If the recent developments in trade are interpreted in regional terms, the possible gains and losses due to the changing character of frontiers are stronger than those at the national level: the production structure of border regions allows for a strong increase in exports. At the same time they become disproportionately vulnerable through import competition in their typical 'low-wage' products: clothing, shoes, and leather. Nevertheless it is possible that the border regions will be better off because of the diversification of their export structure. The former exports were concentrated on a few products coming from cities or industrial regions. Now there are exports in a wide range of products and the border regions are given the chance of exporting, which they hardly had before.

If the development of *joint ventures* are considered as an indicator for cooperation and transborder activities, it must be regarded as a positive sign that the total number of joint ventures with Western participation in the reforming countries rose from about 15 000 in 1990 to 55 000 in 1992.

Even Austrian firms—usually not very keen to cross the border with such activities—dared to take the initiative and undertook direct investments in these countries. About a quarter of the total stock of Austria's foreign direct investments (Sch 65 billion) went to these countries in transition, in 1992 there was an increase from Sch 10.8 billion to Sch 15.6 billion. The strongest target is Hungary with about Sch 11 billion, divided between 2600 joint ventures. This target is about the same in the former CSSR, although the actual amount at Sch 2.2 billion is far below that for Hungary. The investment going to the rest of the former COMECON countries is almost negligible. Most of these joint ventures are concentrated on services, construction, and retail trade (Stankovsky, 1992).

A further indicator used to evaluate the positive and negative effects of the recent changes, and to take into account the very subjective expectations, consists of *surveys*, where entrepreneurs and managers are asked about their general expectations concerning the opening of borders, about their contacts and experiences with the reforming countries, about their need of support, and about their estimation of future developments both on the Austrian side of the border and beyond.

A questionnaire directed at firms close to the southeastern border of Austria, towards Slovenia and Hungary, showed a quite remarkable optimism (Steiner and Sturn, 1992b). The survey concentrated on firms with existing experience in Slovenia, Croatia, and Hungary, and it was assumed that their general appraisals would be less speculative than appraisals from firms without contact. The inquiry was focused on three questions:

(1) the consequences of the opening of borders for the economic development of this southeastern region: only about a quarter of all firms were afraid of staff reduction, more than a third believed in growing markets, almost half of them expected an increasing importance of dispositive functions for local firms in Austria;

(2) the main reasons for successful cooperations. Here low wages scored as the most important factor for half of the firms. Among the other possible factors (highly qualified workers, low rental charges, high-quality products, willingness to cooperate, reliability of the partners) only the 'willingness to cooperate' reached a significant score (21%).

The firms were also asked what kind of support they would prefer (information about the economic and legal structure of bordering regions, information about particular firms, arrangement of cooperation, supply of model contracts, help for technology transfer, supply of infrastructure, help in marketing, installation of border-crossing projects). The emerging tendency was the need for general rather than for specific information: 37% of all firms in the first instance wished for better information about economic and legal structures, but not a single firm favoured specific support such as the marketing of cooperatively produced commodities.

Taken as a whole, the firms questioned appeared to be more optimistic than was to be expected. One additional point deserves a mention: the stronger the existing contact of the firms with their neighbouring regions (that is, firms which were already engaged with concrete economic activities of their own, such as having built up firms, having undertaken joint ventures, and take overs), the more optimistic was their evaluation.

5 Crossing the border with technology?
5.1 Technology/industry parks at the Austrian border
A very special approach for cooperation between regions and across borders at this moment lies partly in the process of realisation, partly in the process of preparation: the idea of building technology and industry parks at the border and even across them.

Three concrete projects—with different degrees of realisation—are currently under consideration along Austria's Eastern border (see figure 1). An international industry park is being constructed at the northeastern border to the (now) Czech Republic, covering parts of Gmünd (Austria) and Ceske Velenice (Czech Republic). The regions on both sides of the border each lack a strong centre; they are peripheral regions with little industry, low wages, and labour-market problems. Yet the potential for research and development is generally higher in Southern Bohemia than in the bordering part of Austria because of research institutions in Ceske Budejovice (65 km from the border); the Austrian counterparts having such

Figure 1. Map of the border locations.

institutions are the (larger) centres of Linz and Vienna which are more than 100 km away. This industry park, therefore, is not for high-tech firms but it is nevertheless hoped that it will contribute to an upgrading of the quality of the firms by alleviating cooperation across the border. It is intended not only for production but also for commercial firms.

A second industry park is being planned for Kittsee, about 50 km east of Vienna, directly on the border with Slovakia and at a distance of 5 km from Bratislava, its capital. The basic intention is to improve bilateral relations between Austria and Slovakia and to give a coherent framework for the economic development of the Vienna–Bratislava axis. This project should also present an incentive to intensify regional East–West trade and should alleviate the transborder transfer of technology. Its realisation depends on how far the site can establish itself as a location for Slovakian (and other Eastern European) firms outside of Vienna.

The third example is in the early stage of consideration: a technology park between Graz and Maribor, the second largest city in (now independent) Slovenia. This third project will be used in section 5.2 as an example for the questions to be asked and the focal points on which depend the positive effects for the bordering regions and, as a consequence, the usefulness of its realisation.

5.2 Some preliminary considerations

The starting point in considering the construction of cross-border industry and technology parks is the actual challenge for Austria to find a position between the economic and political integration in Western Europe on the one side, and the various changes in the East on the other side. In order to avoid in this 'sandwich position' a 'small-country squeeze' it is also necessary to develop an offensive strategy toward the East. This is the background for the feasibility question: can technology/industry parks intensify cooperative and competitive relations to the advantage of both sides?

Such considerations have to start with the fact that until recently these 'dead border' regions were peripheral, agrarian areas. In the past, their development was restricted by the almost complete lack of short-distance relations across borders. The hopes of these border regions to establish economic contacts with their immediate neighbours, thus gaining incentives for growth, is mingled with the fear that the former dead-end street might develop into a fast lane without intermediate stops. This fear is not completely unjustified: the need of the countries in transition for high levels of technology and for production-oriented services can hardly be fulfilled in these regions, which themselves suffer from a lack of such services and functions and of such an immaterial infrastructure. As long as these border regions are not able to offer functions of this kind, and as long as they have no specific qualification, it will be hard to assume new forms of cooperation.

Not far from these borders, the southeastern centres of Austria (Vienna and Graz) are confronted with the challenge to find new forms of trade and cooperation on a higher qualitative level. Whereas the former trade structure between centres of Austria and the East was marked by low-level imports and higher-level exports (the typical comparative trade structure) there is now a chance of a substantial upgrading.

In this situation, a technology park is intended to create an axis between two centres (in this case Graz–Maribor, but basically the same considerations apply for Vienna–Bratislava). The intensification of cooperation should not only strengthen the competitiveness of the cities themselves, but also their 'radiative power'; it should be made possible for these centres to set stronger impulses for their surroundings and, hence, for the border regions.

5.2.1 *Questions to be asked*
To evaluate the probability of this improvement it seems necessary to develop an analysis along three lines. The first consists of the economic situation and the development potential of the border regions; the second is an evaluation of the state of technology, of the existence of industrial clusters, and of the technological know-how of the centres. From these two factors—economic and technological potential—the resulting possibilities for cooperation, its complementary and substitutive components, have to be derived. This will lead finally to recommendations concerning the orientation towards the technology park and its technical emphasis.

5.2.2 *Regional background and potential*
The northeastern part of Slovenia—with Maribor as its centre—is the least developed region of Slovenia with an above average agrarian sector. Maribor itself is far above the level of development, but is, as a centre, too weak to transmit sufficient impulses for its surrounding area. The weaknesses of this region therefore are: a centre with too little economic penetration to the neighbouring regions; a strong dependence on heavy industry and a loss of old markets in former Yugoslavia; the lack of small and medium-sized enterprises; the domination of low-wage industries; exports founded on low wages; and high vertical integration with hardly any horizontal clustering. But there are advantages as well: it has a university town; there is a slow emergence of a small-scale private sector; a high rate of new firms being formed; a high proportion—compared with the rest of Slovenia—of producer-oriented services; an increase in its export orientation; and a spin-off of noncore activities.

On the Austrian side of the border, the situation is different in level (of income, productivity, gross regional product), but similar in structure: again there is a lagging region with a large agrarian sector (up to 40%), long-distance commuting, loss of employment (especially for females in low-wage industries such as textiles, clothing, and leather), external control of plants, and low wages. And again the centre—Graz on this side—is itself strong, with special emphasis on technology and services, but too weak to diffuse its potential very far into the neighbouring areas.

So the questions to be asked concern the similarities in factors relevant for future development: what deficits in material/immaterial infrastructure exist, which are common and complementary strengths, which incentives have to come from the outside?

5.2.3 *Technological potential*

To evaluate this potential within the two bordering regions it does not suffice to use technological criteria in the narrow sense. Two further aspects are needed: human capital resources and the existence of innovative clusters.

To obtain insights about the state of technological development within the two regions under consideration, it is necessary to look at the following indicators: the existence of technology producers such as universities and institutions for applied research; technological centres and technological transfer institutions; technology adoption (firms using high and medium technology); and the qualifications of the work force.

To locate the technological development potential and strength of the regions the following questions have to be answered. How far do technological producers—and takers—cooperate? Are there comparative advantages in specific fields of technology? What technologies possess special possibilities in diffusion and application? Where are the export chances?

An important aspect is the evaluation of innovative clusters: which firms (and groups of firms) are (functionally) integrated and have high information intensity and innovative power? This technological integration in the sense of innovative clusters is materialised in cooperative relations between corporations, in the (common) use of producer-oriented services and of technology transfer institutions. Attention has to be paid to how far there are already existing ties of the peripheral parts to the technological nuclei of the two cities: how strong are input relations, not only in production, but also services, how far are there local reserves of a qualified work force and special labour pools?

5.2.4 *Cooperative potential*

This leads to the final question of the resources for transborder cooperation based on these technological and regional potentials. The following complementarities will have to be considered. What are the chances for common product innovations (cooperation between science and the economy) within small, selected fields? Which relations between technology producers and adopters can be extended? Which affinities in the economic structure exist to improve competitiveness?

These considerations will have important effects for the orientation of a future technology park. It should be concentrated on those fields where, on both sides of the border, technology producers and firms can already rely on experience and success. It should also be focussed on fields with existing links between innovative firms.

6 Conclusions

On first sight, the idea of fostering regional development and cooperation across borders by means of technology and industry parks might seem inadequate. Technology parks are usually seen as an instrument to enforce the technological development in agglomerations, where the information transfer is assumed to work automatically because of the spatial closeness to universities, science, and research and development institutions, where we expect to have a network of specialised suppliers and purchasers, and where the firms have access to qualified labour and services.

The support of border-crossing activities between the Western and Eastern European countries, however, is usually a step taken in order to solve completely different problems: Western European border regions are handicapped because of their geographical situation bordering the former planned economies. They were and are the typical peripheral, backward, mainly rural regions, where qualification levels are low and infrastructure scarcely exists. Enforcing border-crossing activities at a local level is a chance for these regions to become better off in their contact with their neighbours. It is therefore an instrument to aid peripheral and rural regions.

There are some arguments for why a combination of technology and industry parks might be a useful tool of regional policy aimed at different types of regions at the same time.

(1) Not only is the immediate border region affected by the former impermeability of the border and the interruption and separation of economic ties and flows, but so are cities close to these borders. They show dynamic features, such as universities, infrastructural supply, and some high-tech industries, but they bear the imprint of a missing economic hinterland.

(2) The quality of science in the former COMECON countries is quite high. Product development and technical bureaux in Western Europe use them as technology suppliers; for example, they buy their ideas but hitherto without giving them a chance to transform the knowledge into a production process and into the development of new processes and products.

(3) The basic idea of technology parks fits into the new framework of regional policy. It is an approach based both on the concept of reliance on endogenous potential and on the idea of networks linking these potentials. The changing character of Middle European borders creates a new opportunity for linking old networks. Also, in this specific case, the potential resides essentially in small and medium firms which are slowly but steadily emerging in the reforming countries and are in need of complementary services which might be offered in these parks.

(4) A future EC membership of Austria will increase the value of these parks at the border between EC and non-EC members. They might turn out to be the closest location within the EC for the reforming countries. For Western firms it might represent an opportunity to make use of the highly qualified Western infrastructure and of an easy access to the potential of the Czech Republic, Slovakia, and Slovenia.

In the short and medium term these technology and industry parks will benefit from differences between centres and regions on both sides of the border. In the long run there is the hope of economic assimilation in a Middle European context following Leo Tolsoi's dictum, according to which happy families look very similar whereas unhappy ones have to master their afflictions each in their own peculiar way.

References
Amelung T, 1991, "The impact of transaction costs on the direction of trade: empirical evidence for Asia Pacific" *Journal of Institutional and Theoretical Economics* **147**(4) 716–732
Christaller W, 1933 *Die zentralen Orte in Süddeutschland* (The Central Locations in Southern Germany) (Wissenschaftliche Buchgesellschaft, Darmstadt) (reprinted 1980)
Goldstücker E, 1991, "Clenched fists. Central Europe from Prague's point of view" *Was* **66** 9–13
Haass J, Peschel K, 1982 *Räumliche Strukturen im internationalen Handel* (Spatial Structures in International Trade) (Florentz, Munich)
Herrmann M, Schmidtke N, Bröcker J, Peschel K, 1982 *Kommunikationskosten und internationaler Handel. Überlegungen zum Marktverhalten von Exporteuren und empirische Untersuchungen zur Erklärung der Außenhandelsverflechtungen* (Communication Costs and International Trade. Considerations of the Market Behaviour of Exporters and Empirical Studies to Explain the Complexity of Foreign Trade) (Florentz, Munich)
Karner S, Kubin I, Steiner M, 1987, "Wie real war 'Mitteleuropa'? Zur wirtschaftlichen Verflochtenheit des Donauraumes nach dem Ersten Weltkrieg" (How real was 'Central Europe'? The economic complexity of the Danube area after World War 1) *Vierteljahresschrift für Sozial- und Wirtschaftsgeschichte* **74**(2) 153–185
Kubin I, Steiner M, 1985, "The relative integration of Europe's South-East region—a historical comparison", RM-8506, University of Graz, Austria
Kubin I, Steiner M, Kreiner G, 1986, "Die Verflechtung der Alpe–Adria Länder Italien Jugoslawien und Österreich im europäischen Außenhandel" (The Complexity of the Alpe–Adria Countries Italy, Yugoslavia and Austria) *Wirtschaftspolitische Blätter* **1** 69–83
Lösch A, 1940 *Die räumliche Ordnung der Wirtschaft* (The Spatial Order of the Economy) (G Fischer, Jena)
Magris C, 1967 *The Myth of Habsburg in the Austrian Literature* (Müller, Vienna)
ÖIR, 1992 *Szenarien zur Ost-Grenzöffnung und deren Auswirkungen auf die österreichischen Ost-Grenzregionen* (Scenarios after the Opening of the Eastern Borders and the Implications for the Eastern Regions of Austria) (Österreichisches Institut für Raumplanung, Vienna)
Ratti R, 1988, "Development theory, technological change and Europe's frontier regions", in *High Technology Industry and Innovative Environments: The European Experience* Eds P Aydalot, D Keeble (Routledge, London) pp 197–220

Ratti R, 1991 *Théorie du Développement des Régions-frontières* (A Theory of the Development of Border Regions) (St Paul, Fribourg)

Stankovsky J, 1992, "Direktinvestitionen Österreichs in den Oststaaten" (Austrian direct investment in the Eastern States) *Österreichisches Institut für Wirtschaftsforschung Monatsberichte* **8** 415–420

Steiner M, Sturn D, 1992a *Der Außenhandel der Südost-Regionen Österreichs mit Ungarn und dem früheren Jugoslawien* (Foreign Trade of Southeast Austria with Hungary and the Former Yugoslavia) (Bericht für den Wissenschaftlichen Beirat der ARGE Alpe-Adria, Graz, Austria)

Steiner M, Sturn D, 1992b *Offene Grenzen zu Ungarn und Slowenien/Kroatien— Chancen und Gefahren für die steirische Wirtschaft. Eine Umfrage unter steirischen Unternehmen und Betrieben* (Open Borders to Hungary and Slovenia/Croatia— Chance and Hazard for the Styrian Economy. An Inquiry among the Styrian Firms and Companies) (Joanneum Research, Graz, Austria)

Steiner M, Sturn D, 1993, "From coexistence to cooperation: the changing character of Austria's South-Eastern border", in *Theory and Strategy of Border Areas Development* Eds R Ratti, S Reichmann (Méta Edition, Austria) forthcoming

Transborder Cooperation and European Integration: The Case of Wallonia

M Quévit, S Bodson
University of Louvain la Neuve

1 Introduction

Cross-border cooperation initiatives would appear to have become a vital component in the construction of a united Europe. Several factors may explain the growing importance of such initiatives:

(1) the removal of customs barriers on completion of the Single Market will provide greater fluidity for economic exchanges between the countries of the EC;

(2) the measures being applied within the programme set up under the terms of the Single Act are having direct repercussions on neighbouring regions in different European countries, insofar as the purpose of the Act is to do away with protectionist measures which encourage the setting-up of economic activities within national borders to the detriment of cross-border exchanges despite the geographical proximity of these neighbouring zones.

In addition to these two reasons, which are directly related to the general problem of European integration, there is a third factor which we believe is having more direct repercussions: the economies of the industrialised countries are facing a new form of economic competition and consequently find themselves competing more and more against economic forces which are managed on a global scale. In this context, it is important to valorise certain areas to make them progressively more competitive and to seek solutions involving economies of scale or critical mass with regard to material and human resources. In fact the phase we are now going through involves a process of redecomposition of areas, transcending the concept of national borders through initiatives with increasingly specific objectives in the context of interregional and cross-border cooperation, not only in the field of the economy but also in the realm of science and technology.

This twin interactive approach, which takes account of the globalisation of the economy and the completion of the European Single Market, must be envisaged alongside the development of a geoeconomy in which the flow of people, capital, and goods will play a much more direct role involving the search for 'external proximities' which can either be found or developed between regions bordering on two or more countries (Quévit et al, 1991).

Border regions are therefore facing a double challenge: they must make the most of their geographical proximity to build up economic areas with a wider impact, and, at the same time, anticipate the negative consequences of the removal of the borders. They do this by creating incentives to locate within the area to ensure that local companies are not tempted to move away, for reasons related to competitiveness, as part of the general trend which has developed as a result of the setting-up of the Single Market (Maillat, 1991).

The aim in this chapter is not to explore all the aspects of the question of cross-border cooperation but, rather, to examine a number of experiments which have been set up by the authorities in a traditionally industrial region which, by virtue of its central geographical location and the nature of its pattern of production, is directly facing this new challenge. The Walloon region is in fact in a state of constant flux not only at an economic level, as it is forced to carry out a much-needed face-lift of its economy, but also at a political level because the recent federalisation of the country has obliged the Walloon region to take up a more autonomous stance within the framework of a federal state. Indeed, these transformations share common points of reference and are partly the result of the intense programme of cross-border cooperation initiatives set up by the regional authorities well before the launching of the EC initiative INTERREG.

Many important lessons can be learnt from an examination of the forms of cross-border cooperation which have been set up. Such initiatives take many forms and can change radically according to the particular period in which they are launched and according to the socioeconomic nature of the areas in question.

In the first part of this chapter, we shall briefly outline the socioeconomic characteristics of the Walloon region, with an emphasis on the key problems the region is facing, in order to identify more clearly the fundamental objectives of the form of cross-border cooperation which has been set up by the regional authorities.

In the second part, we shall examine the main cross-border cooperation initiatives, including those which began long before the EC initiative INTERREG got under way. We shall concentrate not only on examining the objectives of such initiatives and their scope of action, but also on the institutional and organisational mechanisms on which they are based.

Finally, at a more analytical level, we intend to stress the diversity of the cross-border cooperation initiatives by analysing the two-fold conceptualisation which serves as a basis for the interaction between the EDP (European Development Pole) and the PACTE program (Programme d'Action et de Coopération Transfrontalier Européen—European Cross-border Action and Cooperation Programme). In this context, our objective will be to demonstrate that the choice of a specific approach in the field of cross-border cooperation will depend above all on the possibilities offered by local land management and planning and the nature of the economic problems affecting individual border areas.

2 The socioeconomic position of Wallonia in the context of European economy

The Walloon region can be briefly characterised as follows.

(1) A strategic geographical position: on the regional map of Europe, Wallonia has common borders and links with many regions (to the south, Nord – Pas-de-Calais, Picardie, Champagne-Ardennes, and Lorraine; to the east, the Grand Duchy of Luxembourg, the Rhineland-Palatinate, and the Rhineland of North Westphalia; to the north, the Netherlands and Flanders). By virtue of its highly developed communications network (motorways, rail, and air links), Wallonia is close to the throbbing heart of Europe and the world of international business.

(2) An economic infrastructure which remains dependant on traditional industries (steel-making, plant, and so on), with the emphasis on upstream production. There is consequently little opportunity for the creation of added value. Within Belgium, Wallonia represents 55.2% of the territory and 32.6% of the population, and it contributes 26% to the gross national product.

(3) Insufficient services to enterprises, characterised by an imbalance between consumer, nonmerchantable, and production services: only 16.6% of jobs for salaried employees are directly related to services rendered to companies as against an average of 22.4% for Belgium.

(4) Insufficient company investment in technological research and development (with an index of 100 for the EC, private investment in Wallonia represents 65.6; that is, 29 short of the European average). In addition, this investment is concentrated in the traditional industrial sectors—basic chemical industries (29%), the electrotechnical sector (29%), and mechanical metalworking (21%).

(5) An education system ill-adapted to technological change. This has progressively widened the gap between the world of industry and the classroom at a time when companies are becoming more and more demanding in terms of the qualifications of their workforce, especially in jobs at an intermediate level (technicians, middle management, and so on).

(6) A process of regionalisation which places the regions at the centre of the decisionmaking process in matters as important and diverse as town and country planning, social ethos, economic policy, applied scientific research, infrastructures, and external trade. Since 1980, through the institutional reform laws, regions have been given exclusive responsibilities in the fields mentioned above, whereas under a new institutional reform now taking place, the regions will soon be given broader responsibilities (covering tourism, social policy, and agriculture).

3 Cross-border cooperation in Wallonia

The Walloon region borders many different European regions and has for many years been pursuing a voluntarist policy with regard to cross-border cooperation. In this respect it should be noted that four particular cross-border initiatives predate the EC initiative INTERREG(1):

(1) the European Development Pole for the three borders (Belgium, Luxembourg, France) was an initiative launched in 1985;

(2) the Euregio Project (Provinces of Liège and Limbourg and the regions of Aix-La-Chapelle and the Dutch Limbourg), in which the Province of Liège has been participating since 1982;

(3) the European Cross-border Cooperation Action Programme (Province of Hainaut and the region of Nord–Pas-de-Calais) was implemented, in the initial stages, through a Joint Declaration signed by the region of Nord–Pas-de-Calais and by the Walloon region in 1986, and subsequently updated in 1989;

(4) the Champagne-Ardennes Programme was launched in 1989 through a feasibility study.

3.1 The European Development Pole

Launched on 19 July 1985, through the joint political determination on the part of the three member states concerned and on the initiative of the regions associated with the project, the EDP takes in the steel-making areas close to the French, Belgian, and Luxembourg borders. Indeed, these three areas already had close ties as they were faced with the same problems of industrial reconversion. The initiative was chiefly centred on the French city of Longwy (about 60 km from Metz, the capital of the Lorraine region), the Luxembourg town of Rodange (20 km from Luxembourg, the capital of the Grand Duchy of Luxembourg, an important financial centre with an international airport), and the Belgian town of Aubange (Athus—20 km from Arlon, the provincial capital of the Belgian Luxembourg).

In December 1986, the Commission of the European Communities decided to provide this cross-border project with major support by awarding special status to the International Activity Park thus created and by offering considerable financial backing through the European Regional Development Fund (ERDF). The main thrust of the EDP is the creation of an International Activity Park covering a continuous area beyond the borders of some 400 hectares which were left unused after the demise of the steel-making industry.

In order to achieve the aim of creating new jobs, the action involved an intervention strategy based on six interrelated and integrated initiatives:

(1) to improve the appeal of the environment to offer new investors the incentive to locate in these regions;

(2) to set up a system of financial intervention to encourage companies to locate;

(3) to offer a specific customs regime to the EDP;

(4) to improve road and rail links;

(5) to create joint enterprise services, information desk, advice services, telecommunications;

(6) to offer joint training courses to meet the training needs expressed by the companies locating locally and to enhance the level of training of the local population.

In order to comply with the regulatory constraints of the ERDF, this EC support programme had to be divided into three NICPs (National Community Interest Programmes), each of which is managed at a national level despite the existence of joint coordination structures.

The first NICPs concentrated on financial measures aimed at revitalising the disused industrial sites located in the Chiers Valley and shared by the three countries. At the same time, the attractiveness of this vast International Activity Park was improved through the establishment of a road and rail infrastructure which allowed the site to be opened up. One of the major achievements has undoubtedly been the completion of a major highway across the region serving the site from several directions. A special enterprise support initiative was also launched with the maximum intervention set at 30% of the private investment injected into the site. Furthermore, in order fully to exploit the specific characteristics of the site, a two-fold strategy has guided the initiatives undertaken to prospect for companies likely to locate: on the one hand, activities related to logistics (supply services, storage, grouping, transport) and, on the other hand, industrial production activities most likely to offer practical solutions to overcome the lack of job opportunities in the industrial sector.

The need to capitalise on the endogenous development potential was also an important aspect of this initiative. This potential is now being effectively maximised within the framework of the Joint Services Centre. In practical terms, a joint 'Euroguichet' has been set up on the site, and joint proposals have been accepted by the Commission, with a view to launching a pilot initiative to encourage 'seed capital', with major support from private financial institutions.

Finally, a wide variety of actions have been implemented in the field of training, particularly vocational training courses for specific needs, but which also involve full-time teachers in mainstream education. One initiative in this respect has been the setting up of a European College of Technology entrusted with the task of fostering synergy between higher education institutions, encouraging cooperation initiatives in the field of the new technologies, and providing continuing vocational training for students graduating from mainstream education. The European Social Fund and the COMETT and ERASMUS programmes have been much in demand.

Now, after more than five years in existence (the EDP has been active only since 1987), an assessment can be made: after the initial aim of 8000 new jobs, 2761 were effectively created in the area. Table 1 presents the details of this outcome.

In Wallonia, ten companies were given support within the framework of the project, which created jobs corresponding to 1030 units; that is,

68.7% of the target. It should be noted in passing that the average size of the companies helped is 103 staff. Indeed, this is an indication of the desire on the part of the Walloon authorities to concentrate their efforts on a few large-scale industrial projects which are more likely to create jobs.

In France and in the Grand Duchy the results would appear to be less encouraging with 26.4% and 27.7% of the targets met, respectively. Overall, 34.5% of the job-creation targets had been achieved by December 1992. Half of these results were achieved by companies which existed prior to the EDP and which were able to expand their activities, whereas the other half is represented by newly established industrial enterprises.

Table 1. The creation of jobs in Belgium, France, and the Grand Duchy of Luxembourg [source: General Directorate of Walloon Economy (unpublished data)].

	Belgium	France	Grand Duchy	Total
Number of companies helped	10	37	9	56
New locations (in above figure)	5	17	9	31
Jobs created	1030	1454	277	2761
1995 jobs target	1500	5500	1000	8000
Success rate (%)	68.7	26.4	27.7	34.5

3.2 The Meuse-Rhine Euregio

The Euregio is an area with some 3.6 million inhabitants which extends across the south of the Dutch Limburg, the provinces of Liege and Limburg in Belgium, and the districts of Aix-la-Chapelle, Duren, Euskirchen of the Rhineland Region, and North Westphalia in the Federal Republic of Germany. Action programmes in these areas, which were submitted to the Commission in 1986, are innovatory in the field of cross-border policy and have the following aims:
(a) the removal of obstacles caused by borders;
(b) the improvement of the competitiveness of the area, notably with regard to technology transfer;
(c) to improve the functioning of the job market (liaison between job centres);
(d) the removal of bottlenecks in the road, rail, and air infrastructures.

Another important achievement in 1989 was the drafting of an inventory of technology transfers and the setting up of a databank on the products of regional industries. These actions received financial backing from the EC and the action programme submitted and accepted by the Commission within the framework of INTERREG has extended this cooperation, which centres on seven distinct types of initiative:
(1) the creation of networks, the exchange of information and communications (social Euroguichet, exchanges, and so on);
(2) traffic, transport, and infrastructures;

(3) leisure and tourism (Meuse training centre, tourist-oriented signposting for cycle-tracks, and so on);
(4) training and the job market (postgraduate management training, home health care);
(5) the environment (recycling of building materials, sewage purification plants);
(6) technology transfer and innovation; and
(7) project research and management (development plans).

3.3 The European Cross-border Action and Cooperation Programme

The PACTE, which was launched in 1988 in the form of feasibility studies, is based from a legal point of view on the signing on 30 May 1989 of a joint declaration between the French Government, the Nord – Pas-de-Calais region, the Département of Nord, and the Walloon region, with the participation of the French-speaking community of Belgium. This declaration, which was signed by the representatives of the French and Belgian official bodies concerned, formalised the process of cross-border cooperation and laid down specific objectives, modes of operation, and working practices.

It was thus decided that the PACTE would be accompanied by practical action according to a twofold approach:
(1) to ensure economic revitalisation and to encourage regional development taking account of the need for spatial balance; and
(2) to achieve cooperation on the basis of a partnership between participants who are fully involved in the decisionmaking process.

Similarly, it was decided to establish geographical and thematic boundaries with a view to defining more precisely the scope of action of the PACTE. The joint declaration, which covered, in France, the arrondissements of Avesnes, Valenciennes, Cambrai, and Lille and, in Belgium, West Hainaut, Mons, the Borinage, and the Centre and the Valley of the Sambre as far as Charleroi, provided for the implementation of a joint cross-border cooperation initiative, centring on:
(a) development, modernisation, and economic, industrial, and technological cooperation among companies;
(b) employment, teaching, and training;
(c) communication infrastructures; and
(d) the social ethos, the quality of daily life, and the environment and the image of the region.

Furthermore, in accordance with the joint declaration, an organisational instrument for cross-border cooperation was established on the basis of the preparatory work carried out jointly by the French and Walloon authorities concerned (Rider, 1988). These meetings, which brought together the operational bodies representing the signatories of the joint declaration, provided an opportunity to:
(a) establish seven thematic working parties and three territorial groups which were entrusted with the task of defining and finalising cross-border

cooperation projects which will be submitted to the arbitration of the Permanent Commission; and
(b) define for each group a precise mission laid down in specific work schedules serving as the task description of the working party.
For each of the working parties, around twenty experts, with equal representation from the French and Walloon partners, were selected from both official public-authority circles and from the private sector as well as from professional bodies in the study zone concerned. The remit of these working parties was:
(a) to define practical projects offering short-term results, with the emphasis on projects involving cross-border synergy between the existing capabilities;
(b) to study the feasibility of such projects;
(c) to compile the corresponding dossiers; and
(d) to submit these dossiers in a finalised form to the Permanent Coordination Commission of the PACTE, the relevant cross-border decision-making body.
This led to a cooperation programme consisting of around fifty separate initiatives within the framework of INTERREG. Eight guidelines for action were thus identified:
(1) support for the setting up and the economic and technological development of small and medium-sized enterprises (SMEs);
(2) development of the RTD (research and technological development) potential;
(3) enhancing the image of the zone;
(4) support for human resources and the cross-border job market;
(5) improving the environment and poles of tourism;
(6) social policy;
(7) urban problems; and
(8) coordination and monitoring unit.
As a result of the two meetings of the monitoring committee of the Operational Programme and the in-depth preparatory work conducted jointly on either side of the border, a wide variety of programmes are now being set up on the ground in subjects as diverse as:
(a) technological research and development—consolidation and amplification of the scope of action of the CETT-CERAM (Centre Européen Transfrontalier de Transfert Technologique en Néocéramique—European Cross-border Neoceramic Technology Transfer Centre) and the implementation of a project involving experimentation and demonstrations with wood;
(b) support for the economic and technological development of SMEs—the creation of an enterprise liaison bureau, a cross-border venture capital institution, and a joint structure to provide advice and assistance to young entrepreneurs;
(c) the environment—joint management of a cross-border park, cleaning of waste water, management of cross-border water tables, and so on;

(d) tourism—integrated development plans for the promotion of tourism and cultural heritage;

(e) urban problems—implementation of a joint town and country planning study; and

(f) training in the field of human resources—creating joint training initiatives to provide qualifications in fields as diverse as new materials, jobs in the textile industry and the graphic arts; creation of an interregional coordination structure to harness the training potential on either side of the border (Euroregional Training Pole—project now being set up).

The ultimate aim of these projects is to create an effective network of links and cooperation initiatives involving actions undertaken on either side of the border, and to present the cross-border zone as a region in its own right and not simply as a mosaic of competing enclaves.

3.4 The Champagne–Ardennes Cooperation Initiative

Within the framework of the removal of borders resulting from the completion of the Single European Market, the competent authorities of the French Ardennes Département and the Walloon zone undertook to study the impact of 1993 on the local economy. Indeed, they have been working since 1989 on a concerted and joint development process involving cooperation between the neighbouring provinces of the Walloon region (province of Namur, parts of the provinces of Hainaut and Luxembourg) and the French Ardennes, particularly the arrondissements of Charleville-Mézières and Sedan.

The objectives are, firstly, to initiate strategic orientations within the context of a process of concerted development based on initiatives taken by the local decisionmakers on either side of the border, and, secondly, to speed up the process of networking, ultimately to enable an efficient cross-border action programme. Within this framework, the different economic scenarios, set up as a result of the industrial development and redeployment strategies according to the specific needs of each area in Wallonia and France, have until now been considered as an obstacle to more sustained economic cooperation. This is a situation which has arisen as a result of the lack of administrative and cultural transparency because of the hampering presence of the border. Despite these aspects of the diagnosis of the fabric of economic life, the process of establishing common themes of interest and the achievements of the cross-border thematic seminars have led to the establishment in the various economic, social, and cultural fields of five guidelines for cross-border cooperation and synergy:

(1) to open up the zone by improving accessibility (general study);

(2) to develop new offerings in the field of tourism and culture (such as, valorisation of the tourist potential of the Meuse, protection of cross-border natural resources, sight-seeing railway circuit in the Valley of the Meuse);

(3) to develop human resources (offering new cross-border vocational training initiatives, initiation of research tools, and so on);
(4) to provide support for economic and agricultural development (enterprise partnerships, expansion funds, networks, quality); and
(5) to ensure coordination and monitoring (international technical team).

The programme, which was submitted to the Commission of the European Community at the same time as the PACTE programme, is currently being launched in the zone concerned.

4 Comparison between the EDP and the PACTE
In our analysis of the different cross-border initiatives undertaken by the Walloon region, we feel it is important to stress the many possible facets, by comparing the dynamic cooperation structures which were set up within the framework, of two of the most important experiments: the EDP and the PACTE.

4.1 Initial constraints and resulting strategic choices
By virtue of the fact that the EDP is located on the periphery of the regions which make up the Pole, the objectives of this initiative have had to be quite specific: the creation of jobs in order to offset the massive decline in the number of jobs available in the traditional industries of the area. In this respect, the development strategy which characterises the cross-border area was designed to recreate a pole of cross-border growth in the purest tradition of the Perroux theory of polarised growth.

The reference here to the Perroux theory of polarised growth is based on several elements. First, the cross-border area concerned was traditionally dominated by one single industry (steelmaking) within a rural region located on the periphery of the country. The region has borne the brunt of the crisis within the metallurgy sector as it was unable to fall back on any form of substitute industry or on a solid urban infrastructure. Second, during the period of the generation of the EDP, at the start of the 1980s, no real account was taken of a number of important nonphysical factors within the context of growth. Indeed, the political decisionmakers were basically convinced that, in order to trigger a process of development, it was sufficient to set up physical infrastructures designed to attract companies.

The strategic objectives of the EDP at its inception were:
(1) to revitalise the industrial wasteland resulting from the decline of a viable traditional industry;
(2) to open up the industrial sites by improving communications and access to the International Activity Park;
(3) to encourage foreign companies to locate (European development logic) by granting investment incentives at an advantageous rate (30% of the amount of the investment); and

(4) once the infrastructure work has been completed, to progressively set in place a framework of services to cater for the needs of companies and to offer appropriate training initiatives within the cross-border area.

In contrast, the initiatives undertaken within the PACTE could not be integrated into the logic of the theory of polarised growth. Instead, the approach adopted was one based on the endogenous potential of the area, with emphasis on the theory of innovative environments (Maillat et al, 1993). This approach takes account both of the nature of the patterns of production which characterise the cross-border area and of its geographical location. The EDP was created on the edge of a rural region on the periphery of the country, whereas the initiatives within the PACTE were geared towards revitalising an area of traditional industry with considerable potential from the point of view of the economy, technological innovation, and the training of human resources.

It should be remembered that the PACTE area can in fact rely on the support of the driving force of the two cities which act as the hub of local industry: Lille in France and Charleroi in Wallonia. In addition, the area has modern communication networks: two regional airports, a heliport, a link with the highspeed TGV rail network, and several universities (Lille, Valenciennes, and Mons). It was therefore logical that any cross-border cooperation initiative should be based on the potential offered by existing local facilities. At the same time, this local potential could be enhanced through a process of innovation by valorising the intangible factors involved.

The methods applied within this programme were based on a strategy which involved a tension between making a break with the past and filtration to the existing situation. They were aimed at fostering exchange and cooperation between the various partners in the economic, social, and institutional spheres within the area in order to stimulate a process of modernisation and revitalisation in the economic fabric of the cross-border region (Aydalot, 1986). In this respect, the projects given priority status were operational projects set up with the aim of establishing links between the existing skills bases within the cross-border area, rather than projects designed to set up the heavy infrastructures needed to open the region.

4.2 Limitation of the approach adopted by the EDP and by the PACTE

In addition to the differences between the respective strategies and objectives pursued by cross-border cooperation, we feel a number of remarks should be made regarding the limitations inherent in the different avenues of approach which characterise the EDP and the PACTE.

As regards the EDP, there are four obvious weaknesses.

(1) The financial cost of the process—the EDP has swallowed up investments totalling nearly ecu 250 million for the area as a whole (of which ecu 80 million were provided by the Commission) within an area with less than 300 000 inhabitants. At a European level, it can thus be seen that

this zone has received more than its fair share of support from the Commission.

(2) By virtue of the burdensome financial cost of the EDP, this initiative, despite being to all intents and purposes a test case for the implementation of the European Single Market, is not transferable to other cross-border sites within the EC. Indeed, considering that there are 10 000 km of borders, the overall budget of the ERDF would not be sufficient to cover the needs of such initiatives.

(3) The fact that the territory involved is very small is a further limitation. At a time when the growing internationalisation of the economy has created a need for more and more openness on an international scale and for greater access to technology, the cross-border area defined by the EDP is too small to contain a skills base offering a source of human resources, technology, or services to industry. Indeed, the only way to overcome these shortcomings, a task which has been entrusted to the Joint Services Centre and to the European College of Technology, would be to integrate the EDP more fully within its wider environment.

(4) Within this context, the lack of an urban infrastructure makes the greater integration of the EDP within a wider environment even more pressing. We feel that the reference to a wider environment is essential if we are to make the project sustainable and ensure the continued existence of the industrial enterprises and jobs which are ultimately created.

As for the PACTE, however, we feel that the limitations of the programme are a result of the nature of the cooperation strategy which has been implemented. Because this programme is focused on intangible investments and on rather diffused actions ultimately designed to modernise the economic activity of businesses, the benefits of the PACTE are less apparent and more difficult to quantify; all the more so as the positive impact of the work will only really be felt in the medium term (that is, after five or ten years).

As the PACTE approach is geared towards developing operational projects with a view to setting up a network of links, the objectives of the cooperation initiatives appear to be more 'diluted'. The practical results achieved by such operations are therefore all the more difficult to assess. In this respect, the strategy which has been developed within the framework of the PACTE should be aimed specifically at sectors in which the results can be seen more readily (for example, cooperation on RTD). Furthermore, we must provide an efficient and methodical means of examining the impact of the initiatives undertaken (by implementing a system of program monitoring and by carrying out an audit of the achievements).

5 Conclusions

Several lessons can be drawn from this brief analysis of cross-border cooperation initiatives in the Walloon region. The pressures resulting, on the one hand, from the completion of the European Single Market and, on the other hand, from the globalisation of the economy have been such that all cross-border regions will, in future, be forced to develop competitive facilities by finding external advantages in the area. It is only in this way that these regions will remain competitive in the European economic and technological market.

Cross-border regions are undeniably at an advantage by virtue of their common heritage and the ties which have been formed through history. This is a cultural factor which can in fact become one of the dynamic components of intracommunity exchanges. However, cross-border areas are also seriously handicapped by the fact that they have always played a peripheral role within their respective national economies. For this reason, cross-border cooperation initiatives cannot use any single model as a reference. Instead, they must take account of the specific effects of the peripheral position of the area on its development. Certain cross-border areas are strengthened through cooperation by achieving synergy between the various assets they have to offer (the PACTE, for example), whereas others are experiencing difficulties which can, in fact, be eliminated when those handicaps are shared (the EDP). Each cross-border cooperation initiative is an experiment which has its own particular characteristics determined not only by the history of the region but also by its economic and social potential.

The experience of Wallonia's cross-border cooperation, with more than ten other European cross-border regions having an entirely different institutional status, indicates that the relative success of these experiments lies in the capacity of the respective regions to conduct these experiments autonomously in partnership with local representatives from economic, cultural, and political spheres. From the results of the experiments carried out to date, it appears undeniable that the federal status of Wallonia and that of North-Rhine Westphalia have enabled the French and Dutch regions to act as better partners within the framework of cross-border cooperation than have their national authorities.

Experiments in cross-border cooperation can eventually fade out if they do not succeed in establishing themselves in wider domains by seeking support from external urban and technological factors. Consequently, rather than being introspective, the aim of such experiments should be to become integrated within the wider framework of European regional policy and to act as catalysts for regional development as an active component of the region.

Cross-border cooperation must avoid giving absolute priority to the development of a heavy infrastructure and strike a balance between intangible investments and the establishment of a dynamic local infrastructure. It is essential that these zones achieve a form of accessibility or 'centrality', which is not simply geographical but human, by developing new incentives to locate there, linked to the quality of life in the area and the quality of local human resources. This form of investment, which is essentially intangible despite its more diffused character and the fact that it has a medium-term effect on regional development, must nonetheless be given priority status if we are to offer these areas a real chance of competing against more centrally located regions within the newly formed European Single Market.

References

Aydalot P (Ed.), 1986 *Milieux Innovateurs en Europe* (Creative Environments in Europe) (GREMI, Paris)

Maillat D, 1991, "The attainment of the European internal market and the trans-border regions", in *Regional Development Trajectories and the Attainment of the European Internal Market* Ed. M Quévit (GREMI, Paris) pp 125 – 146

Maillat D, Quévit M, Senn L-F (Eds), 1993 *Milieux Innovateurs et Réseaux d'Innovation: Un Pari pour le Développement Régional* (Creative Environments and Innovation Networks: Encouraging Regional Development) (EDES, Neuchâtel)

Quévit M, Houard J, Bodson S, Dangoisse A, 1991 *Impact Régional 1992: Les Régions de Tradition Industrielle* (Regional Impact 1992: Regions with a Strong Industrial Base) (De Boeck Université, Bruxelles)

Rider, 1988, "Le potentiel de développement de la zone Pacte et la coopération transfrontalière avec le Nord–Pas-de-Calais" (Growth potential of the Pacte region and cross-border cooperation with the Nord–Pas-de-Calais), research report, Interdisciplinary Research Group on Regional Development, University College, London

Transnational Networks and Cooperation in the New Europe: Experiences and Prospects in the Upper Rhine Area and Recommendations for Eastern Europe

R H Funck
University of Karlsruhe
J S Kowalski
University of Münster

1 General considerations

The future Europe will to a large extent be a continent of competing regions and groups of regions. The first signs of growing regional awareness and of growing efforts to shape regionally based alliances, networks, and neighbourhood cooperation can already be seen in various parts of Europe. Cities such as Karlsruhe, Strasbourg, Freiburg, Mulhouse, and Basel on the German–French–Swiss borders are increasingly extending their cooperation from the cultural and educational spheres toward common infrastructural and spatial planning projects. The same phenomena may be observed on the northern fringe of the EC, where the London–Paris–Brussels–Amsterdam–Düsseldorf alliance appears to be gaining strength and to be ensuring, through the planning of modern transportation links, that the future locus of European economic development will be focused there.

These extra efforts and programmes are required not only because of increased competition in the future united European market, but also to address and solve problems of a supranational and supraregional character. Such problems include environmental matters, the majority of the relevant transportation infrastructure projects, and also social and economic issues connected with migration, trade flows, technological cooperation, and so on. Regions cannot cope with such problems on their own: they are unable to fulfil their 'European mission' as single entities. Their respective national governments are usually distant, and their perspective on issues and problems is not always to the advantage of the regions concerned. This means that regions located in geographical proximity are natural partners for cooperation in an effort to solve common problems and ensure at least equal positions in the European framework. But it should be realised that transnational, cross-border cooperations are confronted with special problems and are not easy to implement.

History, institutions, and rules of the game connected with them matter in economic development. To a large extent they determine whether in a given society at a certain moment in time incentive mechanisms have been created which induce economic actors to act efficiently in the economic sense.

They determine if contracts can be negotiated, arrived at, implemented, and enforced with low transaction costs, thus enabling sophisticated, complex, impersonal exchange patterns underlying every modern economically developed society.

Institutions prescribing certain ways of formal behaviour, as well as informal behaviour norms and constraints, which stem from the historical evolution of a given society and from its cultural characteristics acquired in the course of development, are thus predominantly responsible for the success of some nations, regions, and areas in creating modern, mature economies. They also underlie the failures and vicious circles of poverty in other places.

This is a message from the strand of economic theory often labeled 'institutional economics', or 'new institutional economics', and connected with, among others, the names of such prominent scholars as Coase (1988), Williamson (1975; 1985), and North (1990) (for an excellent overview see Eggertson, 1990). These authors extended the traditional economic analysis by looking explicitly at the role of the institutional framework, within which people act as economic actors.

Creating institutions that benefit economic development is a difficult undertaking even in very favourable circumstances. It is not surprising that only a handful of societies have been able to achieve this aim in modern times. It is also obvious that the cultural, historical, and legal differences characteristic of cross-border areas render the task of shaping the institutional framework, reducing transactional costs, and thus fostering economic development even more tedious and complex than in other cases. By definition, the cross-border regions are places where a cultural and social divide is omnipresent. Sometimes the language barrier is absent (when people in different national parts of the transnational region are able to use a similar dialect), but customs, legal rules, and indeed most of the formal and informal rules of behaviour differ.

On the other hand, the enlarged Europe, the prospects for the success of European union, and the implementation of the internal European market, all necessitate a growing degree of transnational and cross-border cooperation. The new pattern of economic flows and exchange must emerge throughout Europe, emanating from the diminished, if not completely eliminated, economic role of the old nation-state frontiers. Seen from this perspective it seems that despite the cultural, legal, and mental barriers, the task of creating institutions and mechanisms for cross-border cooperation has become one of the key linchpins on which the future of project 'Europe' depends.

The strategies aimed at fostering transnational cross-border cooperation must be different and fit specific needs. Cooperation between strong industrial or postindustrial regional economies is focused on synergies which are potentially achievable from technological and financial equal partnerships. Relations between regions at unequal levels of development will necessarily focus more on development – help programmes, which will, however, over a longer period bring measurable benefits to the stronger partners of the deal.

The interregional programmes and regional structural programmes of the EC should, to a larger extent than before, be directed specifically to promoting such regional group agreements and bilateral deals within them. In the next section, we use the example of the Upper Rhine area to demonstrate practical solutions and activities that have been pursued and problems that have been encountered. Later, in section 3, we proceed to formulate advice on transnational and networking cooperation in Eastern Europe, with particular reference to Poland.

2 Experience from the Upper Rhine region

The Upper Rhine region (URR) situated in the so-called 'three countries Triangle' encompasses the German-speaking Swiss region of Basel and parts of the surrounding counties (the so-called Regio Basiliensis) (for some programmes, a part of the canton of Jura is also of relevance), the French region of Alsace (where French is the dominant language, but the older generation especially is still fluent in the dialect, which is well understood in Germany), the western part of the German federal state of Baden-Württemberg up to the Karlsruhe area in the north, and the southern part of the state of Rhineland-Palatinate (see figure 1). Numerous innovative programmes and schemes for transnational and transregional cooperation have emerged in the URR. In particular programmes concerning infrastructure networks, university cooperation, transfer of knowledge and technology, and programmes for intensifying contacts between small and medium-sized enterprises (SMEs) in the Triangle have been developed, but at the same time there are still many obstacles hampering the transnational cooperation.

The cross-border Upper Rhine region does not possess any formal administrative organisation, financial status, or legal basis. It is a forum for cooperation between the respective national authorities, who signed documents of 'goodwill' covering different fields of action. It is also a forum for formal and informal cooperation by various regional institutions, organisations, associations, chambers of commerce, and so on, some of them only local in nature, some covering parts of the Upper Rhine area, and only a few of them encompassing the whole region. On the whole it can be said that the Palatinate part of the URR is on average less involved in the projects covering the whole area, but local initiatives also abound there.

Every two years a large conference involving representatives of the government and of various institutions takes place. The most recent, the fourth Three Countries Congress was held in December 1992 in Karlsruhe.

The whole Upper Rhine area covers about 20000 km² and had about 5 million inhabitants in the late 1980s (Strasbourg, 1992, pages 131 – 156).

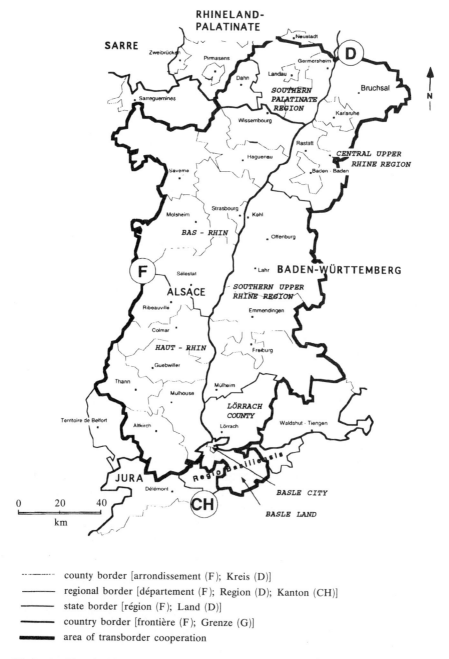

county border [arrondissement (F); Kreis (D)]
regional border [département (F); Region (D); Kanton (CH)]
state border [région (F); Land (D)]
country border [frontière (F); Grenze (G)]
area of transborder cooperation

Figure 1. Transborder area on the Upper Rhine River (source: adapted from Strasbourg, 1992, page 133).

The French part of the region and the Palatinate are, on average, less developed than the Swiss and Baden-Württemberg areas, but in general the URR is one of the most prosperous places in Europe. Manufacturing, especially machinery, chemicals, and electrotechnics, dominated in the past but have since experienced a downward trend in employment and in their share of GDP. The growing share of various services is typical of developments throughout Europe. The region is characterised by an above average share of SMEs in the size distribution of enterprises and by strong dependence of its economic activities upon foreign trade (Funck et al, 1993a).

Transnational cooperation in the URR covers a broad spectrum of issues and activities. As mentioned above there are numerous local undertakings (for example, between schools or sport associations) often extending to both sides of the border. We shall refer here only to the most important ones, especially those that cover the whole, or at least a large part, of the region.

In the field of *environmental protection* the state, regional, and cantonal governments signed agreements for cross-border cooperation, especially on information flows concerning pollution, refuse collection and disposal, common examination of the environmental impacts of the transportation projects, and large real-estate and industrial construction projects. In the lead-up to the Three Countries Congress in 1992, working groups were established, which provided a thorough examination of carbon dioxide and other air pollution in the region. A network of weather research stations and environmental research (the Regional Climate Project and the French–German Institute for Environmental Research) at the regions' universities are examples of the spin-offs from these activities.

In the field of *transportation* the national institutions remain responsible for the planning and implementation of the projects. But the information flow and coordination of the undertakings with neighbouring regions has now become a matter of routine. At least in the field of initiative generation, the conferences of the Upper Rhine area play an important role. But the cross-border transportation links, especially between France and Germany, can still be considered a weakness in the transnational region. The most important developments for the future are the following:
(a) the construction of the North–South motorway on the French side of the Rhine, improvement of the motorway on the German side, and the provision of better links between the two;
(b) inclusion of the region in the high-speed train link between Paris, Strasbourg, Karlsruhe, Stuttgart, and Munich; and
(c) implementation of the Upper Rhine rapid train system, EURORHIN, which is supposed to provide an hourly or two-hourly service between the main centres of the region.

In *telecommunications* the infrastructure networks are good, but the compatibility of the national systems across the borders is not always guaranteed (Funck et al, 1993a, page 157).

With respect to *technology support and transfer* it should be mentioned that the region belongs to the European powerhouses. The research potential is enormous, as prominent technical universities and research laboratories are located there.

Most of the important higher education institutions are members of a university network called EUCOR, which is a cooperation agreement of the universities located along the Upper Rhine river. The University of Basel (Switzerland), the German universities of Freiburg and of Karlsruhe, together with the French universities in Mulhouse, Strasbourg, and Colmar participate in EUCOR. Common institutes, mutual recognition of courses, common curricula (especially in computer sciences and software engineering, robotics, as well as in biology and medicine) are the elements of the EUCOR activities. The EUCOR should probably be extended in the future to include professional colleges (Fachhochschule) in Germany and similar institutions in France and Switzerland.

In order to promote intensified cooperation of enterprises in R&D, the chambers of commerce in Alsace and in Karlsruhe prepared a handbook of research and development in the Upper Rhine area and a handbook on energy use. Both these sources provide information on the enterprises and research units in various fields. A cooperation network for about 250 research units from Germany and Alsace is provided by the French–German Institute for Automation and Robotics (IAR); several similar institutions have been established in other fields.

Nevertheless, support programmes for technology research and transfer still follow predominantly national–regional channels. To a large extent, transnational cooperation is limited to information provision and contact matching. Chambers of commerce and universities play a leading role in this respect in the region. The northern part of the Upper Rhine area is covered by an EC-financed PAMINA project for cross-border enterprise cooperation (for Northern Alsatia, Southern Palatinate, and Central Upper Rhine areas), especially for SMEs and newly established high-technology-oriented firms.

Research on the state of the cross-border transnational cooperations by enterprises points to the strong barriers, legal and mental, hampering this kind of activity (Gemünden, 1993). In those instances where trans-border cooperation is functioning, it is directed more at common access to sales markets and less at collaboration in the development of products and production processes.

3 The opening and transformation of Eastern Europe and the transational regional cooperation

We shall base our reflections in this section on the example of Poland, but most of the issues are of direct relevance to all countries in transition. In the transition period (which may last for a long time) the market economy in Eastern Europe is neither really a market economy in the Western

European sense (many institutions and mechanisms are different) nor the planned one because the old institutional setup has been eliminated.

Apart from these general points, the following aspects must be considered in all programmes of regional development in Eastern European conditions:
(a) physical environment (pollution, water supply, and so on);
(b) supply and maintenance of the residential environment (flats and communal infrastructure such as shops, kindergartens, and schools), utilities, and other services (garbage collection, for example);
(c) cultural environment;
(d) transport infrastructure and distance to and from markets (domestic and foreign);
(e) communications infrastructure;
(f) skill of local labour and labour mobility (determined to a large extent in the countries in transition by the availability of residential space);
(g) regional labour costs;
(h) industrial structure and level of economic development;
(i) volume and quality of fixed capital; and
(j) facilities and conditions for development of science and R&D activities.

In Poland in the past, as in all other Soviet-type economies, investment policy was considered the most important regional development factor. Contrary to the proclaimed doctrine of the regional policy, this view favoured the old well-established industrial regions, and large cities. The official doctrine of regional development emphasised the convergence of economic structures of regions stressing industrialisation, neglecting other aspects of socioeconomic life. These phenomena are extensively described in literature on centrally planned economies (CPEs) (for example, see Gorzelak, 1989; Kowalski, 1990; Zienkowski et al, 1978). A similar paradigm permeated thinking on regional policy in the market economies (for example, see Funck, 1993), although aspects of technological change and innovation activities were given a much more prominent place there than in the literature on the CPEs.

The first three years of the transition process in Poland have shown that systemic transformation results in a dramatic change of sectoral and regional development patterns. The old industrial and mining regions are facing relative decline and enormous social tensions (unemployment, work stoppages, and so on) as a result (Funck et al, 1993b). There are also many instances of urban regions that in the past developed around a single huge industrial enterprise, so that the failure of these enterprises in the transition to a market economy (which is often the case because of their inability to adapt to market conditions) deprives these regions almost totally of their economic base.

On the other hand, border regions that were considered in the past to be peripheral and lagging in economic development show signs of growing entrepreneurship and bottom-up initiatives (and this is recorded not only in regions on the western Polish border with Germany or the southern border with the Czech and Slovak Republics, but also on the eastern fringe from the Baltic states to the Ukraine). In particular, however, the regions adjacent to the former German Democratic Republic seem to be recording above-average rates of growth of new economic activities.

Another important phenomenon observed during the first phase of the transition to a market economy is that regional policy (if not regional thinking) has definitely been relegated to the back position in relation to other economic policy considerations, with the typical justification that change in the economic system is of utmost importance and no regional policy can be simultaneously elaborated and paid for. We (that is, regional economists) know of course that this view is wrong, shortsighted, and dangerous. Regional policy can and should contribute positively to the overall economic efficiency of the national economy (Funck, 1993).

Knowledge of the factors underlying changes in regional development prospects and potentials in Poland is not very extensive. There is some knowledge of a general character (for example, see Korcelli, 1993) but in-depth analysis based on statistical sources is lacking (the regionalised statistics on many facets of economic life, such as the growth of economic activities in the informal sector, are lacking too). Even more importantly there seems to be very little knowledge about the factors determining the medium-term and long-term prospects of regional development, known increasingly in the literature as 'soft factors' (Funck et al, 1992), which will in future gain in importance because of the psychological and socially related barriers of systemic transformation and as a result of the creation of the market economy in Eastern Europe.

It should be made easier for regions from Eastern Europe, which plan to establish regional-cooperation networks, to apply for the EC help. Some initial experience in this field, such as the creation of the 'Carpatian European Transregion' or the efforts to create a transnational region on both sides of the Oder river, seem to be very promising.

We believe that the Polish regions should attempt to create similar network schemes at the regional, city, and community levels as well as between institutions (such as chambers of industry and commerce, universities, and so on). We also think that the efforts of the Polish regions to find partners in Western Europe should not be confined to the most developed, richest regions of the EC. Backwardness is a relative concept. Many regions in what is called peripheral Europe (some parts of Greece, Spain, and Portugal) are certainly able to provide useful assistance in problems concerning management, accounting and financing practices, and the like.

It should be noted here that, on the basis of research on Polish regions, we are of the opinion that the Polish authorities at all levels need more-practice-oriented advice on specific business matters and administrative solutions, than more-general information on the basic principles of the functioning of the market economy. This latter kind of advisory activity seem to have dominated up till now in the projects financed internationally. Networking between regions and communities may be a pragmatic way of redirecting advisory efforts toward these more-practice-oriented questions.

Moreover, the concept of the local area networks, developing around a technologically strong nucleus, seems to us to be a practically relevant strategy for regional authorities in Poland. Poland possesses a well-developed network of universities and technical universities as well as other research institutions. Instead of closing most of them in the period of financial austerity, which seems to be a serious possibility for 1993, they should be used as possible source of spin-offs for the establishment of new enterprises in the surrounding area.

References
Coase R H, 1988 *The Firm, the Market and the Law* (University of Chicago Press, Chicago, IL)
Eggertson T, 1990 *Economic Behavior and Institutions* (Cambridge University Press, Cambridge)
Funck R, 1993, "Regionalwissenschaft" (Regional Science), in *Handbuch der Raumforschung und Raumordnung* Akademie für Raumforschung und Landesplanung, 30161 Hannover, Germany (forthcoming)
Funck R, Kowalski J, 1993 *Baden-Württemberg: A High Technology Region Facing the Future* Institut für Wirtschaftspolitik und Wirtschaftsforschung, Universität Karlsruhe, Karlsruhe, Germany
Funck R, Böttcher H, Kowalski J (Eds), 1993a *Technologie, Wirtschaft und Umwelt im offenen Europa unter Berücksichtigung der speziellen Aspekte der Region am Oberrhein* (Technology, Economy and Environment in open Europe, with particular reference to the special aspects of the Upper Rhine region), Institut für Wirtschaftspolitik und Wirtschaftsforschung der Universität Karlsruhe und Fachschaft Wirtschaftswissenschaften, Karlsruhe, Germany
Funck R, Dziembowska-Kowalska J, Robertson-Wensauer C Y, 1992 *Kultur als Wirtschaftsfaktor in Karlsruhe* (Culture as an Economic Factor in Karlsruhe), Institut für Wirtschaftspolitik und Wirtschaftsforschung, Universität Karlsruhe, Karlsruhe, Germany
Funck R, Kowalski J, Zienkowski L, 1993b *The Role of Small and Medium Enterprises in the Restructuring of the Polish Regions* (Nomos, Baden-Baden) forthcoming
Gemünden H G, 1993, "Grenzüberschreitende Kooperationen kleiner und mittleren Unternehmen" (Transborder cooperations of the small and medium enterprises), in *Wirtschaftsraum Oberrhein—ein Modell in Europa* Regierungspräsidium, Karlsruhe, Koordinierungsstelle für grenzüberscheitende Zusammenarbeit, Schlossplatz 1-3, D-76128, Karlsruhe, Germany
Gorzelak G, 1989 *Rozwój Regionalny Polski w Warunkach Kryzysu* (Regional Development in Poland During the Phase of Economic Crisis), University of Warsaw, Warsaw, Poland
Korcelli P, 1993, "Implication of demographic change and economic restructuring for the Polish urban system", in *The Role of Small and Medium Enterprises in the Restructuring of the Polish Regions* Eds R Funck, J Kowalski, L Zienkowski (Nomos, Baden-Baden) forthcoming

Kowalski J, 1990, "Economic reforms in centrally planned economies and their consequences for regional development", in *Infrastructure and the Space Economy* Ed. K Peschel (Springer, Berlin) pp 391 – 402

Kowalski J, 1993, "Transformation of Eastern European Economies", Discussion Paper, University of Münster, Münster, Germany

North D C, 1990 *Institutions, Institutional Change and Economic Performance* (Cambridge University Press, Cambridge)

Strasbourg, 1992 *Élements pour un Atlas de l'Espace Transfrontalier du Fossé Rhénan* (Elements for the Atlas of the Transfrontier Area of the Rhine Valley), Préfecture de la Région Alsace et Secrétariat Général pour les Affaires Régionales et Européennes, 5 Place de la République, 67073 Strasbourg

Williamson O E, 1975 *Markets and Hierarchies* (The Free Press, New York)

Williamson O E, 1985 *The Economic Institutions of Capitalism* (The Free Press, New York)

Zienkowski L, Kowalski J, Wyżnikiewicz B, 1978 *Badania Porównawcze nad Regionalnym Zróżnicowaniem Dochodu Narodowego* (Comparative Studies of the Interregional Differentiation of National Income), in *Problemy i Metody Ekonomiki Regionalnej* Ed. A Kuklinski (Polish Scientific Publishers, Warsaw), pp 141 – 192

The Atlantic Arc: The Small and Medium-sized Enterprises and the Transfer of Technologies

B Guesnier
University of Poitiers

1 Introduction

The Atlantic Front is made up of the coastal regions of Western Europe. This natural macroregion, belonging to five different European countries, faces many challenges, which have prompted action from local policy-makers. These regions have pronounced features of a peripheral nature which is why there is widespread support for a concerted approach to ensure their development in an ever-changing European background.

The fall of the Berlin Wall, along with the opening of the borders toward the Central European countries, has resulted in a shifting of the EC's centre of gravity eastwards. This evolution made the leaders of the Atlantic regions react in order to avoid a further accentuation of the important marginalising effects caused by their peripheral situation. "Europe, do not forget your Atlantic" said J P Raffarin, President of the regional council of Poitou-Charentes, who wanted to prove that this grouping of the Atlantic regions served a dual purpose: first of all, to defend their rank, their economic future, but also to contribute to the European movement and to participate in its social and economic development. The Atlantic Arc, 'project-territory' of the Atlantic Front, is therefore seen as a way of expressing a strategy of development based on new products and services in a changing world. ['Project-territory' means a space organised so as to promote externalities for projects of new activities (Guesnier, 1992).]

In order to support this political action, an international scientific symposium was organised in Poitiers, in March 1990. Its goal was to evaluate this concept and, through exchanges between researchers and local actors, to enrich the initial elements of an Atlantic dynamic which will be the cement of a lobbying action in the EC.

The birth of the Atlantic Arc (studied from June 1989 onwards by Professor Y Morvan, working for the Association Ouest Atlantique, and commissioned to develop the regional economy of Bretagne, Pays de la Loire, and Poitou-Charentes) was confirmed officially in October 1989 during the Conference of the European Community's Coastal and Peripheral Regions (CRPM), which designated a Specific Internal Commission during its annual session, in Faro, Portugal. From April 1991 onwards, the Atlantic Arc Commission has been based in Rennes and headed by M Guichard, President of the Regional council of Pays de la Loire.

The Atlantic Arc, this European macroregion, was soon to be the object of much attention. Thus, in 1990 the Centre Européen de Développement

Régional (CEDRE) began the first prospective study of the Atlantic regions on behalf of the European Commission, and the Délégation à l'Aménagement du Territoire et à l'Action Régionale (DATAR), in its project 'Prospective et Territoires', chose for its seventh research theme 'the future of the Atlantic Front'. These thorough studies, whose results are now widely available (Beauchard, 1993; CEDRE, 1993), stress some essential characteristics, and it is convenient to recapitulate on them briefly in order to realise fully how important is the future of these regions in the context of the European movement. In the past, the regions grew wealthy thanks to the shipping trade, but now they are affected by quite different situations: these regions are extremely rural and their agriculture (albeit dominant) is heterogeneous. For example, the overall sizes of farms range from 2.5 ha in Portugal to 80 ha in Scotland, whereas the agricultural revenue is seven times greater in Scotland than in Portugal. It may be that the Atlantic regions, being largely nonindustrial (with the notable exception of Northern Spain) and having shifted belatedly toward a manufacturing economy, have been spared an industrial model that still imposes difficult adaptations on many regions. Besides, apart from the industrial reconversion in Spain, most of the Atlantic regions have experimented with development during the 1980s, which can be seen in the ecotourism phenomenon in Ireland, in foreign investment in Portugal, and through the creation of many firms in South West England.

Such is the case for the five French regions of the Atlantic Arc, on which I will base my analysis. Between 1982 and 1990, there was an important development: in the matter of salaried employment, the five regions exceeded the country's overall rating and found themselves on the heels of Île de France, which is itself beaten by the four dynamic regions of the South and the South East (Rhône-Alpes, Provence-Alpes-Côte d'Azur, Languedoc-Roussillon, Midi-Pyrénées). This evolution reveals both a notable success of the regional development policies and an evolution of the behaviour of the small and medium-sized enterprises (SMEs), which have ensured their mutation through their connection to technology transfer networks.

One can observe that those firms that transferred out of Île de France between 1960 and 1975 experienced a substantial amount of restructuring. Some were replaced after the transformation of a unit with 2000 semi-skilled workers to a much smaller technician unit, but many others simply disappeared. Eventually, employment was maintained by an important flow of firm start-ups which generated a diversified economic fabric made of numerous SMEs. Of course, this period (1980–90), characterised by the buildup of small production units must be studied carefully (the subcontracting activities have certainly favoured SMEs) but it is also interesting to observe the creation of a network of Regional Centres for the Information and the Transfer of Technologies (whose French acronym is CRITTs). In 1992, the French Atlantic Front acquired forty-three CRITTs out of ninety-seven. Serving the SMEs, these centres of technological circulation help to further the adaptation of these firms to changes in the industrial system.

The economic evolution, rather positive in employment terms, is above the average for the regions of the Atlantic Arc, and is almost certainly the result of the buildup of SMEs. However, part of this favourable trend is likely to be the result of the related development of productive industrial activities on the one hand and, on the other, services related to these firms, along with an important network of CRITTs, which made the circulation of new technologies easier. An analysis of the changes which affected the structure of intermediary consumption reveals the growing influence of the information flows, a buildup of (immaterial) and a widening use of the services of high value added (SHVAs). The high concentration of SHVAs in the biggest cities, which are quite rare in the Atlantic Front, raises the problem of connecting the small and medium-sized firms and industries to the information network, and thus the problem of the potential role of the CRITTs.

The SMEs encompass a stratum of firms ready for expansion or development. The question arises as to whether it is possible to generate the conditions for another cross-fertilisation in order to assess the potential of these firms, make their projects circulate, encourage their initiatives, and, eventually, determine the problems (obstacles or con-straints) and assess their solutions. To do so, we could base business growth on the development of services used by these firms in general, and on the development of CRITTs in particular.

The analysis of the structural transformations and of the overall rating of the production system since 1970 in the peripheral regions of the Atlantic Front reveals the existence of synergistic effects between the SMEs and the organisations related to the technological transfers. The creation of the Atlantic Arc and its operation are the only way of merging the new economic activities of these regions with those of the European Community, given the important transformations imposed on the produc-tion system by the worldwide exchanges and technological evolution. Thus, partnership and interregional cooperation are the most important tools for intervention in order to further the completion of the Atlantic Art as a real 'project-territory'; that is, a space where economic policy based on alliance strategies and lobbying organisation create conditions favouring a growth of activity.

In the next section, I will describe the origin and rise of the Atlantic Arc project. I will then consider the characteristics and evolution of the economies of the Atlantic regions. Finally, I will examine technology transfer and the mechanisms required to generate innovative productive backgrounds: the importance of the Atlantic Arc.

2 The birth and rise of the Atlantic Arc project

In order to assess the impact of the creation of the Atlantic Arc project (that is, the idea of a mobilisation of regions ranging from Northern Scotland to South Portugal and Andalusia), it is useful to have its historical background. The choice of intervention tools was made with a view to acting on the most essential characteristics of the marginal and peripheral nature of these regions (that is, on the infrastructures) to moderate the effects of isolating these regions, and on the diffusion of knowledge and technology to reduce the effects of dependence on a productive system whose economic conditions were changing rapidly (namely globalisation, international competition, and technical evolution).

In regional science it is possible to identify several different approaches to the concept of region: natural, historial, cultural, economic, and political. In terms of town and country planning (in French, *aménagement du territoire*), it is helpful to classify these definitions. One can distinguish between: a geographic entity, with its natural obstacles; an economic and social entity, a man-made rural, urban, and country space built by people; or a strategic entity, in which the territory is seen as a political mobilisation project. With its goal of taking up the challenge of its marginalisation, the Atlantic Arc, aiming to combine efficiency and solidarity beyond all borders, belongs to this last category.

Despite the fact that the question of an Atlantic decline was raised in 1987 in Santander during a meeting between representatives of Aquitaine and the Cantabrian Heights, the expression 'Atlantic Arc' was used for the first time in a meeting held by the Regional Chamber of Industry and Commerce (CRCI) of Bretagne, in October 1988. Taken up by J Morvan, this expression was adopted by the political leaders and has been widely used from September 1989 onwards by the media, who generate an 'Atlantic Arc' image.

The fall of the Berlin Wall in November 1989 underlines the risks of marginalisation, and makes mobilisation all the more crucial, in order to design a strategy in reaction to the problems raised by this recent revolution for the coastal regions of Europe. So, twenty-three regions met to build their future in and with the EC.

The Atlantic Arc, designed to take up such challenges, is the result of a common political strategy. Eighteen months after its creation, the Atlantic Arc quietly grows stronger: as a mobilising concept, it is the reference or the guideline for many other projects. It has turned into a very useful interregional network. It has already initiated common actions between different regions, it has encouraged a further grouping, and it has obtained support from the EC through budgetary programmes such as PERIFRA and ATLANTIS.

The following chronology demonstrates that the Atlantic Arc is actually a process for a dynamic Atlantic area.

October 1988. The expression 'Atlantic Arc' is first used during a meeting of the CRCI of Bretagne.

June 1989. Y Morvan, of the University of Rennes, begins his study of this subject on behalf of the Association Ouest Atlantique.

September 1989. Y Bourges and O Guichard, Presidents of the Regional Councils of Bretagne and Pays de la Loire, put forward this idea during a biannual meeting held in Rennes.

October 1989. The Maritime and Peripheral Regions Conference creates an Internal Commission during its annual meeting in Faro, Portugal.

November 1989. During the General Meeting of the Association Ouest Atlantique (in charge of the economic promotion of the regions of Bretagne, Pays de la Loire, and Poitou-Charentes), Y Morvan expounds the results of his study.

November 1989. In Nantes, J Chereque, French Minister of Aménagement du Territoire, organises a meeting of his European counterparts. Together, they approve the creation of the Atlantic Arc and confirm the validity of this concept in the context of European Aménagement du Territoire.

November 1989. In Strasbourg, in the European Parliament, the local representatives of the Atlantic regions form a new political group, headed by J P Raffarin, President of the Regional Council of Poitou-Charentes, Member of the European Parliament. This is the birth of the 'Atlantic Group'.

January 1990. In Nantes, delegates from sixteen regions attend the Atlantic Arc's first meeting, highlighting the success of the mobilisation about this macroregion.

March 1990. The President of the Economic and Social Regional Committee (in French, CESR) of the Pays de la Loire puts forward the idea of a permanent conference of all the CESRs.

March 1990. An international symposium, whose theme is 'The Atlantic dynamics by the year 2000', is organised in Poitiers by the Regional Studies Institute (Institut d'Economie Régionale de l'Université de Poitiers). It is supported by many partners, notably the Regional Council Poitou-Charentes, the General Planning Board, and the DATAR. This symposium, under the patronage of B Millan, member of the Commission of the European Community, DG XVI, is an important step toward the conceptualisation of the Atlantic Arc. E Landaburu, General Director of DG XVI, honours the symposium with his presence and announces an invitation to tender for a prospective study of the Atlantic Arc (Guesnier, 1991).

April 1990. In Rennes, representatives of twenty-one regions gather for their first official meeting since Faro, headed by O Guichard. The Atlantic Arc Commission created during this meeting defines five priority orientations: (a) the transportation network, (b) the leading-edge technologies, (c) better cooperation between firms and universities, (d) the financial services, and (e) tourist development. This order of priorities is not fortuitous. The transportation priority reveals the will to remove the isolation of the peripheral Atlantic regions, and the following orientations direct the attention of these regions toward the specific characteristics of their economic fabric, and towards the necessity of intervening specifically in order to make the production system evolve. From the creation of this Commission onwards, the interregional cooperation will be more diversified.

April 1990. In Bordeaux, Presidents J P Raffarin (from Poitou-Charentes) and J Tavernier (from Aquitaine) initiate an interregional programme with the nearby region of Euskadi (Spain), creating Sud Europe Atlantique. This cooperation will be directed at: (a) the communication infrastructures, (b) the transfers of new technologies, and (c) training.

May 1990. During a debate about 'aménagement du territoire' on the floor of the Assemblée Nationale, J Chereque defines seven zones, which include the Atlantic Front, as building blocks for country planning.

June 1990. During their permanent meetings, the CESRs from the Atlantic Arc define three subjects for further studies: infrastructures, education and research, and rural development.

June 1990. In Inverness (Scotland) the Junior Chambers of Commerce (JCEs), during one of their European meetings, agreed to contribute to the creation of an Atlantic Arc whose vocation will be economic, touristic, and cultural. This action is taken up by the National Congress of the JCEs in Bretagne.

July 1990. During the Francofolies in La Rochelle, and with the agreement of the mayor, M Crepeau, a cultural mobilisation is initiated by J P Raffarin in favour of the Atlantic Arc. The Francofolies are renamed 'the Atlantic Festival'.

September 1990. In Bilbao, Sud Europe Atlantique works on its cooperation projects, based on the problems of research and technological transfers. An interregional fund is created, with a budget reaching ecu 200 000. Its objective is to further the contribution of the regions to EC programmes such as INTERREG and, above all, STRIDE, whose goal is to enhance the innovative and technological capacities. Four priority themes are defined: (a) greater awareness of innovations and of the means of technical promotion, (b) the organisation of educational programmes adapted to the introduction of innovations in firms, (c) support for cooperation between educational establishments and small and medium-sized industries, and (d) the development of intermediary organisms of diffusion.

October 1990. In La Baule, the 18th Peripheral and Coastal Regions Conference expresses the desire to benefit from an EC-sponsored Integrated Programme for the Atlantic Arc.

November 1990. The Prospective and Territory programme of the DATAR is announced by J-P Duport, Delegate to Regional Development. Its seventh theme is 'the future of the Atlantic Front'. The essential question, posed by J-L Guigou, is: could the West find itself marginalised?

January 1991. The EC grants ecu14 million to finance a programme of cooperation between the regions of the Atlantic Front: the programme ARCANTEL (for a better communication between sea ports), a preparation for the shipping trade sector, a project of financial engineering, and the development of their maritime resources (through the Association for the Management of the Atlantic Littoral).

At first a simple proposition, the Atlantic Arc soon began to launch its projects of cooperation. The mobilisation in favour of this strategy, creating a movement largely taken up by the media, has enabled the regions to confirm the existence of relations between the local actors along the Atlantic coast. It has also favoured many initiatives, thus furthering the synergistic effects. The important activity engaged in the European Parliament of Strasbourg by J P Raffarin's 'Atlantic Group' has brought acceptance from the authorities of the EC of the idea of starting a prospective study of the Atlantic Arc.

Many cross-cooperation programmes between different partners of the Atlantic Arc have been initiated: as an example, one could cite the agreements between the CRCIs, the Regional Chambers of Agriculture; between the Regional Development Societies (which have created a GEIE—Groupement Européen d'Intérêt Économique); between the Atlantic ports (which initiated ARCANTEL); between one from Andalusia and Pays de la Loire; between the Department of Vienne and Lisbon; between Scottish firms and Bretagne; and between a dairy cooperative from Poitou-Charentes and one from Andalusia (FROMANDAL). Or one could point to the vote by the European Parliament for a budget, PERIFRA, for the peripheral regions affected by the turmoil in Eastern Europe, and the adoption of the ATLANTIS programme aimed at furthering development, especially in tourist matters.

With the increase in the number of products and initiatives and the granting of official status by Brussels, which gave the Atlantic Arc sufficient funds to realise concrete projects, there is no longer any doubt about the reality of the concept of 'Atlantic Arc'. This is definitely new territory, the result of a common political will designed to generate new conditions of development.

3 The strengths and weaknesses of the economies of the Atlantic regions
The marginal and peripheral nature of the Atlantic regions is reflected in the inadequacies of the means of communication and in the specificity of the economic fabric. The industrial fabric evolved from the local transformation of agricultural goods, from the implantation of production activities largely based on execution and assembling tasks, and from the creation of a set of SMES which, during the last decade, displayed a notable dynamism thanks to their flexibility, adaptability, and innovative capacity.

Without going as far as to detail the many characteristics emphasising the heterogeneousness of the economies of the Atlantic regions, one can

define some major point. Despite the predominance of agricultural production activities and their related processing tasks, the productive system
has developed largely into numerous small sectors of activity which are
modernising quickly.

Agricultural activity still makes up 13%–17% of the total economic
activity in the Atlantic Arc. Even though this predominance eventually
has its drawbacks in the context of the evolution of both the GATT and
the PAC, it nevertheless favoured the development of a farm-produce
industry which represents more than one third of French production.

Only a few years ago, the traditional processing activities of, for
example, the wood-processing industry, the furniture, leather, shoes,
textile, or clothing industries still represented the economic base, widely
scattered throughout the regions of the Atlantic Arc. Nowadays, they are
no longer the source of development, employment, and value added.

Since 1965, regional development policies contributed strongly to the
implantation of industrial establishments whose development was ham-
pered in the congested Île de France. This decentralisation of businesses
and firms in the mechanical and electrical industries favoured an industrialisation process by maintaining in these regions a part of the active
population which otherwise would have been driven towards those cities
experiencing a high growth rate (in Northern or Eastern France, and in Île
de France).

The industrial changes, whose effects began to appear in the end of the
1970s, showed themselves in different ways. They generated a fabric of
small and medium-sized firms and industries which first formed to meet
the demand for subcontracting firms, but gradually filled in the promising
market gaps of small-scale production or of export by exploiting a technological niche where local resources, know-how, technical innovation, and
market opportunities were combined. Electronics, aeronautics, chemistry,
plastics technology, or composite materials are examples illustrating this
new industry; even the traditional activities opened up to new technologies, to naval construction (yachting), farm-produce industry, robotics,
biotechnology, and even the clothing industry (small-scale production,
quality controls).

The size distribution of industrial firms in January 1992 shows the
predominance of SMEs in the Atlantic Arc. The largest firms (more than
200 employees) are proportionately more numerous in France than in the
Atlantic Arc (table 1). The only exception is those with 5 to 9 employees.

Another sign of the importance of the SMEs and of a lesser concentration of the productive system in the Atlantic Arc is revealed by the fact
that the proportion of all employers in industry reaches 17%, whereas the
proportion of employees is only 14%. Thus, the evolution of the productive system is characterised by an increase in numbers of small employers
which betrays a dynamic entrepreneurship.

This diversification of the industrial activities in a vast number of small and medium-sized production units was made possible by an increase in numbers and by an unprecedented spatial diffusion of services towards the firms. It is fair to add that the policy of the Ministry of Industry, consisting of the creation, along with the regions, of the Regional Funds for the Advice to Businesses, favoured the expansion in France of advising activities by encouraging local start-ups or the opening of local branches by important firms.

The tertiarisation of the economy of the Atlantic Arc is strongly emphasized, because the numbers of employers and of salaried employees are rising far more steeply than in France (table 2), for all but a few of the tertiary activities. As a matter of fact, the small and medium-sized firms and industries have benefitted the most from such an introduction of 'immaterial'; that is, of knowledge, innovation, organisation, engineering, in the productive process.

The results of these multiple transformations of the productive system are complex. This did not prevent drastic cuts in salaried employment, especially in the big industrial establishments, but one can observe a global progress of the activities which is greater than the national average.

However, the economy of the Atlantic Arc has suffered the effects of the closures of important decentralised plants, representing 2000-3000 employees, but not to the same extent as in the vast industrial restructuring observed in the traditionally industrial regions. As a consequence, one could say that the absence of a massive industrialisation requiring the mobilisation of material, financial, and human resources within the territory could have favoured the emergence of an enterprising spirit expressed through new, original activities. Drawing support from a seam of local resources and a cultural heritage of know-how, the contractors have been

Table 1. Distribution by size of establishments with employees (source: UNEDIC-Institut d'Économie Régionale, University of Poitiers).

Number of employees	Atlantic Arc		France	
	number of employers	%	number of employers	%
1-4	9047	40.36	51490	39.18
5-9	4584	20.45	29417	22.38
10-19	3353	14.96	19282	14.67
20-49	3159	14.19	18488	14.06
50-99	1156	5.15	6097	4.63
100-199	620	2.76	3586	2.73
200-499	366	1.63	2209	1.68
500+	128	0.57	845	0.64
Total	22413	100.00	131414	100.00

able to use original technological knowledge and innovations, without which there would have been no real development of the activity and of employment.

This explains the diversity of the outcomes observed in the various Atlantic regions. Rather than attempting a complete description, I can establish a typology, distinguishing:

(1) traditional activity sites where organisational innovation has emerged (such as the mutual insurance system in Niort, the wood industry in the forest of the Landes in Aquitaine);

(2) sites where localised productive systems, based on solidarity and durability, have been developed such as Parthenay, where entrepreneurs have created an active association to exchange information; and the Choletais, a small region with a small town with many innovative SMEs and great interrelation between firms;

Table 2. Evolution of tertiary activities. For each entry, the top row represent employers and the bottom row salaried employees (source: UNEDIC-Institut d'Économie Régionale, University of Poitiers).

Sector	1979	1991	1991 – 79 growth rate (%)
Atlantic Arc			
Commercial services	67665	99623	147.2
for enterprises	371619	586523	157.8
Transport	5337	7299	136.7
	74843	101682	135.8
Insurance	538	988	183.6
	14839	21710	146.3
Financial organisations	2458	2788	113.4
	45940	49400	107.5
Noncommercial services	14291	23005	160.9
	118611	168189	141.7
France			
Commercial services			
for enterprises	350448	513694	146.5
	2470139	3796026	153.6
Transport	30630	39724	129.6
	473117	584051	123.4
Insurance	2655	5110	192.4
	129325	141879	109.7
Financial organisations	13573	15997	117.8
	334339	351237	105.0
Noncommercial services	54902	94755	172.5
	639037	863116	135.0

(3) sites created thanks to the will of the territorial actors (the IFREMER's activity in Brest; the science park Futuroscope; Sablé sur Sarthe; Nord-Finistère);

(4) sites related to the promotion of research (the Rennes-Atalante Technopole); and

(5) sites created around the concept of technological transfers (biotechnologies in Vannes, plastics technology in Alençon, yachting in La Rochelle, Agropole in Agen).

Combinations of these situations are not ruled out, especially in the most important towns. Assuredly, the conclusion about the role of the immaterial, of their knowledge and their transfer, aiming at the development of economic activity, is an easy one.

The transformation of the techno-productive system, which began two decades ago with globalisation, the worldwide economy, and the importance of immaterial investment is an unprecedented challenge for the economy of the Atlantic Arc and for its local actors, both political and economic. The comparatively good results of the economy of the Atlantic Arc in terms of employment during the 1980s are probably the result of an enterprising spirit expressed through an economic 'milieu' eager to create new businesses and to generate substantially diversified activities.

4 The CRITTs and the future of the Atlantic Front: a useful tool to create innovating productive milieux

The CRITTs were designed to face the needs expressed during a vast dialogue initiated by the Ministry of Research and Technology in 1981, which brought together economic actors and researchers. This dialogue, which took place in every French region and was concluded by a national symposium, underscored the poor links between production and research, and between the firms and the researchers, notably those working in public research organisations dealing with fundamental or practical research developed in the facilities of the Centre National de la Recherche Scientifique (CNRS) or in the universities. The very objectives of the CRITTs was to support this relation between firms and laboratories. They are organisations run jointly by businessmen and the heads of the CNRS or university laboratories. The creation of ninety-seven CRITTs in France during the last decade is a sign of the relevance of the function of these diffusion organisations. We will examine briefly the situation in the Atlantic Arc, and then the conditions for the creation of innovating productive milieux.

4.1 The CRITTs in the Atlantic Arc

It is notable that the French Atlantic Arc, whose economy represents less than 20% of the national economic activity, accounts for forty-three of the ninety-seven CRITTs. The relations established during the dialogue about 'research technology' have greatly furthered the emergence of the CRITTs.

For instance, in Poitou-Charentes, the Association for the Development of Research and Technology, aimed at promoting the dialogue, has followed this generation of isolated CRITTs before the creation of Poitou-Charentes Technologie, which coordinates and manages the activities of the nine CRITTs.

The need to overcome the crisis through connection to information networks, felt throughout the whole economic fabric, justified the rise of a group of diffusion centres. Let us examine their characteristics.

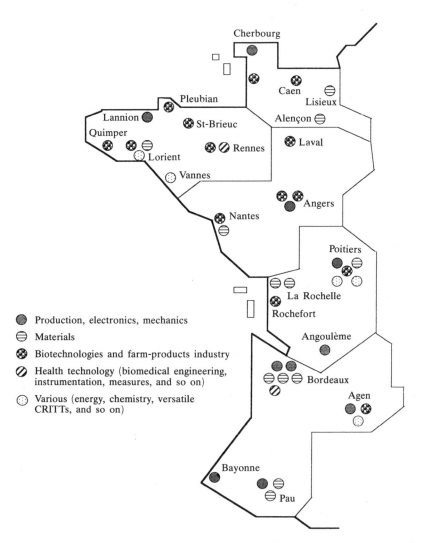

Figure 1. The CRITTS of the Atlantic Front in 1993 (source: Chauchefoin, 1993).

In the first place, the wide range of industrial activities covered by the CRITTs (although this range is rather overshadowed by the grouping) is quite striking (see figure 1). Thus, the range of services proposed throughout the Atlantic Arc matches the variety of the sectors of activity. Second, I will discuss the dispersal of the CRITTs throughout the macroregion. The whole territory is covered, serving to promote diffusion within the economic fabric through proximity relations.

Thus, the dispersal of the CRITTs confirms that the need to connect to information networks via intermediaries is definitely a characteristic specifically related to the predominance of SMEs in the economic fabric. Although the influence of a CRITT cannot be strictly limited to its economic basis, the conditions for a thorough dialogue between SMEs and research laboratories reveals the existence of a vast capacity of enterprising initiative.

One can observe, however, that the number of CRITTs does not match the importance of the industrial activity of each region. Thus, Poitou-Charentes, which represents the smallest industrial sector of the Atlantic Arc, created nine CRITTs. Pays de la Loire, although the biggest industrial sector, has only six. This betrays a strategic attitude that varies from region to region. The comparatively small number of CRITTs in Pays de la Loire is in accordance with the largely noninterventionist policy of the Regional Council. It contrasts with the policy of Bretagne, which is to reinforce the importance of many sites except Rennes, the regional capital of Bretagne. These implantations express the wish to reinforce the emerging productive systems. Funds aimed at developing higher education are also granted to these sites. The objective is to achieve the completion of the vital (or at least necessary if not sufficient) characteristics permitting the generation of an innovative milieu.

4.2 How to generate innovative production systems
That the adaptation and evolution of the Atlantic Arc between 1982 and 1990 cannot be attributed solely to CRITTs is beyond doubt. There is, however, a definite relation between the presence of the CRITTs and the rate of business creation (that is, entrepreneurship) of the activity centres (seventy-nine activity bases throughout the Atlantic Arc).

This observation leads us to confirm the existence of a link, notably in the case of firms specialised in transfers related to the transformation of productive activities on a regional scale. For example, the links between the CRITT for horticulture and agricultural activity (especially begonias in Rochefort sur Mer), the CRITT for polymeric composite materials and the plastics technology sector in Alençon, or between the CRITT of the Research Centre for the Nautical Design Industry (Centre de Recherche pour l'Architecture et l'Industrie Nautique, in short CRAIN) and production for the yachting sector in La Rochelle. Thus, one can envisage the generation of an innovative productive milieu as a tool for economic development and as a strategic plan of action to build (in accordance with the evolution of the European productive system) an original economic fabric based on the exploitation and the promotion of regional natural resources, ensuring its autonomy, diversification, and adaptability.

This reflection is based on the following definition:

"An innovating 'milieu' is the combination of three systems: the productive system, made of production activities and their market, the sociocultural context within which many people will be induced to innovate and the institutional partnership (with the State, territorial administrations, chambers of commerce and industry) which sustains the economy through training programmes, aids to the diffusion of technologies and access to research facilities" (Lemaignan, 1993, page 113).

The validity of a territorial strategy based on such a concept of innovating milieu is easily understandable. The potentialities of the milieux of the Atlantic Arc can be assessed in order to make up for missing elements, mainly by providing the vital connections to the technical information flows, but also by creating enterprise nurseries.

That a dialogue between SMEs can be initiated in every activity site in order to detect the potentialities and eventually to innovate is quite clear. Not only can innovation emerge endogenously from its milieu, it can also originate from external conditions, thus validating the creation of a CRITT when the economic fabric matures. The mission of the CRITT is not limited to the local scale, but the will to create an innovative productive milieu involves a strong territorial complementarity linking the productive activity, an enterprising social context, an institutional partnership, and also education, engineering, and technological diffusion. The synergistic effects can circulate, but one could estimate that the specialisation of a milieu in a well-defined market gap improves the variety of the productive system. However, it can also weaken it, and thus the future of the Atlantic Arc not only involves the generation of innovative productive systems, but also the grouping within a network of CRITTs and all the other research bodies and diffusion centres.

The cross-fertilisation can be renewed by organising dialogues and information exchanges within microregions able to create localised productive milieux. Such milieux, however, become innovative only through the creation of endogenous innovation or through the diffusion of technology from external sources, and can maintain themselves only with a properly interconnected network. Access to the international information and 'immaterial' flows would indeed be quite difficult without proper interconnections between the centres of attraction and the CRITTs of the Atlantic Arc. The interregional cooperation and transnationality presently at work foreshadow the future systems of a development strategy aiming at the integration of the Atlantic Arc to Europe.

5 Conclusion

The integration of this vast Atlantic Front to Europe is a major challenge that has to be taken up. This integration strategy can only be conceived if the Atlantic Front is really a place open to ocean (with the aim of using its cultural background as much as possible), but also to information networks in order to acquire new technologies, made vital by the evolution of the technical and economic paradigm which is essential for the development of specific activities.

In order to meet this expectation, it is essential to create conditions favourable to the diffusion of technological information towards the SMEs, to help them to adapt to the changes provoked by the market, and to innovate in new products designed to create new technologies. Be it the adaptation of local productive systems by the provision of missing services or the creation of innovative milieux, the strategy is to develop the networks charged with diffusing technologies. The recent evolution of the economy of the Atlantic Front is a sign that there is a crucial link between industrial activities, the tertiarisation, and the creation of CRITTs.

Thus, the role of the Atlantic Arc, as a 'project-territory', is to further the creation of conditions allowing modernisation of the productive fabric through the intensification of interregional cooperation, of lobbying actions in the EC, and of the organisation of programmes such as PERIFRA, ATLANTIS, and so on.

The European and international integration of the Atlantic Arc implies the continuation of the diversification of the productive system, which can be effectuated from the enhancement of the value of local or undiscovered resources. It is essential to support all projects of exploitation of these local resources. Thus, it is clear that, in order to manage the growing complexity of the characteristics qualifying the territories and their ability to develop, it is necessary to have a system with increasingly varied modes of intervention.

The organisation of the technological poles and the diffusion centres into networks is certainly the best way to further complementarity and to combat international competition. The current interconnections of CRITTs within the territory is a step, which can certainly be furthered by revealing the seam of potential activity start-ups. A dialogue in every site of activity can lead, through an 'inventive analysis' (Lassus, 1992), to the detection of opportunities for the generation of further entrepreneurship, firm formation, the growth of existing enterprises, or synergies between activities. For example, I point to the horticultural activities based on begonias with the help of the CRITT for horticulture in Rochefort, which illustrates the potential results of a real heuristic action on the part of the local actors (Lassus, 1992, page 19).

The Atlantic Arc, as a mobilising force, thus has a dual lobbyist mission: in the first place, inducing the EC to allocate budgets and intervention funds, and then, creating the structures supporting interregional and even multinational cooperation. The organisation into networks is essential in order to discover development opportunities for local resources. The diversification of the activities, along with the reinforcement of the SMEs' fabric, will be the real signs of a successful integration to Europe.

References
Beauchard J (Ed.), 1993 *Destins Atlantiques. Entre Mémoire et Mobilité* (Atlantic Destinies: Between Memories and Mobility) (Datar/Éditions de l'Aube, La Tour d'Aigues, France)
CEDRE, 1993 *Étude Prospective des Régions Atlantiques* (Prospective Research on Atlantic Regions) (Commission des Communautés Européennes, Bruxelles)
Chauchefoin P, 1993 *Liste des CRITT par Régions* (The Regional List of CRITTs) Ministère de la Recherche et de la Technologie, Institut d'Économie Régionale, Poitiers, France
Guesnier B (Ed.), 1991 *La Dynamique Atlantique. Potentialités et Stratégies de Développement des Régions de l'Arc Atlantique en Europe* (Atlantic Dynamics. Potentialities and Strategies for Development of Atlantic Regions in Europe) Institut d'Économie Régionale, Poitiers, France
Guesnier B, 1992, "L'Arc Atlantique. Un nouveau territoire pour de nouvelles activités" (Atlantic front. A new territory for new activities) presented to the Colloque ASRDLF 'Nouvelles activités, nouveaux espaces', Montréal, 3–5 September 1991; copy available from the author
Lassus B, 1992 *Hypothèses pour une Troisième Nature* (Hypothesis for a Third Nature) (Cercle Charles-Rivière Dufresney, Coralle, Londres)
Lemaignan C, 1993, "Les milieux innovants" (Innovative milieux) in *Destins Atlantiques. Entre Mémoire et Mobilité* Ed. J Beauchard (Datar/Éditions de l'Aube, La Tour d'Aigues, France) pp 113–122

Transborder Cooperation: Regional and Business Development

A Pimpão
University of the Algarve

1 Economic systems and cooperation

1.1 Performance of economic systems

An economic system can be seen as a space where there is a set of economic units establishing relationships in order to achieve certain goals through a rational allocation of resources. In other words, these relationships constitute a process of producing various commodities to satisfy the necessities of the populations living in such a space (region, country, or integrated market).

The economic system needs a regulation process to guarantee the compatibility of preferences of different economic units and at different stages of decision (Pimpão, 1985). For each economic unit D_i we can define a utility preference function $W(x)$. The utility level of each economic unit D_i is $U_i(x)$ for each state of the economy x. The utility level for the central, regional, or local public authority is $W(x)$. From welfare-economics theory, convergence exists when the Pareto optimum is achieved.

In real economic systems, this is a political process where the function $W(x)$ is a problem of public choice. To see the interaction of the several actors and stages of decision we can use figure 1.

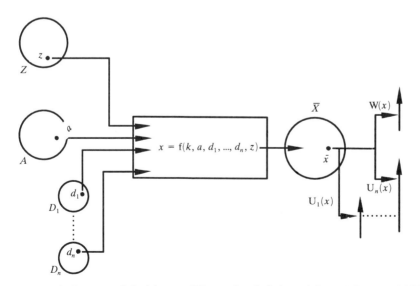

Figure 1. Process of decision at different levels (adapted from Johansen, 1977).

The functions $U_i(x)$ and $W(x)$ have the following definitions:

$$W(x) = W[f(a, d_1, ..., d_i, ..., d_n, z)],$$

$$U_i(x) = U_i[f(a, d_1, ..., d_i, ..., d_n, z)],$$

where a represents regulation instruments; d_i are the decisions of the units i ($i = 1, ..., n$); and z represents exogenous factors. The existence of several preference functions presents a problem of aggregating preferences so that the public authority can make a decision. From an interregional and international point of view, the aggregation of preferences gives rise to an additional difficulty because, instead of a single public authority, there are several of them. The process of decisionmaking can be given a game-theory interpretation. The games can be either cooperative or noncooperative. For the noncooperative games each unit acts independently of the others without contacts or negotiations. Cooperative games allow negotiations and coalitions (Johansen, 1977).

1.2 The internationalisation of economic systems and its implications for cooperation
We will see in the new Europe of the Single Market which kind of game represents the best way for regional development. The construction of the Single Market is the consequence of a worldwide process of international-isation of the economy. The globalisation of markets, the intensity of international trade, and the speed of technical progress are all forcing economic systems to become more open. The economic structure of the system is sometimes the main cause of the internationalisation process, when foreign trade accounts for a large proportion of the product of the economy. In the last 50 years international trade increased 100 fold. From 1945 to 1986 the rates of increase in the volume of foreign trade were 7% in the period 1945–67, 3% in 1967–73, and 3% in 1980–86 (Lafay and Herzog, 1989). The elasticity of foreign trade versus GDP was 1.5 until 1967, after which it rose to about 1.9.

In global terms the interaction of foreign trade and production has increased. In the specific case of the EC the most radical change in cooperation was after 1 January 1993. The reasons for this acceleration in international trade can be analysed according to the contributions of authors such as Smith, Ricardo, Heckscher, Ohlin, and Samuelson, who define the comparative advantages of economics. However, this theory presupposes the immobility of production factors and the absence of technological progress. The examples of Japan, Singapore, Korea, and other Asian newly industrialised countries, and the European Community suggest other interpretations of the necessity of internationalisation and economic cooperation. Before public authorities discovered the way, the firms felt this problem as a strategic motivation and a new concept for business success (Pimpão, 1992a).

1.3 Microeconomic analysis of cooperation

The strategy of cooperation in the case of firms is related to the costs of integration (Ratti, 1992) and to technological, market-related, and financial reasons (Lafay and Herzog, 1989). Normally mergers and joint ventures bring institutional difficulties and costs of concentration. In addition, they imply an irreversible process, which means less autonomy and lower capability to adapt to the new strategic positions in the markets. In contrast, cooperation is more flexible and has fewer costs of organisation.

In some instances, territorial proximity is an important factor in developing cooperation. However, cooperation can arise for other reasons.

(a) Technological reasons. A number of Japanese firms have chosen cooperation as a means to conquer new markets in Europe and in the United States or to prevent a competitive entrance into Japan by foreign firms. Such cooperations include Hitachi–Thompson, Matsushita–3M–Sanyo–Intel, Fujitsu–IBM, and Mitsubishi–Boeing.

(b) Market-related and financial reasons. This type of cooperation permits the dispersal of markets and allows international experience to be gained. The financial agreements have normally resulted in an increase in the share of capital of the foreign partners to control the execution of technological agreements (Rover–Honda, and Nissan–Alfa Romeo, for instance) or to participate in a large international project such as the Airbus project.

Sometimes cooperation is more complex and involves multilateral processes for a joint business development. (A good example is the telecommunication cooperation network between IBM, NTT Japan, British Telecom, Mitsubishi, Mitel Canada, Stet-Italy, and others.)

1.4 Cooperation and integration of economic systems

From a macroeconomic point of view, the cooperation process is a consequence of the internationalisation of an economy with intensive interaction within and between economic systems. The need to bring this interaction into cooperative games leads to the appearance of supranational systems. Within this kind of system it is possible to reconcile different preference functions. It is possible, for instance, to have cooperation to maximise the external economies and minimise the external diseconomies (environmental policy or management of water resources, for instance). It is also the way to reduce uncertainty and increase the diffusion of information.

However, cooperation between the economic units of regions of different national systems has the problem of the border. This can be either a barrier or an opportunity for development. In the EC countries there are two kinds of border: those of the industrialised regions of central Europe with declining activities, and those of the southern countries with characteristics of peripheral regions with underdeveloped economic activity.

Europe is essentially a system of regions and it will be strong as a whole if the regions are also strong. For Portugal and Spain the border is a space with no tradition of contacts and cooperation. On the contrary, these countries used the border as a line of war and suspicion. However, the removal of administrative and fiscal barriers has opened up new possibilities for the economic and social development of border regions. But here the difficulties begin. With no tradition of economic and institutional contacts, cooperation has very little to build upon. For the less developed regions, away from the main cities, cooperation provides a strategy for more independent development with less restrictions from the central public administrations.

2 Transborder cooperation: Algarve – Andalusia

2.1 Two peripheral regions with different levels of economic performance

The Algarve is the most southern region of Portugal and Andalusia is the same for Spain. The border between them is one of the less-developed areas of both regions. However, this zone has some differences from other border regions, because in the southern regions there is a considerable amount of tourism and specialist forms of agriculture. On both sides of the border there are also some differences. The Algarve has an area of 5000 km^2 and 350000 inhabitants, and Andalusia has an area of 87000 km^2 with 6.8 million inhabitants. The nearest zone to the border (the Province of Huelva) in Andalusia has a very important industrial sector, but there is no counterpart to this in the Algarve.

Another important difference is the unemployment rate: at 5% in the Algarve and 25% in Andalusia (and a little higher in Huelva). Both regions have below-average levels of development: 57.5 for Andalusia and 46 for Algarve, compared with an index of 100 for the EC (Pimpão, 1992a). A comparison between the economic structures of Huelva and the Algarve is given in table 1.

The Algarve and Huelva both specialise strongly in agriculture and fishing. Huelva has an important industry, namely metallurgy. The Algarve has very little industry with no economic synergy. On the contrary, all the activities are concentrated on tourism and a number of other service sectors.

Thus, the Algarve and Andalusia have some similarities, but a great deal of variation in their economic activities. The main differences are in respect of industry and urban settlement. Andalusia has cities of 700000 (Seville) and 150000 (Huelva) inhabitants. In the Algarve the most important urban centre is Faro with 40000 inhabitants.

Table 1. The percentage of GDP for sectors in Huelva and the Algarve (source: Pimpão, 1992a).

Sector	Huelva	Algarve
Agriculture, fishing, and forestry	11	14
Industry and construction	40	25
Services	49	61

2.2 The effects of the EC regional policy

The EC regional policy for the border regions is primarily a set of programmes for infrastructures. There are no great differences between the 'normal' regional policy and that for the border regions. The roads and other infrastructures have received important financial support through INTERREG (a Community programme for the development of border regions). A new road is being built from the Spanish border to join the main road to Lisbon, and some roads are also being built on the Spanish side. However, this is not enough. Roads are necessary, but without economic activities there is no development. Transborder cooperation must be seen as a common strategy of complementary activities and not as a context between firms in the same sector on both sides of the border (Pimpão, 1992a).

The regional policy has another limitation. The Algarve and Andalusia are regions of Southern Europe. They have a highly specialised agriculture and a strong tourist sector. This sector receives no support from the European Regional Development Fund (ERDF) or any other EC structural fund. The restructuring of the regional economies of both regions, even with some differences, means new tourist activities, development of the food industry, and training of young people.

To establish cooperation, some special instruments must be created to promote cooperation between firms. In fact, a development strategy implies more income and employment. For that we certainly need roads and other forms of infrastructure, but production and income are the tasks of the productive sector, which means that cooperation between firms and businesses is essential.

2.3 The institutional problem of cooperation and the national strategy for regional development

In the past, the Algarve was one of the less-developed regions of Portugal. Business activity was always very weak, only the cork and food industries provided exceptions to this. In the 1960s, with the increase in tourism, new firms appeared, but most of them had a head office outside the region. There are no regional economic clusters, and the region's tourism has no important links with agriculture or industry.

This fragility gives the region less negotiating power to compete with the interests of the other regions in Portugal or in Spain (such as Andalusia). The attractivity of Seville is not yet a problem because Andalusia is also one of the poorest regions in Europe. However, the new investments in Andalusia, namely for the support of, and directly connected with, the EXPO 92, created a new capacity and good conditions for the localisation of firms and development of new projects.

What is the regional strategy needed to face these problems? The public authorities in Portugal have a vision of regional development from a national point of view. The main goal is to decrease the gap between the Algarve and the other regions of Portugal and the European average.

However, there is no strategy for transborder cooperation. Of course there is the INTERREG, but this is mainly directed towards infrastructure.

To understand the problems of cooperation it is important to describe the principal institutional differences between the Algarve and Andalusia.

(a) The capacity to take decisions at the regional level is very weak in the Algarve because of the lack of a regional government. The regional policy for the Algarve in political terms is decided by the central government. By contrast, in Andalusia there is a regional authority.

(b) Business activity in Andalusia is supported by strong economic associations. In the Algarve the association of firms is not significant compared with that in Andalusia or the other Portuguese regions, namely those of Lisbon and Oporto.

(c) The cities are much smaller in the Algarve than in Andalusia. This reduces the power of the municipalities of the Algarve in the context of the two regions.

2.4 The strategy for development and firm cooperation

The Algarve and Andalusia are closer to each other than to Lisbon or Madrid. This geographical proximity is a very good basis for cooperation. The problem of transport costs is minimised. However, other factors must be analysed: language, legislation, cultural values. This means that cooperation is possible if there is a policy directed towards the prior resolution of these problems. But this resolution must be seen within the context of the development strategy of the two regions with two main characteristics:

(1) programmes implemented according to the basic necessities of the region; and

(2) programmes of common interest fo facilitate cooperation between firms in the two regions.

The main effect of a stronger integration of the regional economies is the expansion of the market. Currently, cooperation is very weak even between the public authorities. Only the CORINE programme has projects on both sides of the border.

First of all, public authorities must agree to create conditions for cooperation between firms. A system of incentives for joint projects would be welcome, as would support for pilot projects in certain areas. Some new ventures could be planned in the marketing of tourism, agriculture, and fishing. Andalusia and the Algarve are typical regions of Southern Europe. This image could be projected in the products of these sectors. To support this cooperation, the public authorities and the economic associations of both sides should consider the formation of an institute for economic cooperation.

A regional policy directed towards transborder development would include the following elements.

(1) Cooperation in *tourism*. In the Guadiana River (boat tours, fishing, food, and culture), mountain tourism (excursions, gastronomy, and hunting);

tourism for young people, cultural and heritage tourism, and integrated packages with international tour operators. One of the outcomes of this cooperation must be the creation of an interregional tour operator.

(2) Cooperation in *agriculture* has three main aspects: diversification in production and complementary development [for example, Andalusia (Huelva) with oranges and the Algarve with dried fruits], associations for trading companies (the Algarve has some difficulties in entering the agricultural markets in Europe, whereas the firms in Andalusia generally have a greater capacity to do so), and regional sweet production (the Algarve and Andalusia have the raw materials and capacity to create a thriving sweet industry).

(3) Cooperation in *fishing*. In this sector the conflicts were very strong but both governments achieved an agreement on the fishing rights on both sides. However, the firms have not yet established agreements for the development of this sector.

(4) Cooperation in *industry*. The Algarve has a weaker position in industry. For some sectors, such as construction materials, wood, cork, and furniture, joint ventures could be established to provide a greater production capacity and to explore new markets.

(5) Cooperation in *training and research*. This is a sector where the public authorities have the main responsibilities. Both regions have experienced great difficulties in achieving a skilled work force. The Universities of the Algarve (Faro), Seville, and Huelva have potential capacity for training and research. Possible areas of cooperation include technological centres, an economic observatory, and exchanges of students and academic staff.

(6) Cooperation in the *environment*. In the Algarve and Huelva there are many important ecological areas. In Huelva industrial pollution could damage the tourist resorts and the quality of life in general. For a good tourist 'product' it is necessary to establish agreements for the preservation of the environment.

(7) Cooperation in *accessibility*. Roads, railways, airports, and other transport infrastructure provide the physical support for trading, tourism, and communications between firms. A number of projects could be implemented: new border crossings on the Guadiana River, the upgrading of roads near the border, and links between the airports of Seville and Faro to make feasible the Faro–Seville railway.

3 Conclusions
The new reality in Europe has changed the traditional relationship between regions and increased the scope for interregional cooperation. Regional problems must be seen not only at the national level but also at the international level.

Analysis of the relationship between the Algarve and Andalusia suggests that development in both regions will benefit from interregional cooperation. However, there is no previous experience in this field. Firms are torn between competition and cooperation. In theoretical terms, this involves a choice between a cooperative game and a noncooperative game. The first approach will permit firms to establish cooperation so that they can engage in complementary business initiatives.

Two peripheral regions, such as the Algarve and Andalusia, must benefit from cooperation in order to establish a strong competitive position vis-à-vis the more developed regions of North and Central Europe. Intensive economic competition, even in agriculture or tourism, will result in an overall loss of competitive position in the markets of Europe and in the rest of the world.

In the past, EC regional policy for transborder development failed to provide sufficient means for the support of programmes of cooperation, particularly between firms. The most recent INTERREG programme financed some important infrastructures such as roads and bridges but was not concerned with productive activities. There are, however, encouraging signs that the next INTERREG programme will be more directly linked with the prospect of development and cooperation.

References
Johansen L, 1977 *Lectures on Macroeconomic Planning* volume 1 (North-Holland, Amsterdam)
Lafay G, Herzog C, 1989 *Commerce International: La Fin des Avantages Acquis* (International Trade: The End of Special Favours) (Economica, Paris)
Pimpão A, 1985, "Planeamento macroeconomico e planeamento empresarial" (Macroeconomic planning and business planning), PhD thesis, Universidade Tecnica de Lisboa, Lisbon
Pimpão A, 1992a, "Estudo do desenvolvimento da regiao fronteirica the Algarve–Andaluzia" (A study of the Algarve–Andalusia border region), final report, University of the Algarve, Faro
Pimpão A, 1992b, "Cooperation and development. A new concept of business", paper presented at the Conference on Cooperation in Pearl River Delta, University of Macao, November 1992, Macao; copy available from the author
Ratti R, 1993, "How can existing barriers and border effects be overcome? A theoretical approach", in this book, pp 60–69

What Makes an Interregional Network Successful?

P Brenner
European Centre for Regional Development, Strasbourg

1 Introduction

The importance of cooperation between regions is a well-recognised fact in the Europe of 1993. Since 1988, the Commission for the European Communities has been cofinancing interregional cooperation activities under Article 10 of the European Regional Development Fund (ERDF); that is, INTERREG, RECITE, and EEP (Experience Exchange Programme). The activities carried out within these programmes are aimed at furthering scientific and technical cooperation between regional authorities within the European Community and strengthening economic and social cohesion, thus overcoming disparities between the more-successful regions of the EC and the less-prosperous ones. However, it must be pointed out that EC regional policy is laid down by the member states and not by the regions themselves, which explains why EC programmes for regions account for 1% of the ERDF.

2 How are interregional cooperation networks set up in practice?

Setting up cooperation between regions implicitly means forming a network, the members of which become partners in a common project. There are various ways of initiating cooperation: for example, several regions, looking into the possibility of creating a network project, come together at the start to examine topics on which to base their future cooperation and draft a network proposal to the European Commission. If the project is successful, it is extended to other regions at a later date.

Once the 'initiating' regions or 'donor' regions have been identified, in other words those which are to play the role of leaders in the network by virtue of their resources and skills, the following stage involves finding the right contact points in these regions; that is to say, singling out the persons in regional authorities and development agencies who are responsible for and interested in setting up network projects. The choice of coordinator is also a critical step. Experience gained over the past few years has taught us that the quality and success of a given network cooperation project depends to a great extent on the abilities and skills of its coordinator to carry out the role of pilot and manager of the project.

One of the network coordinator's tasks at this stage is to help the initiating region to identify potential partners; that is to say, those with complementary skills. Then the 'beneficiaries'—regions to which the information and know-how are to be transferred—must be found, ideally among less-developed regions of the Community such as those under Objective 1, 2, or 5b (that is, those lagging behind the rest of Europe in terms of development).

Certain key factors must be taken into consideration at this particular stage, such as the feasibility of the future cooperation. Is the cooperation network of mutual benefit to those involved? Which valuable information is transferable? Can the various partners involved work together effectively in practice? Indeed, there is absolutely no point in forming a group of individuals who are incapable of working as a team.

3 Drafting an interregional network proposal and methodology

The subject of the network cooperation proposal must be carefully defined at the outset. The proposals that receive funding are those that have clearly demonstrated their worth and shown they are beneficial to all the regions taking part. The proposals must reflect a true desire to make the regional partnership work and a strong desire to cooperate. Three key criteria are to be borne in mind when drafting a network proposal: innovation, methodological rigour, and richness of content.

All proposals must be attractive and portray a good image of the network. Whether laying down network objectives, defining network activities, or planning work schedules, it is essential to avoid rhetoric. Proposals must be clear, concise, and businesslike. They must get their message across without resorting to highly technical language and jargon. A good, clear description of the situation at hand bears witness to the fact that the network has carried out enough preparatory work to ensure that its project will complement and not duplicate other networks' efforts. The intrinsic value of any network proposal resides in its ability to achieve concrete regional development. To this end, it should situate regional problems in terms of their relevance to regional development or transnational problems.

Also, it is important that the work involved be shared out among all those involved in the network so as to encourage a 'team spirit', which is vital should problems arise. Any proposal must clearly lay down the practical operations that the network undertakes to carry out. These operations must be feasible both in terms of forecasted achievements and in terms of available funds.

Methodology involves such activities as collecting useful information, organising seminars or meetings on specific topics, taking part in business-exchange forums or trade fairs. All sources of information, as well as particulars on the partners involved and proposed cooperation techniques, are to be indicated. The cooperation network should be as pragmatic as possible and prove that it can handle the technical aspects the project entails.

4 The role of the network coordinator: a key factor in the success of a cooperation network

Coordinating an interregional cooperation network requires the coordinator to be both adaptable and persistent as he or she is the central figure in charge of 'orchestrating' the partners and managing a project which must be brought to a successful conclusion. As good communication is a crucial aspect for the smooth running of interregional cooperation networks, the coordinator must keep the partners well informed of the project's progress.

A coordinator must be well acquainted with the subject at hand, monitor the proceedings and trends, and head the project, manage it with the interests of all those involved in mind, and, more important still, never lose sight of the schedule and the network's objectives. He or she must be in a position to assess the degree of success of a project and find indications on the basis of which to evaluate the activities that have been carried out.

Another important task for a network coordinator is that of financially managing the network programme. He or she is responsible not only to the regions involved in the network but also to the European Commission for managing and allocating the available funds.

5 Problems which arise

If the partners involved in the network do not have a sound knowledge of each other at the outset (that is, if the project has not been sufficiently well researched) problems will inevitably arise. Similarly, if the objectives of the network and the commitments of those involved are not clear right from the early stages, the network will be impossible to manage.

In interregional cooperation networks, one must never lose sight of the fact that one is dealing with regions, and therefore with regional authorities. People change or get promoted or even lose interest in the programmes, which means that they fall behind schedule or even grind to a halt. Certain partners may not be pulling their weight and personalities and ideas may clash. This is where the importance of a team spirit comes into play in order to rekindle enthusiasm and revitalise projects. Other problems which cannot be avoided are those related to daily administrative problems: language barriers, communications, red tape, and so on. One of the main qualities of a coordinator who has to deal with minor problems of this kind is patience.

6 Contractual provisions of interregional cooperation networks

Once the network proposal has been accepted by the Commission of the European Communities, contractual obligations must be laid down between all those involved in the network project in the form of a 'cooperation agreement'. This cooperation agreement with the Commission defines the implementation terms of the network project, the obligations of those involved, as well as their responsibilities as regards funding.

One of the key characteristics of regional funding is that EC money is no longer handed out to regions in the form of subsidies but as cofinancing and therefore has to be backed up by a contribution from the regions themselves. The proportion of EC to local funding is laid down in the cooperation agreement and varies according to a region's needs and resources. EC funding is paid out in several instalments, and is tied to the submission of reports: progress report, financial report, and final report.

A certain number of indications are compulsory when drawing up a cooperation agreement, such as the names of the regions involved and their official representatives, the purpose of the cooperation and the operations which are to be carried out. The network project may be given a title, such as EUROCERAM or EURORAI.

Generally speaking, a project coordinator is appointed for the duration of the project. He or she officially represents the partners and is responsible for managing the project.

It is of the utmost importance to lay down the legal ground rules for a cooperation agreement insofar as they ensure that a given network programme is carried out in a satisfactory way. To this end all agreements must be clear, concise, and operational; their terms must be propitious, motivating, and lay down all the rights, obligations, and sanctions of all the parties involved.

7 Cooperation in practice

Since 1988, around 100 cooperation projects have been set up in 120 regions of Europe, thanks to the EEP of the European Community. The number of projects submitted each year to the Commission is steadily rising, which bears witness to the increasing interest of regions in cooperation activities. The topics covered vary from environmental issues, agriculture, and technology transfer, to ways of dealing with the problems of industrial wasteland.

I have chosen to present three highly successful networks to illustrate the way in which such programmes work.

Example 1 setting up a cooperation network between Regional Centres for Consumer Affairs
This particular network programme, which was focused on working out a policy on quality for agricultural produce, was conducted with the region of the Asturias (Spain). To this end, a training course was organised in Lille in April 1991 for representatives from the Asturias (companies, distributors, Chambers of Commerce, trade unions, consumers, and representatives of local and regional authorities). Our highly motivated partners were given a theoretical, technical, and practical approach to ways of working out a policy on the quality required to create a 'seal of quality' for regional produce, as well as a certifying body.

The partners then returned to the Asturias to set up a Regional Commission on Quality. This also involved pinpointing methods with which to set up Local Centres on Price Information for which the trainees had to carry out real price surveys on shops in the region. The results of these surveys will be published and available from Town Halls in the region.

The success of this particular programme can be expressed in terms of interregional solidarity and knowledge of the regional partners involved, their needs, abilities, and skills. Thanks to the EEP, this project was granted EC funding to enable the initial contacts to be made between new partners and to launch new activities which were carried through to a successful conclusion.

Example 2 the Union of Southern European Foresters: a transfer
of know-how in the field of the protection and development of forests
This programme was aimed at the exchange of know-how in the area of forestry between regions of Southern Europe and the facilitation of the circulation of ideas and information between local and regional authorities. The first steps carried out took the form of informal contacts between regions in southern France and northern Spain from which was born a real desire to cooperate. This gave rise to the creation of the Union of Southern European Foresters (USSE).

The objectives this group of regions set itself were to provide and distribute information to its members, work out a forest management policy, contribute towards finding new techniques with which to tackle forest fires, and achieve economic unity for the large forests represented by each member. Following an important meeting held in Santiago de Compostela in 1991, the activities of the USSE began to take shape: the need to define a forestry policy common to all the regions of Southern Europe, and a desire to find ways of cooperating together effectively through the creation of vocational training schemes.

The progress of operations was hindered by geographical and cultural problems at the outset. However, thanks to the meetings that were organised, the determination of all those involved, and the concrete nature of the network, the USSE initiative has proved to be highly successful.

Example 3 Technology Transfer to Southern Europe (SITEF)
Since 1989, by virtue of the international symposia, meetings, and conferences that it has organised, this network has enabled priority regions of the EC to benefit from the numerous international contacts that have been made in the fields of technology transfer, biotechnologies, environmental technologies, and automation. The activities of this network are centred around singling out transferable technologies originating from regions of Southern Europe and promoting concrete exchanges of a commercial or industrial nature, or those involving the search for partnerships between regions of Europe.

To this end, an International Business Centre on technology transfer was set up during the course of the SITEF event (International Forum on Technology Transfer) which is held in Toulouse, to assess the existing supply and demand for technology and encourage the signing of agreements between companies, research laboratories, and regional authorities in Southern Europe. Workshops were also organised to follow up the offers for technology transfer and illustrate the different types of action which contribute towards the success of operations involving technology transfer. By way of an example, in 1989 alone, SITEF generated a potential of 5000 offers and demands for transferable technologies.

Thanks to this 'matchmaking service' for supply and demand, a number of European networks have been brought into contact, new links have been forged between network managers, and new opportunities have been opened up. Indeed, in the future, the activities of this network may well have the effect of lessening the disparities that exist between regions of the European Community. This is truly an example of a network which has contributed in a concrete way to achieving the objectives set out in the European policy on regional development.

8 Conclusion
Interregional networks are possible and they work, thanks to a great deal of effort in the preparatory phases of network creation and commitment in implementation. EC regional policy sows the seeds for interregional cooperation networks and acts as a network incubator. Within this framework, the role of European network programmes is to consolidate the lines of progress in existence, bring about cooperation, match supply and demand, and develop a strategic outlook for such programmes in the medium and long term.

Index

Accessibility 57–58, 119–120
Administrative regions 2, 35–36
Aland Islands 42–43
Algarve 234–238
Alpe-Adria working community
    157–167
Andalusia 236–240
Archipelago Europe Study 24–25
Asymmetric barrier effects 52
Atlantic Arc 27, 102–104, 217–232
Atlantic Axis (Eixo Atlantico) 97
Austria 59, 77–79, 184–188, 189

Barents region 43–45
Barrier effects
    asymmetric 52
    linguistic differences 56–57
    symmetric 52
    telecommunications 56–57
    time-related 50–51
    typology 48–52
    use of railway network 54–55
Baltic region 38–43, 135–155
Baltic States 149
Bazaar economy 149, 151, 152–154
Belgium 194–196, 197–204
Blue Banana area 25, 27, 37, 144–145
Border regions 47, 49
Borders
    as a barrier 62
    as a contract factor 61
    as a filter 62
    as a separation factor 61
    national 10, 57–58
    open borders 62
    spatial analysis 66
    theory of 63–68
Champagne-Ardennes Programme 194,
    199
Channel Tunnel 116–133
Coastal regions 47, 116–133
Cooperation
    cross-border 89–94, 128–132
CRITTs 216–217, 226–230
Croatia 159
Czech Republic 184, 189

Development trends 31–35

Eastern Europe 15, 80, 135–142,
    144–155, 178–189
East Germany 152
Economically developed regions 18

Economically lagging regions 15,
    18–19, 98–114, 234–238
EC regional policies 16, 111–113,
    235, 239–240, 244
Endogenous regional development 78
Ethnic and cultural values 34–35, 38
EUCOR 210
EUREGIO region 37, 89, 91–95, 194,
    196
EURES 132
EUROMETROPOLIS 106
European Community Support
    Frameworks 18, 98, 143
European Cross-border Cooperation
    Action Programme (PACTE) 194,
    200–202
European Integration 21–27,
    141–142, 191
European Investment Bank 117–118
Europe of regions 6

FAST Programme 26
Fiscal federalism 89
Four motors of Europe 37–38, 108
Frontier concept 60–61
Functional regions 37, 41–45, 49

Game theory 232, 238
Germany 91–95, 207–210
Green Banana area 37

Historical regions 2
Homogeneous regions 2, 49
Hungary 157–175, 180

Identity regions 38, 40, 42–43
Infrastructure 42, 50, 57, 99, 111,
    112, 155, 161
Infrastructure networks 4, 5, 52–55,
    120–125, 132, 209, 235, 237
Institutional integration 8
International
    common objectives 78–79
    conditions for creating 77–78
    continuity and success 80–81
    obstacles to 79–80
    typology 83–86
Interregional network proposal 240
Italy 159

Kalaningrad 142
Kent 118–133

Leningrad 142
Luxembourg 194–196

Maastricht Treaty 21, 34, 36, 111, 142
Meso regions 2-3, 18, 143-149, 155
Middle Europe 177-189

Nation 32-33
Nation state 32-33
National borders 10, 57-58
Netherlands 91-95
Network coordinator 239-241
Norden 36, 38-45, 135-149
Norte (Portugal) 96-114

Objective 1 regions 25, 98, 110-111
Open borders 62
Organisational forms 8

Pas de Calais 118-133
Poland 210-213
Portugal 96-114, 234-239

Randkerne regions 138-144
RECITE Programme 5, 11, 27, 106,
    107, 110, 113, 239
Regional clusters 23-24
Regional development
    endogenous 78
    trajectories 97-99
Regions
    administrative 2, 35-36
    border 47, 49
    coastal 47, 116-133
    economically developed 18
    economically lagging 15, 18-19,
        98-114, 234-238
    functional 37, 41-45, 49

Regions (continued)
    historical 2
    homogeneous 2, 49
    identity 38, 40, 42-43
    meso 2-3, 18, 143-149, 155
    Objective 1 25, 98, 110-111
    Randkerne 138-144
Research and development 24-25,
    212

Schema Directeur Autoroutier 121
Single European Market 5, 6, 11, 16,
    33, 102, 191-192
Slovakia 185, 189
Slovenia 158, 185-186, 189
Small and medium-sized enterprises
    (SMEs) 151-155, 216-230
Spaces of flows 22, 28-29
Spaces of places 22, 28-29
Spain 96-114, 234-238
Subsidiary principle 8-10, 36, 38, 43
Symmetric barrier effects 52
Switzerland 158, 207-210

Technology and industry parks
    184-186
Time-related barrier effects 50-51
Transfer of know-how 107-111, 113,
    155, 187-188, 210, 239, 243

United Kingdom 118-133
Upper Rhine region 205-210
Urban networks 97, 101, 114

Wallonia 191-204